Landmarks in European Literature

TO POPPY
(for later)

Landmarks in European Literature

Philip Gaskell

Edinburgh University Press

© Philip Gaskell, 1999

Edinburgh University Press
22 George Square, Edinburgh

Typeset in Futura and Sabon
by Bibliocraft Ltd, Dundee, and
printed and bound in Great Britain
by MPG Books, Bodmin

A CIP record for this book is available
from the British Library

ISBN 0 7486 1280 7 (paperback)

The right of Philip Gaskell to be
identified as author of this work has
been asserted in accordance with the
Copyright, Designs and Patents Act
1988

Contents

Preface   *ix*
Acknowledgements   *x*
Abbreviations   *xi*

Introduction   1
A European canon
Reading foreign literature in translation
The availability of translations
How this book is arranged

I   **Dante and Petrarch**   8
    Italy in the early fourteenth century   8
        Dante (1265–1321)   9
            The Divine Comedy, 1307–21   11
        Petrarch (1304–74)   15
            Love Lyrics, 1327–58   16

II **Villon, Ronsard, and Montaigne**   19
    France from the late Middle Ages to the
        Renaissance   19
    Metre and sound in French verse   20
        Villon (1431–63+)   22
            Poems, 1456–61   22
        Ronsard (1524–85)   25
            Poems, 1550–85   26
        Montaigne (1533–92)   29
            Essays, 1572, 1588, 1595   30

III   **Cervantes and Molière**   35
Spain and France in the seventeenth century   35
     Cervantes (1547–1616)   36
       Don Quixote, 1605–15   38
     Molière (1622–73)   41
       Tartuffe, 1664, 1669   42

IV   **Voltaire and Rousseau**   46
France before the Revolution   46
     Voltaire (1694–1778),   47
       Candide, 1759   49
     Rousseau (1712–78),   51
       Confessions, 1766–70   54

V   **Goethe and Schiller**   59
German-speaking countries in the eighteenth century   59
     Goethe (1749–1832)   60
       Faust, Part One, 1775–1808   63
     Schiller (1759–1805)   67
       Wallenstein, 1798–9   70

VI   **Púshkin and Lérmontov**   75
The Russian Empire in the nineteenth century   75
     Púshkin (1799–1837)   80
       Eugene Onégin, 1831   82
     Lérmontov (1814–41)   85
       A Hero of Our Time, 1840   87

VII   **Balzac and Flaubert**   91
France: Restoration and the July Monarchy,
     1815–48   91
     Balzac (1799–1850)   93
       Le Père Goriot, 1834–5   94
     Flaubert (1821–80)   97
   Women and adultery in the nineteenth century   98
       Madame Bovary, 1856–7   103

VIII Baudelaire and Rimbaud   107
      France: Second Republic and Second Empire,
         1848–71   107
            Baudelaire (1821–67)   109
               Les Fleurs du Mal, 1857, 1861, 1868   111
            Rimbaud (1854–91)   114
               Poems, 1870–3   117

  IX Turgénev, Tolstóy, and Dostoévsky   121
      The great age of the Russian novel, 1856–80   121
            Turgénev (1818–83)   123
               Fathers and Children, 1862   125
            Tolstóy (1828–1910)   128
               Ánna Karénina, 1875–7   130
            Dostoévsky (1821–81)   134
               The Brothers Karamázov, 1879–80   137

   X Ibsen, Strindberg, and Hamsun   142
      Scandinavia in the nineteenth Century   142
            Ibsen (1828–1906)   144
               A Doll's House, 1879   146
            Strindberg (1849–1912)   149
               Miss Julie, 1888   152
            Hamsun (1859–1952)   154
               Hunger, 1890   157

  XI Chékhov and Górky   160
      Russia at the end of the Old Régime   160
            Chékhov (1860–1904)   162
               The Cherry Orchard, 1903–4   164
            Górky (1868–1936)   166
               The Lower Depths, 1902   169

 XII Zola, Fontane, and Proust   173
      France and Germany at the end of the
         nineteenth century   173
            Zola (1840–1902)   175
               Germinal, 1885   179
            Fontane (1819–98)   181
               Effi Briest, 1895   183
            Proust (1871–1922)   184
               Swann's Way, 1913   187

XIII   **Mann and Kafka**   192

The central powers before 1914   192

Modernist fiction   193

     Mann (1875–1955)   194

     Death in Venice, 1912   196

     Kafka (1883–1924)   199

     The Trial, 1914, 1925   202

XIV **Pirandello and Brecht**   206

The years of *l'entre deux guerres*   206

     Pirandello (1867–1936)   208

     Six Characters in Search of an Author, 1921   210

     Brecht (1898–1956)   212

     The Threepenny Opera, 1928   214

Appendix A: Translating Flaubert   217

**Appendix B: Quotations from original texts
     and selected translations**   223

**Appendix C: The form and pronunciation
     of Russian names**   238

**Appendix D: The value of money in the
     mid- to late-nineteenth century**   240

Copyright Acknowledgements   242

Index   243

Preface

This book, which aims to introduce thirty-two key works of European literature in translation to ordinary readers, with some account of their authors and their times, has not as far as I know been attempted in quite this way before. Books longer than this one can be written – and in most cases have been written several times over – about each of the works treated in it; and it is obviously not intended for specialists or advanced students of these works. But no one is a specialist in all thirty-two of them, and I make no apology for this attempt to enrich the lives of those who want to investigate for themselves some of the greatest European authors writing in languages other than English. What this book is not, and could not be even if I were that impossible multi-specialist, is a substitute for reading the thirty-two works I have chosen: the translations are there, nearly all of them in easily available, well-edited paperback editions: and my intention is simply to encourage people to get hold of them, to read them, and to enjoy them.

Acknowledgements

I am most grateful for help and advice generously given by Simon Barnard; Laurence and Paul Bunyan; Anne Cobby; Margaret Gaskell; Jackie Jones; Jean Khalfa; Roger Paulin; Adrian Poole; Kitty Stidworthy; Ella Westland; and the staff of Helston Public Library. Above all I owe thanks to Alison Sproston, Sub-Librarian of Trinity College, Cambridge, who has answered an unreasonable number of questions and requests with unfailing competence and good nature.

Abbreviations

...	ellipsis in the original
[...]	editorial ellipsis

Caveat Lector

No formula which expresses clearly the thought of one
generation can convey the same meaning to the generation
which follows
(Bishop B. F. Westcott)

A translation [. . .] cannot be the same thing in another
language, producing the same effect on the mind
(G. H. Lewes)

Translations are like women:
when they are beautiful they are not faithful, and when
they are faithful they are not beautiful
(sexist French saying)

Introduction

A European Canon

Readers and students of literature are familiar with the idea of a canon of great authors, those authors who are generally agreed to have produced work of exceptionally high quality that has been an unavoidable influence on their successors. Harold Bloom in his *The Western Canon* (London 1995) offered a list of twenty-six canonical authors from Dante to the present day, writing in Europe and the Americas; while in *Landmarks in English Literature* (Edinburgh 1998) I suggested that eighteen British authors up to the early twentieth century met these criteria, and that a further thirty-six were close runners-up. What is attempted here is something similar but not quite the same: the aim is to identify and discuss the key works of a canon of European authors, thirty-two of them, writing in languages other than English, from Dante to Brecht. It will be understood that canonical lists are essentially personal – my list, although it might be generally acceptable to many people, would not correspond in every particular with a list compiled by another critic – and that they are liable to change as new writers emerge and critical sensibilities are modified in each new generation of readers.

There is also the problem of which particular work (or works) of each canonical author should be chosen for discussion. While readers who already know something about a particular author would probably be pleased if the choice fell on something other than that author's best-known, most-anthologised work, this would not serve the best interests of those who know little or nothing about that author. To take particular examples from the first two chapters, there is no question but that the choice for Dante must be *The Divine Comedy*, and in any case there is always something more to be learned about this enormous work however well the reader knows it already. But for Petrarch, Villon, and Ronsard, most of whose poems were relatively short, different criteria must apply. Petrarch's *canzoniere* are not well known in detail, so any good example might be chosen; but in the cases of Villon and Ronsard, although their work is not generally familiar, there is one poem by each of them which is particularly well known and often quoted: the *Ballade des dames du temps jadis* (with the refrain *'Mais où sont les neiges d'antan?'*) by Villon, and the sonnet beginning *'Quand vous serez bien vieille, au soir, à la chandelle'* by Ronsard. Readers who are already well acquainted with Villon or Ronsard might prefer another choice for discussion here; but I have taken the view that these relatively well-known poems are intrinsically so good, and also so influential, that it would be wrong not to choose them, for the reason that the majority of readers know them, if at all, only by repute or by the few words that I have quoted here. Similar considerations apply to many of the choices, mostly of longer works, that I have made later in the book: for Voltaire, *Candide*; for Turgénev, *Fathers and Children*; for Ibsen, *A Doll's House*; and so on.

Despite all these difficulties, I believe that the attempt to identify the key works of European literature and to read and discuss them is worth while; to ignore them is to miss not only the mutual influence between them and English literature, but also contact with some of the most original thinkers of all time – including Dante, Montaigne, Rousseau, Goethe, Tolstóy, and Ibsen – together with the aesthetic and intellectual rewards offered by their major works. Although the canonical masterpieces in English – *Hamlet*, *Paradise Lost*, *Lyrical Ballads*, and so on – are reasonably familiar to serious readers of literature, the works of the great European masters are not so well known. This is not only because we are inclined to regard them as a less important part of our literary heritage than literature in English, but also because we are relatively unfamiliar with their national, literary, and historical contexts; and not least because they are written in foreign languages and must usually be read in translation.

Reading foreign literature in translation

The British are notoriously monoglot. Not many of us can read even one foreign language fluently; very few but language specialists can read two or three; and we are usually obliged to see the great works of European literature through the distorting glass of translation.

This is not to disparage translators, to whom we owe a great debt, but they themselves would be the first to acknowledge that translation is an imperfect medium for the transmission of even the simplest literature written in prose, and that it is especially inadequate for expressing the poetry of one language in terms of another.

Only the basic words for material things (such as English 'dog', French *chien*, German *Hund*) translate directly between languages without some distortion of meaning; and even simple words tend to have subsidiary senses that differ from language to language. For instance, the French noun *livre* is generally a 'book' in English (but not a 'book' in betting or a 'cheque book' or a 'match book', for which we look to *pari*, *cahier*, and *carnet* in French); while *livre* also means a 'pound', weight or sterling. Then in German there is *Buch*, but also *Teil*, *Band*, *Heft*, and *Block*. As for abstract nouns such as the French *amour* and German *Liebe*, the translator has to consider a number of English words with different shades of meaning, such as 'love', 'desire', 'passion', 'amorousness', 'affection', 'fondness', 'friendship', and 'liking'. These are simple examples which do not touch on the possible traps to be found in the homonyms, the synonyms and near-synonyms, and the strange idiomatic usages that lurk in every language.

There is also the question of which sort of English is preferred for the translation. A British reader, for instance, who is comfortable with a translation into British English might be put off by a translation into American English; and vice versa.

For poetry the situation is even worse. The rhythms, sounds, puns, nuances, and emotional charges of poetry simply cannot be translated from one language to another, and cannot easily be mimicked in the inevitably different modes of another language. One solution is to construct something like a parallel poem in English – preferably by a translator who is also a poet and can do it in verse – which gives as well as it can the meaning of the original, and suggests its devices and characteristics by means of comparable usages in English.[1] Nevertheless, as G. H. Lewes put it definitively in his biography of Goethe in 1855:

> A translation [of a poem] may be good *as* a translation, but it cannot be an adequate reproduction of the original. It may be a good poem; it may be a good imitation of another poem; it may be better than the original; but it

---

[1] The texts of some French, German, and Italian poems in Appendix B may be compared with the English versions given both there and in the relevant chapters of this book.

cannot be an adequate reproduction; it cannot be the same thing in another language, producing the same effect on the mind.[2]

Another way of translating poetry is to attempt a literal prose translation. But 'can there be any such thing?' asks Robert M. Durling, an able translator of Petrarch:

> Granted [he goes on] that one omits the expressiveness of rhyme and play of forms, granted that one often has to disentangle periodic, subordinating syntax into simpler, coordinating structure, there are three other principal difficulties. Petrarch is obscure, he is ambiguous, and he is refined and even precious in his diction. There are many passages where the meaning is doubtful [...] or disputed [...] Many of Petrarch's words bring with them a wealth of associations [...] derived from earlier use. These associations can almost never be conveyed in English, and sometimes there is no English word with even a reasonably similar denotation. (*Petrarch's Lyric Poems*, trs. by R. M. Durling, Harvard University Press 1976, pp. ix–x)

I would add that, having read all the translations that I could find of the poets treated in this book, most of the translations in verse (especially of French poetry) seem to me to lose more in verbal accuracy than they gain in verbal music. But, although I personally tend to prefer the prose versions because they are closer in meaning to the originals, I have included examples of both sorts of translation so that readers can make up their own minds about which they prefer.

There are other questions. For one, how should the translator represent in English the personal prose style of a foreign author? Should he attempt to follow his subject's sentence structure or should he simply ignore it? For another, is it better to read a translation of an early work made soon after the time of its composition, which will suggest the flavour of its period; or to have a modern translation in the English of our own time, which will avoid the misapprehensions that can result from reading older forms of our own language? – for there is something to be said for either course. Do we, in short, think that Dryden is right when he says of his translation of Juvenal, '[I] have endeavour'd to make him speak

---

[2] *The Life and Works of Goethe*, Everyman's Library, 1908 and reprints, p. 483. Lewes's pronouncement goes to the heart of the matter; but valuable discussions of the problems of translating poetry are to be found in the Introduction to David Luke's translation of Goethe's *Faust* Part One, Oxford World's Classics 1987, pp. xlix–lv; in ch. 1 of A. D. P. Briggs's *Púshkin: Eugene Onégin*, Cambridge University Press 1992; and in the Note on the Translation in James E. Falen's version of Púshkin's *Eugene Onégin*, Oxford World's Classics 1995, pp. xxv–xxx. The philosophy of translation is considered at greater length in George Steiner's erudite *After Babel*, rev. edn., Oxford University Press 1991.

that kind of English, which he wou'd have spoken had he liv'd in England, and had written to this Age'?[3]

A bleak, dismissive answer is given by the novelist and critic Vladímir Nabókov, who writes in the Foreword to his version of Lérmontov's short novel *A Hero of Our Time*,[4] (1840, translated 1958):

> This is the first English translation of Lérmontov's novel. The book has been paraphrased into English several times,[5] but never translated before. The experienced hack may find it quite easy to turn Lérmontov's Russian into slick English clichés by means of judicious omission, amplification, and levigation;[6] and he will tone down everything that might seem unfamiliar to the meek and imbecile reader visualised by his publisher. But the honest translator is faced with a different task.
>
> In the first place, we must dismiss, once and for all, the conventional notion that a translation 'should read smoothly', and 'should not sound like a translation' (to quote the would-be compliments, addressed to vague versions, by genteel reviewers who never have and never will read the original texts). In point of fact, any translation that does *not* sound like a translation is bound to be inexact upon inspection; while, on the other hand, the only virtue of a good translation is faithfulness and completeness. Whether it reads smoothly or not depends on the model, not on the mimic. (Mikhail Lérmontov, *A Hero of our Time*, trs. by Vladímir Nabókov, Oxford World's Classics 1984, pp. xii–xiii.)

An entirely different view is taken by Norman Denny, also a novelist, who translated Victor Hugo's long – he thinks over-long – novel *Les Misérables* (1862, translated 1976, now a Penguin Classic). He writes:

> It is now generally recognised that the translator's first concern must be with his author's *intention*; not with the words he uses or with the way he uses them, if they have a different impact when they are rendered too faithfully into English, but with what he is seeking to convey to the reader. [Denny then explains that in *Les Misérables* Hugo is frequently long-winded, extravagant in his use of words, sprawling and self-indulgent; that this adversely affects his readability; and that the translator can:] 'edit' – that is to say abridge, tone down the rhetoric, even delete where the passage in question is merely an elaboration of what has already been said.

---

[3] Juvenal, *From the Satires*, translated by John Dryden (1693), from the Dedication. (Dryden made the same remark, slightly amended, in the Dedication to his translation of Virgil, 1697.) A comparison of an eighteenth-century with a twentieth-century translation of *Don Quixote* can be made on pp. 39–40 and 228–9 below.

[4] See p. 87 below.

[5] Nabókov identifies five previous versions; there have been others.

[6] To 'levigate' is to make a smooth paste of something.

I have edited in this sense throughout the book, as a rule only to a minor degree, and never, I hope, so drastically as to be unfaithful to Hugo's intention. (Victor Hugo, *Les Misérables*, Penguin Classics 1982, pp. 11–12).

According to the ability and attitude of the translator, then, versions of the same foreign text can differ from each other in their degree of verbal accuracy, and in their capacity to convey the style and tone of the author, and the feeling of the place and period of the original work. To show how markedly translations of the same work can differ from each other in these ways, Appendix A, pp. 217–22, lgives a paragraph from the original French of Flaubert's *Madame Bovary* (1857), which was written with scrupulous attention to vocabulary and style, together with five different translations of it, and detailed criticism of short passages taken from these translations.

But, however able the translator, we have to accept the fact that translations of foreign works of literature are certain to be imperfect representations of the originals. There is little that we can do about this but be aware that it is so; and be thankful that we do have translations, however defective, rather than not being able to read the great works of European literature at all.

The availability of translations

Three series of translated classics published in Britain are outstanding: Everyman Classics, Oxford World's Classics and Penguin Classics. The Everyman and Oxford series were begun as pocket hardbacks before the First World War, and the Penguin series had its first big success in 1946 with the publication of E. V. Rieu's prose translation of Homer's *Odyssey* in paperback. Everyman changed from hardback to paperback in the 1960s, but has now returned to the more expensive hardback form, with mostly new, annotated translations. Oxford went on with its pretty and convenient little pocket hardbacks until the 1980s but then changed permanently to paperbacks (which have recently been changed again to a slightly larger format). Oxford has been careful to keep its classic texts up to date with the latest scholarship, and they are now generally the best translated and best edited, as well as usually the cheapest, of all. The Penguin Classics have always been in paperback,[7] but they too have now changed to a larger format; the translations are in many cases

[7] A few Penguin Classics were reissued in hardback in the 1960s.

older than those of the Oxford series, and lack Oxford's annotations and other apparatus, but new, annotated translations are being substituted for the old ones (some of the old ones being reprinted in the ultra-cheap Penguin Popular Classics series). Of these three series, Penguin has the widest coverage of titles: of the twenty-three pre-twentieth-century works examined in this book, Penguin currently has in print translations of nineteen (one in duplicate, and one as selections); Oxford has fourteen (one as selections), and Everyman eleven (two as selections).

There is also the great series of Methuen Drama (or Methuen World Classics), paperback collections of the works of over fifty major dramatists (some of them in several volumes) from Aeschylus to the present day.

How this book is arranged

The thirty-two works that I have chosen are gathered into fourteen chapters in approximately chronological order, those in each chapter having some connection with each other. Each chapter is prefaced by an introduction outlining the national, historical, and literary contexts in which the two or three works it contains were written. This is followed by a short biography of the author of each work; a cultural and critical discussion of the work itself; a note on the problems of translating it; and suggestions for further reading. As far as possible I have used and referred to the easily available paperback translations in the Penguin Classics and Oxford World's Classics series mentioned above.

I have not been consistent in using the English or the foreign forms of the titles of particular works, but have used whichever is more familiar, citing, for instance, *The Divine Comedy* and *Death in Venice*, but *Les Fleurs du mal* and *À la recherche du temps perdu*.

Quotations in the text, which are kept short, are mostly taken from English translations; and a selection of quotations in French, German and Italian, are given, with some additional English translations, in Appendix B.

Appendix C concerns the form and pronunciation of Russian names, which puzzle some readers; while Appendix D attempts to give the value in today's money of mid- to late-nineteenth-century pounds, francs, roubles, marks, and kroner, as an aid to interpreting aspects of nineteenth-century European fiction.

1 Dante and Petrarch

Italy in the early fourteenth century

Between the fall of the Western Roman Empire and unification in the nineteenth century, Italy was divided into a number of separate states, which from time to time changed hands, added territory and lost it. At the beginning of the fourteenth century the Kingdom of Naples occupied the southern half of the peninsula; then, under the nominal rule of the Holy Roman Emperor, came a central group of Papal States running north-eastwards from Rome; and a further fifteen states in the north of Italy. Of these last, the city-republic of Florence, where Dante, and Petrarch's father, were born, was one of the most prosperous and influential.

In the early fourteenth century a sensational cultural revolution, the Renaissance, was under way in northern and central Italy, especially in such centres as Florence. It was here that the poetry and thought of the classical world were in the process of being newly appreciated after the ignorance and neglect of the Dark Ages that had been inflicted upon western and southern Europe by successive Germanic invasions. It was a time of exhilarating intellectual and artistic discovery and advance, and it was taking place in the cultural centres of the same sunny, beautiful Italy in which the poets and thinkers of Rome had lived and thrived a thousand and more years before; it was a wonderful time to live and love and be a poet. As Wordsworth wrote of a later revolution, 'Bliss was it in that dawn to be alive,/But to be young was very heaven!'

But for Dante and Petrarch the Renaissance was not an uninterrupted bliss of sunshine and classical enchantment, even when they were young, for the beliefs of Western Christianity oversaw all moral and intellectual processes, while the political instability of the Italian city-states gave a dangerous edge to everyday living. Two great Italian saints at opposite ends of the religious spectrum, Francis of Assisi and Thomas Aquinas, had died as recently as 1226 and 1274; while the spiritual authority of the Church was absolute everywhere. To a degree that is almost impossible for us to comprehend today when the sea of faith has retreated nearly out of sight, the religious beliefs of Christianity and the Catholic Church were central and inescapable elements in everyone's lives, inner as well as outer.

The monolithic stability of the Catholic faith was not evident in the political institutions of the quasi-independent states of the north. The people there were mostly indigenous Italians, but there was also an Italian-speaking upper class of German-Gothic descent which was divided into two main political parties, the Ghibellines (who believed in autocracy) and the Guelphs (who preferred con-stitutional government). The two parties were in frequent conflict, sometimes one seizing power in a city, sometimes the other. In Florence the conflict had been running since 1215; the Ghibellines gained the upper hand in 1248, the Guelphs in 1258, the Ghibel-lines again in 1260. The Guelphs finally chased the Ghibellines out and took control of the city in 1267; but later still they themselves were to split into two factions, the Whites and the Blacks, who jockeyed for power in their turn. It could be a matter of life and death whether you were, so to speak, a Montagu or a Capulet.

Neither was Rome itself immune to change. Following desperate factional strife there the Papacy removed to Avignon from 1309 to 1377, leaving the eternal city half in ruins and bereft of its authority.

Dante Alighieri, 1265–1321

Dante was born in 1265 to a respectable Guelph merchant family, two years before the final expulsion of the Ghibellines. A defining moment of his life occurred at the age of nine, in 1274, when his father took him to a party at the house of Folco Portinari, and he met the Portinaris' daughter Beatrice, herself aged only eight. He fell in love with her on the spot, but what seems to have happened to him was something more extraordinary than simply falling in love: the vision of Beatrice, a pretty little girl in a red dress, appeared to Dante as a vision of the wonder and goodness of God, activating in him a transcendental experience that permanently changed his perception of creation and of his own place in it.[1] He saw her not merely as a human being whom he could idolise, but as a 'God-bearing image', an aspect of the divine that was to inspire him for the rest of his spiritual life. What Beatrice thought about it we do not know; Dante said later that she mocked and rebuffed him. At any rate, she married a banker in 1287, and died a widow in 1290, when she was twenty-four and Dante was twenty-five. He related the story of his passion in *La vita nuova*, written in about 1292.

Dante, who had been orphaned when he was twelve, was acting as head of his house by the age of eighteen; and for some years he engaged in a course of study that was to immerse him in both ancient classical literature and modern scholastic philosophy. In 1289, aged twenty-four, he served in the cavalry of a Florentine army that beat the Ghibellines at the battle of Campedino. In 1298, when he had joined a Merchant Guild and was taking a part in the administration of the city, he married Gemma Donati. Two years later he was elected to City office, but at the same time a feud broke out between the White and Black factions of the Florentine Guelphs. Sent on an embassy to Rome in 1301, Dante and his companions – who were Whites – were accused by the Black faction in Florence of fraud and corruption; and early in 1302 Dante was heavily fined and exiled for life, not for any real wrongdoing but for the crime of belonging to the wrong faction. Dante never returned to Florence or saw his wife again, for the Donatis were Blacks, and Gemma stayed behind to bring up the children. Dante was then thirty-six.

For the next twenty years Dante roamed all over Italy, writing poetry and tracts and moving on, for much of the time in great poverty. His two sons were exiled in their turn for being his children, and joined him in 1314. In 1317 he ended his wanderings in Ravenna, where he died in 1321, at the age of fifty-six.

Although Dante's other late works are of interest to specialists, it is for *The Divine Comedy* that he is celebrated as one of the greatest and most influential poets of all time. This towering religious epic – the first major work of literature by an Italian author written in his own vigorous, everyday language – which was begun in about 1307

---

[1] Most mystics, and many ordinary people, have reported having such transcendental experiences. As to their connection with falling in love, see Tolstoy's *Anna Karénina* (which is discussed in ch. IX below), pt IV, ch. 15, where Lévin, whom Kitty has just accepted as her fiancé, sees the ordinary world in an extraordinary light in the paragraph beginning: 'And what he then saw he never saw again.'

and which occupied Dante for most of the rest of his life, is an allegory of man's spiritual journey from worldly sin through redemption to ultimate salvation.

The Divine Comedy, 1307–21

The Divine Comedy,[2] Dante's masterwork, is the story of a journey that takes the poet from the Hell of human sinfulness (*Inferno*), through the Purgatory of cleansing redemption (*Purgatorio*), to the Heaven of union with the divinity (*Paradiso*). The story begins when the narrator is thirty-five (at the mid-point of a man's three-score years and ten), which in Dante's case was the year 1300, and before rather than after his expulsion from Florence. Having lost his way, the narrator – whom it will be convenient to call 'Dante' – finds himself in a 'dark wood' of sin, where he catches sight of a sunlit mountain which he must climb from the 'right road'. Three beasts, a leopard, a lion and a wolf (traditionally believed to be images of the sins of lust, pride, and avarice[3]), leap suddenly out of the wood to confront and prevent him from doing so. The leopard and the lion pass on, but the wolf is still threatening Dante when a human form crosses his path, which turns out to be the shade of Virgil, the greatest of pagan poets. Having acknowledged Virgil as his master, Dante is told that he must take another road to escape from the dark wood, and that he should follow his new-found guide through deepest Hell to reach the gates of Purgatory.

So the great journey begins:

> In the middle of the journey of our life I came to myself within a dark wood where the straight way was lost. Ah, how hard a thing it is to tell of that wood, savage and harsh and dense, the thought of which renews my fear! So bitter is it that death is hardly more. But to give account of the good which I found there I will tell of the other things I noted there.[4]

Virgil the guide, seen as the central figure in classical art, represents what is finest in human intelligence and understanding; he is the one who can help the traveller to grasp his sinful nature and to find the strength to overcome it. The path they take leads

---

[2] 'Comedy' (Italian *commèdia*) simply meant a story that was not a tragedy; the word did not imply something amusing or satirical.

[3] Mark Musa prefers to identify them with fraud, violence, and lust respectively (*The Divine Comedy: Inferno*, trs. by Mark Musa, Penguin Classics 1984, p. 73).

[4] Prose translation of *Inferno* I. 1–9 by John D. Sinclair, Oxford University Press 1939. The original Italian of this passage, and four verse translations of it, are given in Appendix B, pp. 223–4 below.

first to Hell, the place where the souls of those guilty but unrepentant of mortal sin go after death. There the damned remain without hope, in eternal torment, in a freezing pit below the surface of the earth in the shape of an inverted cone, lodged in seven circles or galleries according to the wickedness of their crimes.

After Hell the travellers come to Purgatory, a conical mountain rising up at the opposite side of the earth's surface from Hell, which is the temporary home of the souls of sinners who have repented. There is first an ante-purgatory leading up to Peter's Gate, then seven cornices or ledges, each appropriate to one of the seven deadly sins. Here the souls, having repented, can expect eventual salvation, but first they must undergo the punishment appropriate to the sins committed during their lives.

Pagan art and understanding can go only so far on the Christian path to God so, part of the way through Purgatory, Virgil has to leave Dante in the care of another and higher guide. This guide is 'the God-bearing image', a reawakening of the great transcendental experience of Dante's life, which now appears as his redeemer in the form of Beatrice. Having rebuked Dante for his shortcomings, Beatrice leads him upwards from the top of Mount Purgatory through ten successive Heavens in which dwell the souls of the saved under the signs of the Moon, the six Planets (including the Sun), the Fixed Stars, and the Prime Mover; until finally they attain the Empyrean, the fiery Heaven, where Dante and Beatrice reach their joint apotheosis in the presence of God.

This bare outline of the story of the *Comedy* does not of course give any idea of the fascinating detail and intellectual attraction of Dante's extraordinary poem; Dante has to be read extensively if justice is to be done to the inspiration of his vision and the mastery of his story-telling. Fortunately there are several good translations of the whole and – just as important – valuable commentaries to elucidate the obscurities resulting from our remoteness from Dante and his intellectual world; though even the best translations (see below) cannot convey the beauty and power of Dante's language and versification.

Here is a passage from Canto V of *Inferno* – less obviously symbolic than the first extract – in the blank verse translation by Tom Phillips. Virgil and Dante have passed down into the second circle of Hell where the lustful are punished, and here Dante becomes particularly interested in the shades of Francesca and her brother-in-law Paolo. The two of them were caught in bed in

1290 (when Dante was twenty-five) and killed by her husband, Paolo's elder brother. Now Dante asks Francesca how it was that they had succumbed to temptation, and she explains:

> One day for our amusement we began
> to read the tale of Lancelot, how love
> had made him prisoner. We were alone,
> without the least suspicion in our minds:
> but more and more our eyes were forced to meet,
> our faces to turn pale by what we read.
> One passage in particular became
> the source of our defeat: when we read how
> the infatuated lover saw the smile
> he'd longed to see and kissed it, this man here
> who never shall be parted from my side,
> all trembling as he did it, kissed my mouth.
> The book was Gallehault,[5] a go-between
> and he who wrote it played that role for us.
> That day we read no further word of it.[6]

Francesca is presented in this Canto as being superficially sympathetic, but hard and disingenuous underneath, hostile to the unhappy shade of Paolo who is eternally coupled with her; and it is implied that it was she (as it was Guinevere in the story, and before her Eve) who initiated their sin by being the tempter, even though it was Paolo who made the first move. And because Francesca seeks to exculpate herself by blaming the overwhelming power of courtly love, Dante is both pointing out its seductive dangers and reminding us that we have a choice, that we do not have to succumb to temptation.

Another reason why it is worth reading *The Divine Comedy*, or substantial parts of it, is that Dante's work is one of the two great nodes or meeting points in the development of Western literature (the other one being Shakespeare); the points at which the influences of the writers of the past are drawn together in the work of one great writer, and then spread out from his work to influence the writers who are to come.

---

[5] Gallehault (or Galehot or Galehaut) was the intermediary between Lancelot and Guinevere in a French version of the Arthurian legend, and his name came to stand for a pander or go-between.

[6] *Inferno* V. 127–38, trs. by Tom Phillips (1985); in *A TV Dante*, Channel 4 Television Publication 1990, p. [34]. The Italian text of this passage (p. 225 below), gives some idea of the brilliance and concise clarity of Dante's exposition.

Translations

The Divine Comedy was written in Italian *terza rima*, groups[7] of three five-stress (decasyllabic) lines of which the first and the third rhyme with each other, and the second rhymes with the first and third of the next group, and so on: *aba/bcb/cdc/* . . . [8] This is a metre that takes advantage of the wealth of rhymes available in Italian, and in which the rhyme-scheme leads the reader on from group to group.

The most easily available translations are in two three-volume Penguin Classics sets, and a single-volume translation in the Oxford World's Classics. The older Penguin set, translated by Dorothy L. Sayers (published 1949–62), mimics Dante's *terza rima* in English, complete with rhymes; the more recent one, by Mark Musa (1971–84), is in five-stress blank verse divided into three-line groups. Musa benefits by not having to search frantically for English rhymes, while Sayers, I feel, has a livelier metrical sense; however, neither of them are primarily poets and it does show. The World's Classics version (1980) is translated by C. J. Sisson in the same rhymeless arrangement as Musa's translation but, although Sisson was a published poet, his version is not notably more inspiring than the others. In the end, which of these translations one prefers is a matter of personal taste.[9] All three are equipped with the extensive introductions, commentaries, maps and notes that are essential if the non-specialist reader wants to reach a fuller understanding of Dante and his poem.

There is an earlier and even better translation of the *Divine Comedy* into English *terza rima* by the poet Laurence Binyon; it was originally published 1933–43, but is no longer in print.

H. F. Carey's early-nineteenth-century version in Miltonic blank verse has a strength and authority which is lacking from most modern translations – for Milton was the poet who, after Dante, was most certain that he could not be wrong – and it may suit those who enjoy its slightly archaic usages; second-hand copies can usually be found.

There is a modern blank-verse translation by Tom Phillips (see p. 13 above), from which an extract was shown on Channel 4 as

---

[7] I call the three-line units 'groups' rather than 'stanzas' because they are often printed without white lines between them; they are also known as 'tercets'.

[8] In this system the rhyme first encountered is labelled *a*, the second *b*, the third *c*, and so on.

[9] For a sample of each see pp. 223–4 below.

A TV Dante in 1990, with stimulating performances by Bob Peck and Sir John Gielgud and much computerised TV magic.

Finally, the reader who wants to get closest to the literal meaning of Dante's poem should use the three-volume parallel-text prose translation, quoted above, by John D. Sinclair (Oxford University Press 1939–46 and later editions).

Petrarch (Francesco Petrarca), 1304–74

Petrarch's father, a notary called Petracco, was exiled from Florence a few months after Dante in 1302, and moved forty miles south-east to Arezzo; Petrarch was born there two years later. While he was still a boy the family moved on, first to Pisa, and finally (when Petrarch was eight) to Carpentras near Avignon, which from 1309 had been the new headquarters of the Papacy. From then until shortly after Petrarch's death, when the Pope moved back to Rome, Avignon was the diplomatic and intellectual centre of the Renaissance world, and a magnet for men of talent and ambition. Here Petrarch grew up, studying the classics at home and at the University of Bologna, and living as a young man in an atmosphere of political intrigue and classical learning; and while he came to detest the corruption of the Papal court, he embraced the classics with passionate devotion.

Dante was a supremely gifted poet who was very well read in classical literature and philosophy; but Petrarch was by nature and inclination just as much a scholar and critic of classical literature as he was a poet. He was enthralled by the outlook and style of the great writers of Augustan Rome, especially Virgil and Cicero; and he plunged with a scholar's dedicated enthusiasm into the recovery and restoration of classical texts that were then known only in disorganised fragments. His notable works of scholarship included the rediscovery of Cicero's letters to Atticus, and of a considerable part of Livy's history of Rome, for which his glosses and notes are still of interest to classical scholars. As his reputation grew, so did his influence, and he travelled as a celebrity to universities and courts in France, Flanders, and Germany; finally achieving his keen ambition to be crowned Poet Laureate in Rome in 1341. Latterly he was able to live in a country retreat outside Avignon in Vaucluse; but in 1353 he returned at last to northern Italy, where he lived successively in Milan, Venice, Pavia, and Padua until his death just before his seventieth birthday in Arquà, south of Padua, in 1374.

Petrarch made a note in his favourite manuscript of Virgil that, in 1327, he caught sight of a woman called Laura in the church of St Clare in Avignon. Nothing is known of her except Petrarch's claim that he fell deeply in love with her, that she died of plague in 1348, and that his pure love for her remained constant though unfulfilled for the rest of his life. There is in fact no certainty that Laura ever actually existed, although she probably did. Petrarch's love for her was idealised from the first, and it became increasingly spiritual as the years passed, but there is no indication that seeing her induced in him the sort of transcendental awakening that I suggested Dante experienced when he met Beatrice.

Whatever sort of love it was, it inspired Petrarch to write a large number of love lyrics, the majority of which were sonnets, the form which was to become archetypal in Renaissance (and later) love poetry. The poetry of the Italian Renaissance, and of Petrarch in particular, had a great and lasting effect on the development of poetry elsewhere, especially in France and England. Petrarch was only forty years older than Chaucer (*c.* 1345–1400), who was certainly aware of what he had written; and Chaucer influenced in turn those English poets of the sixteenth century who, in their love poems and sonnet sequences, were the conscious heirs of the Italian Renaissance: Wyatt, Surrey, Sidney, Spenser, and Shakespeare.

Love Lyrics, 1327–58

Petrarch's *Vernacular Fragments* (*Canzoniere*, *Rime sparse*, or *Rerum vulgarum fragmenta*) is a collection of 366 poems, ranging from *canzoni* of a hundred or more lines down to fourteen-line sonnets and even shorter 'madrigals'. Petrarch did not invent the sonnet form, but he brought it to a height of perfection that ensured its survival.

The Italian sonnet, as it came to be known, was divided into two unequal groups of rhyming five-stress lines, the eight-line 'octave' and the six-line 'sestet'. The octave was rhymed in a scheme such as *abba abba*, while the sestet might be rhymed *cdc dcd*; and there was some change of sense or direction between the octave and the sestet.

Although their chief inspiration can be traced back to Petrarch, the great majority of sonnets written in English from the sixteenth century to the nineteenth end with a rhyming couplet, which gives them a flourish or punch lacking in their Italian model; and they do not always have a break between the octave and the sestet. Here, however, is a translation from the Italian of a sonnet

by Dante's friend Guido Cavalcanti, which mimics the Italian form
in English:

> Who is she coming, whom all gaze upon,
> Who makes the air all tremulous with light,
> And at whose side is Love himself? that none
> Dare speak, but each man's sighs are infinite.
> Ah me! how she looks round from left to right,
> Let Love discourse: I may not speak thereon.
> Lady she seems of such high benison
> As makes all others graceless in men's sight.
> The honour which is hers cannot be said;
> To whom are subject all things virtuous,
> While all things beauteous own her deity.
> Ne'er was the mind of man so nobly led,
> Nor yet was such redemption granted us
> That we should ever know her perfectly.
> ('A Rapture Concerning His Lady', trs. by D. G. Rosetti)

Here the rhyme scheme is *abab baab cde cde*; and the question
which is pondered in the octave is answered in the sestet.

There have been similar attempts to translate Petrarch's sonnets
into English, but they inevitably diminish the fire of his original
Italian, and a fine translation into English prose of one of the
sonnets about Laura may give a better sense of what the poet was
attempting, allowing Petrarch's pace and excitement to burst
through the barrier of language:

> [octave]
> Blessed be the day and the month and the year and the season and the time
> and the hour and the instant and the beautiful country-side and the place
> where I was struck by the two lovely eyes that have bound me;
> and blessed be the first sweet trouble I felt on being made one with Love, and
> the bow and the arrows that pierced me, and the wounds that reach my
> heart!
> [sestet]
> Blessed be the many words I have scattered calling the name of my lady, and
> the sighs and the tears and the desire;
> and blessed be all the pages where I gain fame for her, and my thoughts,
> which are only of her, so that no other has part in them!
> (*Vernacular Fragments* 61, trs. by Robert M. Durling; the original
> Italian text, and a verse translation, are given in Appendix B,
> pp. 225–6 below)

Whether or not Laura really existed, the theme of Petrarch's love
poems is the position and attitude of the poet as lover; and what is

original about them is not the theme but its treatment. Love poetry had always been about such things as love at first sight, the lover's lovesickness and frustration, his obsession with the image of the lady, her virtue, her early death, and so on. Petrarch's originality lay in the fresh intensity of his treatment of these well-worn subjects; in the range and flexibility of the language and form of the verse; and in his making a collection of his love poems in a sequence that follows the psychological progress of the lover.

Translations

Though Petrarch has had many imitators among the English poets, there are few translations of his whole collection of love lyrics. As has been suggested above, Robert M. Durling's prose translation (Harvard University Press, 1976) offers a scholarly but vivid entry into Petrarch's world; it has the Italian text of the poems on the right-hand pages, the translations opposite them on the left, and an admirable Introduction to Petrarch's life and work. The Oxford World's Classics translation of *Selections from the Canzoniere and Other Works* by Mark Musa (1985) gives the poems in five-stress blank-verse.

Further reading

The Dante literature is huge, but the most accessible short biographies and sets of explanatory notes are in the two three-volume Penguin translations by Dorothy L. Sayers and Mark Musa mentioned above. See also *The Cambridge Companion to Dante*, Cambridge University Press 1993; and Robin Kirkpatrick, *Dante: The Divine Comedy*, Cambridge University Press 1987.

For Petrarch (who also has an enormous literature) the standard short biography is E. H. Wilkins, *Life of Petrarch*, Chicago and London 1961. Nicholas Mann's *Petrarch*, Oxford University Press 1984, is a good short introduction to the work; see also Robert M. Durling's Introduction to the translation recommended above.

II Villon, Ronsard, and Montaigne

France from the late Middle Ages to the Renaissance

In a series of short, well-fought campaigns in 1449–53, the French brought the Hundred Years' War to a brisk conclusion by defeating the English in battle and regaining first the huge area of northern France that had been taken by Henry V, and then Gascony, parts of which had been an English possession since the twelfth century; only Calais and the Channel Islands were kept by the English, and Calais was to be regained just over a hundred years later. This was the beginning of the consolidation of the kingdom of France. It was to take another two centuries before most of the semi-autonomous French-speaking regions were brought under central control, but the modern map of France was already within sight.

The end of a long war could leave a country, however encouraged by victory, in political and economic disarray, and with its people suffering from want and disease. Since the coming of the Black Death to France in 1347, moreover, plague and recurrent famine had combined with the endemic warfare to reduce the population of France from about seventeen million to about twelve million, a catastrophe of epic proportions; and although the trend was about to be reversed and the population and the economy were shortly to enter a period of growth, this fact was not yet known to those whose only memories were of generations of spoliation and early death. Such was the feudal, still medieval, France of the mid-fifteenth century in which Villon was born and lived his life. The country was politically unstable, with great magnates and their followers vying with the Crown for control of their fiefs; the Church was notably corrupt, yet indispensable at a time when religious belief touched on every aspect of life, and especially for intercession in times of trouble; and no rank or group of people felt really secure in its way of life.

Ronsard and Montaigne, on the other hand, born half a century or more after Villon's death, found themselves in a France that had recovered from these disasters, and was already well on its way to becoming a major European power. More than this, France's writers – with the encouragement of the advent of printing (which had reached France in 1470) and of increasing literacy – were in the process of throwing out the tired traditions of medieval thought and art, and of replacing them with the exciting new culture of the Renaissance. But, although sixteenth-century France was no longer ravaged by foreign wars, and plague and famine had decreased, its internal organisation was disrupted in a different way by the inflation and unemployment that resulted from the rapidly increasing population. There were also the effects of the Reformation: disputes between French Catholics and Protestants, under a weak and equivocal monarchy, flared up in the second half of the century into several episodes of all-out civil war. Despite these difficulties, writers of the first rank emerged during the sixteenth century – including Rabelais as well as Ronsard and Montaigne – and were able to work without persecution or serious interruption.

Metre and sound in French verse[1]

Before considering Villon's and Ronsard's poems, it should be explained that French poetry – and we shall be looking at a good deal of it in the course of this book – is technically different from most English (and much German and Russian) poetry in that its metre is based, not on patterns of stressed and unstressed syllables, but on the numbers of syllables in the lines.[2] This is because multisyllabic words in French are spoken without much inherent stress, so that where in English we say *frácture* with stress on the first syllable and *insénsible* with stress on the second, the French say *fracture* and *insensible* with the syllables more or less equally stressed (although, of course, rhetorical stress may be used to emphasise a word or phrase in the course of speaking a sentence in French). There is something called *accent* both in spoken French and in French verse, but it is not what we mean by stress; *accents*

---

[1] This section may be compared with the description of English versification in my *Landmarks in English Literature*, Edinburgh University Press 1998, pp. 70–81.

[2] Not that poets writing in stressed languages were necessarily indifferent to syllable-counts, but that patterns of stress were their prime metrical device.

are points within the line that are marked by some change in pitch or vowel-sound, and which derive from its semantic and grammatical structure.

Thus, we refer to English *six-stress* (or *hexameter*), *five-stress* (or *pentameter*), and *four-stress* (or *tetrameter*) lines, but of French *alexandrine* (= twelve-syllable), *decasyllabic*, and *octosyllabic* lines. Syllable counts, which were strictly observed in French verse until the later nineteenth century, and by many twentieth-century French poets as well, were subject to elaborate rules governing the counting of mute and semi-mute *es* and the counting of separate vowels in diphthongs; generally speaking, *es* that are mute in spoken French are counted as syllables in a line of verse if they precede a consonant. Thus in the first two lines of the Villon *ballade* quoted below in modernised spelling (*Dites-moi où, n'en quel pays, / Est Flora, la belle Romaine,*) eight syllables are achieved in each line by counting two syllables each for the words *Dites*, *pays*, and *belle* (but two, not three, for *Romaine*). There would probably be *accents*, in the French sense, on *où*, *pays*, and *Romaine*.

The rhythm of French lines, especially *alexandrines* and *decasyllabics*, is generally assisted by the insertion of a *caesura* – a slight pause, or sometimes a grammatical accent – in the middle, dividing them into two halves; similarly the end of the line – which is normally a rhyme word – also produces a slight pause or variation.

The great majority of French classical poetry was rhymed, for there was no tradition of blank verse as there was in English poetry. French rhymes differ from English rhymes, again because of the lack of inherent stress in French words. An English rhyme must include a stressed syllable plus any sounds that follow it, whereas a French one consists of sounds alone; and again there were rules governing what did and did not constitute acceptable rhymes in French verse. It is worth mentioning one possible source of confusion: in English verse a 'masculine rhyme' is one that ends with the stressed syllable (explóde/corróde), and a 'feminine rhyme' is one that ends with an unstressed syllable (explósive/corrósive), but in French verse a rhyme is called 'feminine' when it ends with a mute syllable (*la mère/amère*), and 'masculine' when it does not (*la mer/amer*); and it was considered wrong to pair a feminine with a masculine rhyme in French even though they might sound exactly the same, as in the masculine/feminine pair *la mer/ amère*.

François Villon, 1431–1463+

Villon was born in the year that Joan of Arc was burned to death by the English and their French collaborators. The son of poor parents, Villon was adopted by a Parisian priest called Guillaume de Villon, from whom he took his name. He had the best education that was available, graduating BA from the University of Paris in 1449, and becoming MA in 1451 when he was twenty-one, shortly before the end of the Hundred Years' War. But although he was now well qualified for an honourable career in the law or the Church, his life was in fact to take a very different course: a life of violence, theft, and probably pimping for which there is no obvious explanation.

He himself tells us of his riotous behaviour in the years immediately after 1451, but it is in surviving legal and other documents that there is the clearest evidence of his wrongdoing. In 1455 he killed a priest in a quarrel and fled the capital, but his plea of self-defence was accepted and he was acquitted. The next year he took part in a robbery, ran away from Paris again, and wandered about France for four years. He is next heard of in prison in the Loire district under sentence of death, from which he was released in an amnesty of 1461. Back in Paris he was arrested again as one of a gang which had robbed the Collège de Navarre. Freed on a promise to return his proceeds from the robbery, he was imprisoned yet again in 1463, when he was thirty-two, for being involved in street fighting. This time the authorities in the capital appear to have had enough of him, and he was sentenced to death a second time; but he was reprieved once more and banished from Paris for ten years instead. At this point the record comes abruptly to an end, and nothing more at all is heard or known of him. Considering his propensity for getting into trouble bad enough to be recorded, and that the flow of his verse ceased at the same time, it seems unlikely that he lived for long after 1463.

Poems, 1456–61

Villon's output of poetry was not great – less than 3,400 short lines in all – and not all of it was excellent; but at its best it was poetry of the very highest quality. There is first the relatively unimportant *Lais*, written just after the robbery of 1456, a tongue-in-cheek testament of 320 lines in which ridiculous bequests are made to his friends and acquaintances. Next, after the amnesty of 1461, comes his most substantial work, *Le Testament*, which is ostensibly another mock will in verse like the *Lais* but which far exceeds its predecessor in length (2,023 lines), emotional power, and technical skill; its eight-line stanzas are occasionally interrupted by short poems in *ballade* (see below) and other forms. In *Le Testament* Villon considers the very real possibility that his own death is imminent, and reviews the waste and suffering of his short life with regret and some self-pity. Finally there is a group of twenty-seven miscellaneous short poems totalling just over 1,000 lines, eleven of them written in thieves' slang, of which a small handful are outstandingly good.

Here we shall look first at a lyric in *ballade* form from *Le Testament*, and then at one of the best of the miscellaneous *ballades*. The usual *ballade*, which was not invented by Villon although he was certainly one of its most skilful practitioners, had three stanzas of eight octosyllabic lines, rhyming *ababbcbc*, and with an optional half stanza, or *envoi*, to end with; and the last line of the first stanza was repeated as a refrain at the end of each of the others.[3] (There were several variants of the *ballade*, and other conventional poetic forms such as the *rondeau*, the *villanelle*, and the sonnet, which were commonly used by French poets in the late Middle Ages and early Renaissance.)

The famous *Ballade des dames du temps jadis* ('The Ballade of the Ladies of Bygone Days', the one that asks where the beauty, love and heroism of the past have gone, and which has as its refrain the striking image *Mais où sont les neiges d'antan?* ['But where are last year's snows?']) presents a particular difficulty because Villon gives his octosyllabic lines an enchanting lilt which is untranslatable. Even if you can't understand the French words, you can probably hear their rueful music simply by saying this first stanza out aloud, pronouncing the internal *es* that would not be sounded in modern French to achieve eight syllables per line, and half-pronouncing the final *es* that would normally be mute (I have modernised the spelling; *es* that would nowadays be mute in ordinary speech but which are sounded in the poem are marked *ë*):

> *Ditës-moi où, n'en quel paÿs,*
> *Est Flora, la bellë Romaine,*
> *Archipiadès ne Thaïs,*
> *Qui fut sa cousinë germaine,*

---

[3] See the complete *ballade* by Villon given on p. 226.

> *Echo parlant quand bruit on mène*
> *Dessus rivière ou sur étang,*
> *Qui beauté eut trop plus q'humaine.*
> *Mais où sont les neigës d'antan?*

This is the whole poem in a modern prose translation:[4]

Tell me where, in what land, is Flora, the beauty of Rome, Archipiades[5] or Thaïs so much like her, Echo speaking when a noise is made over river or lake, whose beauty was more than human. But where are last year's snows? Where is the very wise Heloïse, for whom Peter Abelard at St Denis was castrated and made a monk? For his love he suffered this torment. Similarly, where is the queen who ordered Buridan to be thrown into the Seine in a sack? But where are last year's snows?

Queen Blanche, white as a lily, who sang with a siren's voice, Bertha Flatfoot, Beatrice, Alice, Arambourg who held the Maine, and Joan the brave maid of Lorraine whom the English burned at Rouen. Where are they, where, sovereign Virgin? But where are last year's snows?

Prince, do not ask this week, or this year, where they have gone, lest I bring you back to you this refrain: But where are last year's snows?[6]

But Villon's mood in this *ballade* is not simply one of nostalgic melancholy for the lost beauties of classical times, for in the second stanza he turns unsentimentally to relatively recent examples of the cruelty that can be caused by love, and in the third to recalling heroic women, including Joan of Arc (martyred within living memory) and the Virgin Mary, greatest of all women. Finally the *envoi*, or conclusion, addressed to an unnamed Prince, reiterates that there is in fact no answer to the question: the beauty, love, and glory of the past are gone forever, as irrecoverably as is last year's snow. So although its verbal beauty has often caused it to be sentimentalised, this much-anthologised *ballade* is not a sentimental poem, but is resolutely clear-eyed.

More obviously unsentimental is Villon's decasyllabic *Ballade des pendus* ('The Ballade of the Hanged Men'), in which, speaking as the bones of a corpse as it hangs on a gibbet alongside four or five other unfortunates, he appeals to those still living for sympathy and

---

[4] The original French text of this and the following poem is given on pp. 226–7 below, together with D. G. Rosetti's verse translation of the *Ballade des dames du temps jadis*.

[5] 'Archipiades' was thought in the Middle Ages to have been the name of a beautiful woman, but in fact the word was a corruption of 'Alcibiades', the Greek soldier.

[6] Translated by John Fox in *Villon: Poems*, Grant and Cutler, London 1984, pp. 47–8.

tolerance, and for their intercession with God for absolution of the dead men's sins (the refrain is *Mais priez Dieu que tous nous vueille absouldre* ['But pray to God that he will absolve us all']). This is the first stanza:

> Brother men who live after us, do not have your hearts hardened against us, for if you have pity on us, God will the sooner have mercy on you. You can see us strung up here, five or six of us. As for the flesh which we fed only too well, for a long time now it has been eaten up and rotten, and we, the bones, are turning to ashes and dust. Let no-one mock our plight, but pray to God that he will absolve us all.[7]

The visual impact of this poem is striking, as it describes a scene that was grimly familiar to fifteenth-century Parisians. It is also a poem of poignant suffering as the speaker implores the living, in their Christian charity, to help him and his fellows to find God's mercy and forgiveness, sinners though they are; and we can hear Villon's own despair in the pathos of its plea, written as it may well have been when he himself was under sentence of death.

Translations

Of all the works considered in this book, the *Poems* of Villon and of Ronsard are the least well served by easily available translations, there being no versions of either currently available in Penguin Classics,[8] Oxford World's Classics, or Everyman Classics. However, there is a good prose translation of selections from Villon by John Fox in Grant and Cutler's Critical Guides to French Texts: *Villon: Poems*, 1984.

Pierre de Ronsard, 1524–85

Ronsard, unlike Villon, was a gentleman and a courtier, known for his good looks, good manners, learning, and intelligence. Born in a small château near Vendôme on the Loire, he was taken to the court of François I by his father (a landowner and man of letters) while he was still a child. There he became a page, first to the Dauphin (who died when Ronsard was eleven years old), and then to the Duc d'Orléans who eventually succeeded to the throne in 1547 as Henri II. Meanwhile Ronsard attended the court of James

---

[7] Translated by John Fox in *Villon: Poems*, p. 96. The French text is given on p. 227 below.

[8] There was a selected *Villon* in Penguin Classics, but it is now out of print.

V of Scotland, returned to France in 1540, and made a second journey abroad, to the Scottish and English courts. Then, when he was in his mid-twenties, an illness left him partially deaf, and he decided in 1548–9 to give up his life at court and settle down to write.

He had indeed written verse from an early age, but now – together with half-a-dozen fellow-writers of like mind who proclaimed themselves the *Pléiade*, after the seven stars of the Pleiades – Ronsard began the serious work that was to make him France's greatest pre-nineteenth-century poet. Based in Paris, but with regular visits to the country, he was inspired at first by classical models, especially the Odes of Pindar from 1550 to 1553, and the work of Anacreon, Horace, and Catullus from 1554 to 1560. Then followed a variety of court and public poetry from 1560 to 1574; and finally, in the last decade of his life, from 1574 to 1585, he wrote mostly lyric poems, notably the superb sequence of Pertrarchan *Sonets pour Hélène*.

Poems, 1550–85

For all its verbal magic, the greater part of Ronsard's considerable output of poetry is inevitably obscure to us today, coming as it does from an intellectual world that has completely passed away: a world of philosophical, scientific, religious, and political beliefs and ideas and preoccupations in which Ronsard lived and wrote, but which most of us cannot now recapture, and which even specialists in the period can find difficult. This leads us to the later poems that have a timeless quality, especially the amorous sonnets of *c*.1574 addressed to Hélène de Surgères, Maid of Honour to Catherine de' Medici (the dowager Queen of Henri II). Perhaps the finest – and certainly the most anthologised – of these lovely poems is *Quand vous serez bien vieille*.

For reasons that will be explained, this is a particularly difficult poem to translate, so we will start with the French text. (Not all readers will understand the French, but there are certain phrases in it which have to be referred to and, as with the Villon, it is satisfying to say the poem aloud; *e*s that would nowadays be mute in ordinary speech but which are sounded in the poem are marked *ë*.)

> *Quand vous serez bien vieille, au soir, à la chandelle,*
> *Assise auprès du feu, dévidant et filant,*
> *Direz, chantant mes vers, en vous émerveillant:*

'*Ronsard me célébrait du temps que j'étais belle.*'   4
Lors vous n'aurez servante oyant tellë nouvelle,
Déjà sous le labeur à demi sommeillant,
Qui au bruit de Ronsard ne s'aillë réveillant,
Bénissant votrë nom de louange immortelle.   8
Je serai sous la terre, et fantômë sans os;
Par les ombrës myrteux je prendrai mon repos;
Vous serez au foyer unë vieille accroupie,
Regrettant mon amour et votrë fier dédain.   12
Vivez, si m'en croyez, n'attendez à demain;
Cueillez dès aujourd'hui les rosës de la vie.
(*Sonets pour Hélène*, V, 1574)

In this sonnet Ronsard puts a traditional idea to his beloved, but
with cunning ambiguity he makes it refer to the present as well as to
the future. He says, for the present, that what she is not giving him
now she will regret later; and, for the future, that when she is old
and he is dead and buried, she will remember his verses and regret
that she had not gathered rosebuds while she might. A prose
translation might go:

(Lines 1–4) When you're quite old, sitting beside the fire in the evening by
candlelight, spinning and reeling up the thread, you'll say, as you recite
my poems, filling you with wonder: 'Ronsard sang my praises in the days
when I was beautiful.'
    In saying '*dévidant et filant*' Ronsard puts these actions the other way round,
'reeling up the thread and spinning'; but the thread has to be spun before it can
be reeled up.
    '*en vous émerveillant*', 'filling you with wonder', refers both to Hélène's
present beauty that the sequence of poems celebrates, and to the wonder she will
feel when she reads them later.

(Lines 6–8) Then you won't have the maid hearing this story – who,
already half asleep after her work, can't be woken up by Ronsard's
noise as he blesses your name with immortal glory.
    vous n'aurez servante [...] *Qui* [...] *ne s'aillë réveillant*, 'you won't have the
maid [...] who can't be woken up', can refer both to the maid you have now
who can't be woken up by Ronsard's *bruit*, noise, blessing your name – and
perhaps making love – and to the maid you will have in old age who won't hear
Ronsard's *bruit* (which can also mean 'rumour' or 'news').

(Lines 9–12) I shall be under the ground, a boneless ghost, I shall be
taking my rest in the myrtle's shadows; you will be an old woman
crouching by the hearth, regretting both my love and your proud
contempt for it.

(Lines 13–14) Live now, believe me, don't wait till tomorrow: pick life's
roses today.

('*si m'en croyez*' might also be translated 'this is my advice', 'take my word for it', 'in my opinion'.)[9]

This was not the first time that the ideas proposed here by Ronsard had been used by poets, nor was it to be the last: the staying power of the poet's work had been celebrated fifteen hundred years earlier by Horace,[10] and was to be celebrated again by Shakespeare in Sonnet 55 (amongst others); while the prediction that the beloved would look back on the poet's pleas and regret her coldness, and the advice that she should accept the love he offered while she was still young, were commonplaces of European poetry, especially in the sixteenth and seventeenth centuries – used by Shakespeare again, and by Marvell in 'To His Coy Mistress'. Ronsard's sonnet is outstanding, first, because of the sheer beauty of his French verse (which is untranslatable); and secondly because of the poignancy of his vision of the lovely Hélène de Surgères grown old, crouching beside the fire in the evening and the candlelight that symbolise the evening and dim remaining light of her life, wondering at the praise Ronsard had so prodigally showered on her, and thinking sadly of the love that she had then proudly rejected.

Cueillez dès aujourd'hui les roses de la vie has an obvious connection with Herrick's exhortation *To Virgins*: 'Gather ye rosebuds while ye may,/Old Time is still a-flying [. . .]';[11] but Ronsard's sonnet was also imitated in a much looser way by Yeats, who wrote an equally original poem – not a sonnet, but three four-line stanzas – on the same theme:

> When you are old and grey and full of sleep,
> And nodding by the fire, take down this book,
> And slowly read, and dream of the soft look
> Your eyes had once, and of their shadows deep;
>
> How many loved your moments of glad grace,
> And loved your beauty with love false or true,
> But one man loved the pilgrim soul in you,
> And loved the sorrows of your changing face;

---

[9] My translation (with help from Jean Khalfa). See p. 228 below for a loose verse translation by Nicholas Kilmer.

[10] *Exegi monumentum aere perennius* [. . .], 'I have raised a monument more lasting than bronze [. . .]'; Horace, *Odes*, III, 30.

[11] Robert Herrick, *Hesperides*, 1648.

And bending down beside the glowing bars,
Murmur, a little sadly, how Love fled
And paced upon the mountains overhead
And hid his face amid a crowd of stars.[12]

Translations

Poems of Pierre de Ronsard, trs. by Nicholas Kilmer, University of California Press, Berkeley and London 1979.

Michel de Montaigne, 1533–92

The Seigneur de Montaigne, a well-born but not notably intellectual Bordelais of merchant stock, was determined that his third son should be thoroughly well-versed in Latin, the language of philosophy and learning. He therefore ordered things at the Château de Montaigne in Périgord so that, when the infant Michel was learning to talk, he should be spoken to only in Latin, hiring a foreign tutor who knew no French, and insisting that he himself, the child's mother, and the servants should all have enough Latin to enable this experiment in humanistic education to be carried through.

> As for me [Montaigne wrote], I was six years old before I knew French any more than I know the *patois* of Périgord or Arabic. And so, without art, without books, without grammar, without rules, without whips and without tears, I had learned Latin as pure as any schoolteacher knew – for I had no means of corrupting it or contaminating it. (Montaigne, *Essays*, I, 26, p. 195[13])

And, although he did not retain the early fluency of his spoken Latin, his father's régime ensured that Montaigne read Latin as easily as he read French for the rest of his life. This strange early .education was followed by a conventional school, which he disliked, and then the arts course at the Collège de Guienne in Bordeaux from the age of thirteen, followed by a legal qualification in Toulouse. Not much is known about this period of his life, but in 1557, when he was twenty-four, he became a counsellor (a legal appointment) to the *Parlement* of Bordeaux. He was married to the well-dowered Françoise de Chassaigne in 1565; three years later his father died; and, his two elder brothers also having died, he was sufficiently well-off to be able to retire in 1571 to the life of a

---

[12] W. B. Yeats, 'When You Are Old', in *The Rose*, 1893 (*Collected Poems*, 2nd edn., Macmillan, London 1950, p. 46).
[13] This and the following quotations from Montaigne's *Essays* are from M. A. Screech's translation, Penguin Classics, 1993.

country gentleman at the Château de Montaigne. Here he lived and read and wrote for the rest of his life, except for visits to Paris and a tour abroad, and for such interruptions as were caused by his being twice elected Mayor of Bordeaux. And here, from 1572 until his death at the age of fifty-nine in 1592, Montaigne wrote and continually revised – by means of adding to the text rather than by altering it – his great collection of *Essays*.

Essays, 1572, 1588, 1595

In his *Essays* Montaigne made the revolutionary decision to write, frankly and simply, about himself, and about his own reactions to life and literature; writing first as an antidote to the depression that struck him at about the time of his father's death, and then simply because he found that he enjoyed doing it. The *Essays* were first published in 1580; a revised and enlarged edition appeared in 1588; and a final edition, further revised and enlarged, came out in 1595, after Montaigne's death. Each of the 107 essays, which are of varying lengths, is concerned, more or less, with a particular subject; but there are copious supporting quotations from the classics – an especially pertinent one being Terence's *Homo sum, humani nil a me alienum puto* ('I am a man; I count nothing concerning mankind foreign to me')[14] – digressions, and occasional remarks on any related topic that happened to occur to Montaigne. Despite their free and easy construction, the *Essays* were immediately recognised and appreciated as the work of an extraordinary mind: a questing, sceptical, highly original intelligence; conservative in politics and religion, but broad in its sympathies, tolerant in its morality, and fearless in its criticism.

More than this, the *Essays* were and are appealing for their sheer readability, and for the immense pleasure they offer of contact with this intelligent, kindly, and sympathetic man, with whom the sympathetic reader seems to make friends, and who – extraordinarily for someone who is writing about himself – is never a bore. Montaigne was of course a man of the sixteenth century, just as Ronsard was, and necessarily shared the general outlook of the time; but in challenging its interests and values he stepped out of his time, and is able to speak to us as clearly and as relevantly as he did to his contemporaries. The text of the closely-printed Penguin Classics translation of *The Complete Essays* fills more than

---

[14] *Heauton Timorumenos*, I, 1, 2nd century BC.

1,260 pages, but it is wonderfully and easily readable; and it is, amongst other things, the perfect bedside book.

Montaigne's determination to know himself, and to share what he discovers, is demonstrated in 'On Some Lines of Virgil', a late essay that is mostly about physical sex, and in the final essay 'On Experience'. In the first of these essays Montaigne writes as an old man – though he was only in his mid-fifties – about the difficulties of coping with the sexual impulses that continue to be trouble-some in later life, and suggests that physical sex is really best left to the young. At the same time he rambles off into various related topics, such as this sardonic comment on men's feelings about their wives' sexual morality compared with their feelings about their own:

> Let us admit it: there is hardly one of us who is not more afraid of the disgrace which comes to him from his wife's immorality than from his own; hardly one who is not so amazingly charitable that he worries more about his dear wife's conscience than he does about his; hardly one who would not rather commit theft or sacrilege – or that his wife were a murderer or a heretic – than to have her be no chaster than he is. (p. 972)

Or this about the jealous man's self-destructive urge to discover his wife's infidelity:

> Curiosity is always a fault; here it is baleful. It is madness to want to find out about an ill for which there is no treatment except one which makes it worse and exacerbates it; one the shame of which is spread abroad and augmented chiefly by our jealousy; one which to avenge means hurting our children rather than curing ourselves. You wither and die while hunting for such hidden truth. How wretched are those husbands in my days who manage to find out! (p. 982)

Or this joke about his own lack of virility:

> Perhaps we are right to condemn ourselves for giving birth to such an absurd thing as a man; right to call it an act of shame and the organs which serve to do it shameful. (It is certain that mine may now properly be called shameful and wretched.) (p. 993)

But he concludes, contrary to the received opinion of his time,[15] that men and women are really much the same as each other:

[15] An anonymous *Disputatio nova contra mulieres, qua probatur eas homines non esse* ('A new argument against women, in which it is demonstrated that they are not human beings' [because they do not have souls]) was published as late as 1595, probably in eastern Germany, and was several times reprinted.

I say that male and female are cast in the same mould: save for education and custom the difference between them is not great. [...] It is far more easy to charge one sex than to discharge the other. As the saying goes: it is the pot calling the kettle smutty. (p. 1016)

The final essay, 'On Experience', is Montaigne's summing up, in which he reaches the end of his search for knowledge of himself and therefore of all men. (I say all 'men' because, although he believes that men and women are in the end equals, Montaigne has been writing as a man about his own kind.) Let him speak here for himself:

We tell ourselves all that we chiefly need: let us listen to it. Is a man not stupid if he remembers having been so often wrong in his judgement yet does not become deeply distrustful of it thereafter? (p. 1218)
The fact that my memory so often trips me up precisely when I am most sure of it is not lost to no purpose: it is no use after that its swearing me oaths and telling me to trust it: I shake my head. (p. 1219)
What shall we do with those people who will receive only printed testimony, who will not believe anyone who is not in a book, nor truth unless it be properly aged? (p. 1227)
A young man ought to shake up his regular habits in order to awaken his powers and stop them from getting lazy and stale. And there is no way of life which is more feeble and stupid than one which is guided by prescriptions and instilled habit. (p. 1229)
When I dance, I dance. When I sleep, I sleep; and when I am strolling along through a beautiful orchard, although part of the time my thoughts are occupied by other things, for part of the time too I bring them back to the walk, to the orchard, to the delight of being alone there, and to me. (p. 1258)
What great fools we are! 'He has spent his life in idleness,' we say. 'I haven't done a thing today.' – 'Why, have you not lived? That is not only the most basic of your employments, it is the most glorious.' – 'I would have shown them what I can do, if they had set me to manage some great affair.' – If you have been able to examine and manage your own life you have achieved the greatest task of all. (p. 1258)
Can I feel something disintegrating? Do not expect me to waste time having my pulse and urine checked so that anxious prognostics can be drawn from them: I will be in plenty of time to feel the anguish without prolonging things by an anguished fear. (p. 1243)

And so this extraordinary book comes to an end. Montaigne claimed no more of it than that 'all this jumble that I am jotting down here is but an account of the assays of my life' (p. 1224); and he ends it thus:

The noble inscription by which the Athenians honoured Pompey's visit to their city corresponds to what I think: *D'autant es tu Dieu comme / Tu te recognois homme.* [Thou art a God in so far as thou recognisest that thou art a man.]

It is an accomplishment, absolute and as it were God-like, to know how to enjoy our being as we ought. [...]

The most beautiful of lives to my liking are those which conform to the common measure, human and ordinate, without miracles though and without rapture.

Old age, however, has some slight need of being treated more tenderly. Let us commend it to that tutelary god of health – and, yes, of wisdom merry and companionable. (pp. 1268–9)

Translations

Montaigne's text was complicated by his successive revisions for new editions, but their various layers have been identified and can be indicated editorially. This is done in the Penguin Classics translation of *The Complete Essays* by M. A. Screech (1993), which has a fine Introduction, together with footnotes and index, and which is much the best version currently available.

Further reading

For the general background, see Roger Price, *A Concise History of France*, Cambridge University Press 1993; and Robin Briggs's *Early Modern France 1560–1715*, Oxford University Press 1977. Metre in French verse is explained by Clive Scott in *French Verse-art: a Study*, Cambridge University Press 1980; and *The Penguin Book of French Poetry 1820–1950* (1990)[16] has a lucid summary of the technicalities of French verse by William Rees on pp. xxix–xxxv.

It is also worth mentioning, in connection with all the French writers treated in this book, that Lytton Strachey's *Landmarks in French Literature* (written originally for the Home University Library in 1912, and subsequently reprinted) is a perceptive and very readable introduction to the whole of French literature from the Middle Ages to the later nineteenth century.

John Fox, *The Poetry of Villon*, Nelson, London 1962, is chiefly concerned with Villon's technique; but the same author's *Villon: Poems*, London 1984 (in Grant and Cutler's 'Critical Guides to French Texts') is a critical guide to a selection of Villon's best work, with prose translations.

---

[16] This is an admirable anthology with prose translations by William Rees, the only fault of which is that the poems in it are not dated.

For Ronsard, *Ronsard the Poet*, ed. Terence Cave, Methuen, London 1973, is a useful collection of essays about various aspects of the poet's outlook and work.

The introduction mentioned above to M. A. Screech's Penguin translation of Montaigne's *The Complete Essays* is recommended; as is chapter 6, on Montaigne and Molière, of Harold Bloom's *The Western Canon*, Macmillan, London 1994. See also Peter Burke's excellent short study *Montaigne*, Oxford University Press 1984.

III Cervantes and Molière

Spain and France in the seventeenth century

Spain in the later sixteenth century, when Cervantes was growing up, was at the height of its imperial power, in the New World, in Flanders, and in the Mediterranean; but, for all its wealth and ebullience, the Spanish Empire was not at ease with the world around it. Wrangling and fighting – with France, with England, with the Papacy, and above all with the Turks – was a constant burden on the energies and the finances of Philip II (reigned 1556–98). His offensive and defensive operations were only possible because the greater part of the treasure received from America was used to support the extensive military and naval forces that were needed for them. The decisive defeat of the Turkish forces at Lepanto in 1571 relieved Spain of its greatest present danger; but then the continuing drain of the fighting in the Netherlands, the massive inflation resulting from the import of precious metals from the New World, and above all the defeat of the Armada against England in 1588, brought the country's expansion to an end, and began its long decline.

The end of the sixteenth century and the beginning of the seventeenth was a particularly bad time for Spain, with state bankruptcy, failed harvests, further military defeats, and the onset of plague which killed 15 per cent of the population. The austere Philip II died in 1598, to be succeeded by the weak and colourless Philip III (reigned 1598–1621); and the government came under the sway of court favourites and an ascendant aristocracy. Nevertheless, the early seventeenth century was also the time when the quality of Spanish culture and art started on its climb to the heights reached by such men as the dramatists Lope de Vega (1562–1635) and Pedro Calderón (1600–81), and the painter Diego Velásquez (1599–1660) – and of course the first and greatest of them, the novelist Miguel de Cervantes (1547–1616).

As Spain declined, France, its civil wars of religion concluded by the decisive defeat of the Protestants, grew in self-confidence. The Treaty of Westphalia, which ended the Thirty Years' War in 1648 (a religious conflict involving most of north-west Europe that ended as a struggle for dominance[1]), left France the predominant power in Europe, as well as its richest and most populous country. At the same time France's overwhelmingly agricultural economy stagnated, and its population and (so far as it can be estimated) its domestic product were much the same at the end of the seventeenth century as they had been at the beginning. Its methods of farming were not improved (as they were, for instance, in England and the Low Countries), and its autocratic political system was not sympathetic to any useful form of social or economic reform.

During this period the conviction grew among the French that they were the most gifted and the most civilised people on earth; that they were moreover blessed with the most beautiful of languages, and produced the world's finest poets and dramatists; opinions that most Frenchmen continued to hold, despite competing claims made by other peoples, until the Second World War, and which linger in many French hearts yet. This growing national self-confidence – the very opposite of Spain's national despair – seems to have encouraged the great French writers of the seventeenth century: Corneille, la Fontaine, Pascal, Racine, and our subject Molière. Sustaining it was the centralised absolutism of the Sun King, Louis XIV (who reigned, astonishingly, from 1643 to 1715), Molière's patron and protector. Under Louis the monarchy imposed a hierarchical system that gave it a monopoly of power throughout the state; and the King himself acted as the ultimate patron and representative of seventeenth-century French art and culture.

Miguel de Cervantes Saavedra, 1547–1616

Few writers of any period had careers as full of great achievements and devastating setbacks as did Cervantes, the story of whose life reads as strangely as any fiction. He was born at Alcalá de Henares, a few miles from Madrid, where his father – although from a family with some pretensions to gentility – was no more than an impoverished surgeon. After a patchy education, Cervantes went to Italy

---

[1] See pp. 70–1 below.

in 1569, when he was twenty-two, and enlisted as a common soldier in the Spanish service. Two years later he fought with distinction at the battle of Lepanto, the crucial naval and military defeat of the Ottoman forces in the Gulf of Corinth, where he was severely wounded. He had recovered sufficiently by 1572 to be involved in further military actions – though his left hand was permanently maimed – but in 1575 he met with disaster. Returning by sea from Italy to Spain, carrying letters from his commanders recommending him for promotion, Cervantes was captured by pirates, and taken to Algiers where he was held as a slave in the expectation – because of the letters he carried – that he would be worth a large ransom. In fact his family was far from being well off, and Cervantes remained captive for five years (during which he made four daring but unsuccessful attempts to escape) before enough money was begged and borrowed to ransom him in 1580.

Back in Spain he attempted to earn a living over the next seven years by writing, chiefly plays of a traditional kind that was to be put out of fashion by the younger playwright Lope de Vega. Cervantes married Catalina de Salazar in 1584; and, finding it increasingly difficult to make ends meet, he gave up literature in 1587 and left home to take up a post in south-west Spain as a government commissioner of supplies, initially for the forthcoming Armada against England. Being an unusually honest man, he found the compulsory requisitioning of corn and oil from communities that could ill afford to give them up both difficult and distasteful, and he did not enrich himself by exploiting the opportunities for fraud and bribery that the job offered. Nevertheless he continued as a commissary until the commission was disbanded in the spring of 1594, though he was harassed (and once briefly imprisoned) for 'debts' to the government which were actually the result of torpid bureaucracy and incompetent accounting by others. In 1594–5 Cervantes was re-employed by the government as a collector of taxes, still in the south-west of the country, when he got into even worse trouble because a merchant with whom he had deposited money from tax receipts went bankrupt. The result was that in 1597–8 he found himself in prison again for debt to the government, this time for six months. The matter was finally sorted out, he was released, and at the age of fifty-one he was once more an unemployed writer.

Cervantes had published a pastoral romance, *La Galatea*, in 1585; and he had never stopped writing plays (most of them lost) and occasional poems. In 1602 there was a brief friendship with the younger and more successful playwright Lope de Vega, which deteriorated into jealous mutual animosity. But it was in the period immediately before the year 1605, in the middle of Spain's constitutional, economic, and psychological crises that Cervantes found at last the means of expressing his genius, for in that year Part I of his masterpiece *Don Quixote* appeared (Part II following in 1615). There were to be other writings in this last blaze of his creativity: novellas and short stories, and another tale of adventure, *Persiles y Sigismunda* (published posthumously in 1617), some of which Cervantes may have preferred; but it was *Don Quixote* that made an instant hit, and it is *Don Quixote* by which he, and the art and culture of early seventeenth-century Spain, is remembered everywhere.

Cervantes died in his sixty-ninth year, recognised as a great writer but still poor, in 1616.

Don Quixote, Part I, 1605; Part II, 1615

The story of *Don Quixote* – a burlesque that also touches the essence of realist fiction – is the tale of a crazed knight, who is deluded by the romances he has read into thinking that he is following in the footsteps of the knight-errants of the age of chivalry; assisted by his shrewd rustic squire, he lurches incompetently from one absurd adventure to another, mistaking windmills for giants and inns for castles. Beyond this there is no plot or structure, for the episodes follow each other without much connection between them, and are interrupted with digressions and separate tales not involving Don Quixote. It is a loose, 'episodic' form of fiction, which continued to be popular until late in the eighteenth century. The appeal of the great original lay in the engaging authenticity of the story's characters, the absurdity of its tales, its racy style, and its ironical humour; indeed, it is still a wonderfully good read, despite its considerable length – although some may find its digressions and separate tales less gripping than the rest – and despite the numerous inconsistencies of detail which Cervantes could not be bothered to put right.

The strength of *Don Quixote* lies – as it must in any successful novel – in its main characters: Don Quixote himself, who develops from being the butt of everyone's jokes into a lovable idealist whose dreams, however ludicrous, have dignity and influence; and his counterpart, the squire Sancho Panza, a peasant realist, fixer, and wit, whose hard eye for the main chance is softened by his genuine admiration and affection for his master. Their contrasting characters are shown and developed both by what they say and do, and by the author's commentary.

It is never quite clear who is telling the story. Sometimes it is simply 'I'; sometimes it is 'I' repeating a tale he has heard from 'Cid Hamet Ben Engeli' who 'was a very curious and very punctual historian in all things' (Part I, ch. 16); but most of the time we are in the presence of a third-person omniscient narrator, who keeps generally to the points of view of Don Quixote and Sancho Panza. It is this familiar narrative technique, along with plain, unsophisticated dialogue in direct speech, that makes *Don Quixote* – now nearly four hundred years old – still so easy for us to read. It was translated into English by Thomas Shelton as early as 1616; it has attracted distinguished illustrators, such as Gustave Doré; and it has held the imagination of readers throughout the western world ever since its first appearance.

Here is the famous description of Don Quixote's attack on the windmills:

As they were thus discoursing, they perceived some thirty or forty windmills that are in that plain; and as soon as Don Quixote espied them, he said to his squire:

'Fortune disposes our affairs better than we ourselves could have desired; look yonder, friend Sancho Panza, where you may discover somewhat more than thirty monstrous giants, with whom I intend to fight, and take away all their lives: with whose spoils we will begin to enrich ourselves; for it is lawful war, and doing God good service to take away so wicked a generation from off the face of the earth.'

'What giants?' said Sancho Panza.

'Those you see yonder,' answered his master, 'with those long arms; for some of them are wont to have them almost of the length of two leagues.'

'Consider, Sir,' answered Sancho, 'that those which appear yonder, are not giants, but windmills; and what seem to be arms are the sails, which, whirled about by the wind, make the millstone go,'

'One may easily see,' answered Don Quixote, 'that you are not versed in the business of adventures: they are giants; and, if you are afraid, get aside and pray, whilst I engage with them in a fierce and unequal combat.'

And so saying, he clapped his spurs to Rosinante, without minding the cries his squire sent after him, assuring him that those he went to assault were without all doubt windmills, and not giants. But he was so fully possessed that they were giants, that he neither heard the outcries of his squire Sancho, nor yet discerned what they were, though he was very near them, but went on, crying out aloud:

'Fly not, ye cowards and vile caitiffs; for it is a single knight who assaults you.'

Now the wind rose a little, and the great sails began to move: which Don Quixote perceiving, he said:

'Well, though you should move more arms than the giant Briareus, you shall pay for it.'

And so saying, and recommending himself devoutly to his lady Dulcinea, beseeching her to succour him in the present danger, being well covered with his buckler, and setting his lance in the rest, he rushed on as fast as Rosinante could gallop, and attacked the first mill before him; and running his lance into the sail, the wind whirled it about with so much violence that it broke the lance to shivers, dragging horse and rider after it, and tumbling them over and over on the plain, in very evil plight. Sancho Panza hastened to his assistance, as fast as his ass could carry him; and when he came up to him, he found him not able to stir; so violent was the blow he and Rosinante had received in falling.

'God save me,' quoth Sancho, 'did not I warn you to have a care of what you did, for that they were nothing but windmills; and nobody could mistake them, but one that had the like in his head.'

'Peace, friend Sancho,' answered Don Quixote; 'for matters of war are, of all others, most subject to continual mutations. Now I verily believe, and it is most certainly so, that the sage Friston, who stole away my chamber and books, has metamorphosed the giants into windmills, on purpose to deprive me of the glory of vanquishing them, so great is the enmity he bears me; but when he has done his worst, his wicked arts will avail but little against the goodness of my sword.'

'God grant it, as he can,' answered Sancho Panza; and, helping him to rise, he mounted him again upon Rosinante, who was half shoulder-slipped.[2]

Don Quixote was enjoyed first of all as an affectionate parody of the absurdly unrealistic romances of chivalry which were the most popular form of fiction in sixteenth-century Spain; but its multi-layered complexity can be – and has been – read in many other ways as well. It is for a start a very funny as well as a deeply moving story, whether or not the reader is acquainted with what it parodies. Another way of reading it, popular in the nineteenth century, was to see Don Quixote himself as a romantic hero, with flashing eyes and floating hair, carrying the burden of poetic insight. Classifiers have seen it as a pivotal work that saw off the Renaissance and introduced Neo-classicism. But above all, *Don Quixote* was the first modern novel, the direct ancestor of, and continuing influence upon, the realistic, psychologically penetrating fiction that has increasingly dominated the literature of the nineteenth and twentieth centuries.

[2] *Don Quixote*, Pt I, ch. 8, trs. by Charles Jarvis (1742), Oxford World's Classics.

Translations

Oxford World's Classics offers the interesting option of reading *Don Quixote* in an early translation: namely that by Charles Jarvis, first published in 1742, and now reprinted with Introduction and Notes by E. O. Riley (1992). It is fluent, and faithful to the Spanish text in terms of its eighteenth-century English, and it suggests the antiquity of the original without being artificially quaint. J. M. Cohen's translation in Penguin Classics, 1950, is a handy modern, version; it has an introduction but no notes. The extract given above is from Jarvis's translation, which can be compared with the equivalent passage in Cohen's translation on pp. 228–9 below.

Molière (Jean Baptiste Poquelin), 1622–73

Jean Baptiste Poquelin's relatively short life – he died in harness when he was only fifty-one – divides into four clearly defined phases. He was born in Paris to bourgeois parents (his father was a furniture upholsterer) who provided him with a comfortable upbringing and a good education. But in 1643, when he was twenty-one, Jean Baptiste left home to join a troop of actors (consisting mostly of the Béjart family), and with them set up a company called *Illustre Théâtre*, taking 'Molière' as his stage name.[3] The new company worked hard in Paris for two years, but did not succeed with the public; and in 1645 they packed up and left for the provinces where they played all over the country for the next twelve years, the third major phase of Molière's life. This long spell of touring was a vitally important experience for him, for it provided him both with the theatrical professionalism and with the intimate knowledge of people of all sorts that were to be essential elements in his later success. For great success followed at last in 1658 when he returned to Paris with the company, of which he was now actor-manager, and began the final fifteen years of his career.

The breakthrough came when Molière's company was invited to perform before Louis XIV, and a farce by Molière amused the King. Royal favour and royal patronage were accorded to them, and it became first the *Troupe de Monsieur* ('Monsieur' being the King's brother) and then in 1665 the *Troupe du Roi*; they played first at the

---

[3] Persons of good family who went on the stage commonly took a stage name, but Jean Baptiste's reason for choosing this particular name is unknown; he could have been remembering a novelist called Molière d'Essertines (1600–24).

Petit-Bourbon and later at the Palais Royal, and Molière's position as the leading dramatist to the court was established. Royal favour was essential to Molière, as we shall see when discussing *Tartuffe*, for it was his only protection against the malice of jealous and powerful people who felt themselves to be belittled or insulted by his hard-hitting comedies. During this period he wrote more than twenty plays, many of them in five acts and in verse, including (besides relatively trivial farces to please the court) his masterpieces *Tartuffe* (1664) and *Le Misanthrope* (1665).

In 1662 Molière married Armande, the youngest Béjart girl (then only seventeen), and they had a son in 1664 to whom the King graciously stood godfather. Although he was outstandingly successful as a playwright, Molière appears to have been melancholy in temperament, but sympathetic and tolerant; at any rate his company of players was consistently loyal to him. In 1673 he was taken ill on stage while playing the lead in his latest piece (which was, ironically, *Le Malade imaginaire*, 'The Imaginary Invalid'), and died soon afterwards.

Tartuffe, or the Impostor, 1664, 1669

When *Tartuffe* was first staged in 1664 – perhaps as a shorter, more farcical piece than the later published version – there was, as Molière said in his Preface to the 1669 edition 'a great deal of fuss' made about it. The King liked it, but powerful forces with religious pretensions objected so strongly that he felt bound to approve a ban on its production or printing that was to last for five years. To continue with Molière's Preface:

> Noblemen, pretentious women, cuckolds and doctors have all submitted to being put on the stage and pretended to be as amused as everyone else at the way I portrayed them, but the [religious] hypocrites would not stand for a joke: they took immediate alarm and found it strange that I had the audacity to make fun of their antics or to decry so numerous and respectable a profession.[4]

The particular sort of religious hypocrite that Molière was attacking is described early on in the play itself:

> I know nothing more odious than those whited sepulchres of specious zeal, those charlatans, those professional zealots, who with sacrilegious and deceitful posturings abuse and mock to their heart's content everything which men hold most sacred and holy; men who put self-interest first, who

---

[4] This and the following quotation are from John Wood's translation of Molière's *The Misanthrope and Other Plays*, Penguin Classics 1959, pp. 99, 119

trade and traffic in devotion, seek to acquire credit and dignities by turning up their eyes in transports of simulated zeal. I mean the people who tread with such extraordinary ardour the godly road to fortune, burning with devotion but seeking material advantage, preaching daily the virtues of solitude and retirement while following the life of courts, shaping their zeal to their vices, quick, revengeful, faithless, scheming, who when they wish to destroy, hide their vindictive pride under the cloak of religion. (*Tartuffe*, I.)

It is plain enough why prominent people around the court of Louis XIV who made a show of their piety should have objected so strongly to *Tartuffe*; for Tartuffe himself displays all these unpleasant characteristics with searing clarity. Perhaps not all of the objectors were hypocrites, but there will have been enough who were, and it will have been the hypocrites who made the most fuss.

The play is ingeniously constructed, the whole of the first two acts being taken up with the Orgon family's reactions to Tartuffe's effect on their lives, while Tartuffe himself does not appear until Act III. We learn that Tartuffe has succeeded in convincing Orgon and Orgon's mother that he is a man of exemplary character, poor but holy, who has been misjudged and misprised; and that Orgon has charitably taken him into his household and is proposing to marry him to the unwilling daughter of the family. By the end of Act II we have a good idea of how creepy and dangerous Tartuffe is; but when he does appear in person he is found to exceed our worst expectations, being a hypocrite of the most odious kind. Here is his first entry:

TARTUFFE [*seeing the maid* DORINE]　Laurent, put away my hair shirt and my scourge and continue to pray Heaven to send you grace. If anyone asks for me I'll be with the prisoners distributing alms.

DORINE　The impudent hypocrite!

TARTUFFE　What do you want?

DORINE　I'm to tell you ...

TARTUFFE　For Heaven's sake! Before you speak, I pray you take this handkerchief. [*Takes handkerchief from his pocket*]

DORINE　Whatever do you mean?

TARTUFFE　Cover your bosom. I can't bear to see it. Such pernicious sights give rise to sinful thoughts.

Immediately after this exchange Tartuffe is seen attempting to seduce Orgon's wife; and when Orgon's son attempts to warn his father of what Tartuffe is up to, Orgon threatens to disinherit the young man. The scene ends:

TARTUFFE   Let me go and by going hence remove all occasion for them to attack me.

ORGON   No. No. You shall stay. My very life depends upon it.

TARTUFFE   Well then if it be so, I must sacrifice myself. But if you would only . . .

ORGON   Yes?

TARTUFFE   Let it be so. We'll speak of it no more but I know now what I must do. Reputation is a brittle thing: friendship requires that I should forestall every whisper, every shadow of suspicion. I must forswear the company of your wife and you will never see . . .

ORGON   No! You *shall* see her in spite of them all. Nothing gives me greater joy than to annoy them. You shall appear with her constantly and – to show my defiance, I'll make you my sole heir. I'll make a gift to you in due form of all my goods here and now. My true, dear friend, whom I now take as my son-in-law, you are dearer to me than son or wife or kin. Will you not accept what I am offering you?

TARTUFFE   Heaven's will be done in all things.

ORGON   Poor fellow! Let us go and draft the document at once. And let the whole envious pack of them burst with vexation at the news![5]

Having thus become legal owner of Orgon's property, Tartuffe arranges not only to have his benefactor and his family evicted from their home but also to have him jailed for protecting a dissident friend. Orgon is about to be arrested when intervention by the king pardons him and has Tartuffe arrested instead.

Perhaps *Tartuffe* in its final version would have been an even more powerful indictment of religious hypocrisy if Tartuffe's scheming had been less obviously criminal, and if the end of the play saw him still succeeding as a hypocrite, just as Alceste at the end of *Le Misanthrope* storms off still convinced of his misanthropy. But that would no doubt have been too much for the religious element at Court to stomach in the 1660s: and besides, audiences prefer fictions (such as Miss Prism's in *The Importance of Being Earnest*) in which the good end happily and the bad unhappily. At all events, *Tartuffe* is still a play of extraordinary strength and authority, with a protagonist of sinister power; and when it was staged in its revised form in 1669 (with Molière playing Orgon), it

---

[5] *Tartuffe*, III, 853–62, 1163–84, trs. by John Wood, Penguin Classics, pp. 134–5, 143. The French text of these quotations is given on pp. 229–30 below.

was an instant and enormous success, running for an unprecedented twenty-eight successive performances, and continuing to be the company's main attraction, both before and after Molière's death.

Translations

The most easily available translations of ten of Molière's plays are in the two Penguin Classics volumes, *The Miser and Other Plays* (1953) and *The Misanthrope and Other Plays* (1959), trs. by John Wood (*Tartuffe* is in the second volume, along with *The Misanthrope*, *The Sicilian*, *A Doctor in Spite of Himself*, and *The Imaginary Invalid*). Wood's translations are clear and spirited, and have good introductions and notes. See also, in Methuen Drama, Molière. *Five Plays* (*The School for Wives*, *Tartuffe*, *The Misanthrope*, *The Miser*, and *The Hypochondriac*), well translated (1982) by R. Wilbur and A. Drury.

Further reading

For the general background, see Melveena McKendrick, *A Concise History of Spain*, Cassell, London 1972; Roger Price, *A Concise History of France*, Cambridge University Press 1993; and Robin Briggs's *Early Modern France 1560–1715*, Oxford University Press 1977.

For Cervantes, Melveena McKendrick's critical biography *Cervantes*, Boston 1980, is particularly recommended. A. J. Close's *Miguel de Cervantes: Don Quixote*, Cambridge University Press, 1990 is scholarly, sensitive, and sophisticated.

For Molière, see W. D. Howarth, *Molière and his Audience*, Cambridge University Press, 1982, an erudite and readable account of Molière and his theatre; and John Wood's introductions to the two Penguin Classics translations mentioned above.

IV Voltaire and Rousseau

France before the Revolution

Despite its central importance to the history of ideas, eighteenth-century France was in other ways an unhappy country. The War of the Spanish Succession (1702–13) established Britain for the first time as a potent competitor with France for power in Europe; and the relative standing of the two countries gradually altered in Britain's favour during the rest of the eighteenth century, a change that was the result as much of differences in their economies and political institutions as of their military prowess. The structure of the French state was in many ways – and remained until the Revolution – an anachronistic survival from much earlier times. An absolute monarch stood at the head of a hierarchical system in which a numerically insignificant nobility had a monopoly of all offices and posts of influence, both civil and military; owned about 20 per cent of all the land; were forbidden to engage in manual labour or trade; and were exempt from taxation. Under them came, on one side, the clergy of a wealthy Church, owning about 10 per cent of the land and also tax-exempt; and on the other, a bourgeoisie of intellectuals, professionals, merchants, higher artisans, and prosperous farmers, moderately taxed, who owned about 30 per cent of the land and who might under exceptional circumstances move up into the less-prestigious ranks of the nobility. Under all were the rural peasants, 85 per cent of the population, who owned the remaining 40 per cent of the land and were the most heavily taxed and tithed of all. It was a system that was not only manifestly unjust but was also economically inefficient; and it was state bankruptcy, resulting from excessive borrowing – in 1788 interest on government debt absorbed *half* the state's revenue – that led indirectly to the final collapse of the whole antique system.

That things were very wrong was apparent by the middle of the century to many young, educated Frenchmen, including some nobles and bourgeois as well as most intellectuals. There were many calls for an 'Estates General', a meeting of representatives of the various sections of the nobility and bourgeoisie to discuss matters of common interest such as taxation, but they were ignored. Intellectuals – *philosophes* – believing in reason and humanity as the supreme values, were signed up by Denis Diderot (1713–84) to produce the *Encyclopédie*, published from 1751 to 1776 in thirty-five large volumes. This great collaborative project, which was begun as a simple translation of Ephraim Chambers's *Cyclopaedia* of 1727, became the central text of the Enlightenment, in which 150 contributors used their articles on philosophy, religion, law, education, and so on, to argue for change based on human reason, and to deny the traditional authority of Church and state. It was in this atmosphere of new thinking in an old, failing culture that Voltaire and Rousseau flourished and amazed, first France, and then the world.

Rousseau was not in fact French, but French-Swiss, coming from the Calvinist republic of Geneva, a few miles from the French border. However, the cultural links between France itself and the other French-speaking communities in the western Alps – principally in French Switzerland and in Savoy (which was then part of the Kingdom of Sardinia) – were very strong, so that French speakers from these districts did not feel or seem as foreign in France as did their non-French-speaking compatriots, however conscious the French-speakers might be of their Swiss or Savoyard nationality.

Voltaire (François-Marie Arouet), 1694–1778

F. M. Arouet was born in Paris, the son of a lawyer, and was educated from 1704 to 1711 at the Jesuit Collège Louis-le-Grand. His father hoped that he would enter public service, and he spent some months in 1713 at the Hague as assistant secretary to the French Ambassador, and some months more the following year in a law office in Paris; but his eyes were already fixed on poetry and the theatre. He quickly gained a reputation for wit, vanity, and outrageous behaviour. A scandalous poem about the Regent resulted in temporary exile from Paris in 1716; and further poems attacking the government got him eleven months' imprisonment in the Bastille (1717–18). While he was in prison he revised his play *Oedipe*, and began an epic poem on the religious conflicts in the reign of Henri IV. *Oedipe* was a huge success when it was performed in 1718 – even the Regent rewarded the author – and François-Marie Arouet began to call himself Voltaire.[1]

From 1718 to 1726 Voltaire flitted about Paris, writing plays and poems, always on the edge of trouble, but the early development of a sharp financial sense made it possible for him to support himself in doing what he wanted without depending on his father or anyone else; besides investing wisely, he was concerned in a scheme for manipulating the State lottery and he loaned money at interest. Not that he needed much help, for *La Ligue* (later retitled *La Henriade*), the epic poem about Henri IV which was eventually completed in 1723, was another triumphant success.

In 1726, however, Voltaire quarrelled with an aristocratic courtier, the Chevalier de Rohan-Chabot, who humiliated Voltaire by having him beaten in public and imprisoned once more in the Bastille. He was released on condition that he would go immediately to England; he did so and was a great success in the society of leading politicians and intellectuals (1726–9). Later, when he was allowed to return to France (1729–34), he recorded his impressions of England in *Letters Concerning the English Nation* (or, in its French version, *Lettres philosophiques*, 1734). The book was promptly banned and burned by the French authorities, but five clandestine editions appeared in France in its first year of publication.

It was clearly better that he should leave Paris, and from 1734 Voltaire made his main base with the Marquise du Châtelet, a bluestocking whose lover he had become with the acquiescence of her husband, at the Château de Cirey near St Dizier, half way to the French frontier. He stayed there – writing, entertaining, and paying occasional visits to the capital – until Madame du Châtelet died in 1749. He then returned briefly to his feverish life in Paris, but the following year he accepted the invitation (which had been several times repeated) of Frederick the Great of Prussia to join his court in Berlin. It was inevitable that Frederick and Voltaire, both being clever, wily egotists, would quarrel sooner or later, but the visit did last for two-and-a-half years (1750–3), and had its pleasures as well as its pains for both of them.

---

[1] There are two possible reasons for his choice of this name, one being that VOLTAIRE is an anagram of AROUET L[E] J[EUNE] (Arouet the younger), with V substituted for U, and I for J; and the other being that in French *volter* is to make a quick movement in fencing to avoid a thrust, and *voltiger* is to flit about, or to perform acrobatics, both words suggesting Voltaire's intellectual agility.

Voltaire's next and final move was to the border between France and Switzerland where he lived from 1755 (when he was over sixty) until his death at the age of eighty-three in 1778, scarcely more than ten years before the Revolution. He was by now a rich man – his financial acumen had not deserted him – and he settled first on the Swiss side of the border, and finally, from 1759, at the Château de Ferney on the French side, where he was effectively out of reach of the French authorities but near enough to Paris not to be out of touch. Here he continued – despite claiming throughout the last twenty years of his life to be on the point of death as a result of ill health – energetically to write, to entertain, and to outrage the French establishment. In fact these last years turned out to be some of his most productive, in which he wrote, besides thousands of letters and dozens of minor works, the *Essai sur les mœurs et l'ésprit des nations* (1756), the *Dictionnaire philosophique* (1764, based on his articles for the *Encyclopédie*), and some of his short novels which were really philosophical tracts in disguise, the most memorable of which is *Candide*.

Voltaire made one last, triumphant visit to Paris at the beginning of 1778, but it was too much for him in his eighty-fourth year, and he died there 'worshipping God, loving my friends, not hating my enemies, and detesting superstition'[2]

Candide, ou l'optimisme, 1759

Ostensibly the entertaining and slightly improper story of the journey through the early part of his life of an ingenuous young man, *Candide* operates on several levels. There is first the story itself, a hilarious travelogue which begins with Candide being thrown out of the castle of his patron in a tiny German state for kissing Cunégonde, the daughter of the house, for whose hand he is – in the opinion of her father and brother – insufficiently well born. After a series of unpleasant adventures, he meets his old tutor, Dr Pangloss, now also in trouble, who appals Candide by telling him that the castle has been sacked by soldiers and the whole family killed. Candide and Pangloss continue on their way together through a series of difficulties and disasters which the tutor – in a travesty of Leibniz's philosophy – explains away as being all for the best in the best of all possible worlds. But then Candide learns that

---

[2] Written to placate a friend who reproached him for becoming reconciled to the Church at the beginning of his final illness. at the end of May.

Cunégonde is still alive, and he determines on a quest to find her. At first he is impressed by Pangloss's consoling explanations of their troubles, that what appears to be a disaster in one place is in fact a benefit somewhere else; but they become gradually less convincing as the horrors follow hard on each other's heels. The two part company for a while, and Candide continues his journey in the company of Martin, another philosopher, who, instead of parroting a lunatic optimism, is cynically suspicious of everyone and everything. Candide and Martin visit a genuine utopia in South America, but Candide's longing for Cunégonde and Martin's vain scepticism ('one is as badly off wherever one is') lead them to leave El Dorado and carry on with their journey. By degrees, overcoming seemingly endless difficulties, they eventually arrive at Constantinople, where they come together with Pangloss (as absurdly optimistic as ever), Cunégonde (now grown ill-favoured and shrewish), and Cunégonde's brother (still objecting on grounds of caste to Candide's pursuit of his sister). Candide, who is now – as a result of his experiences – neither optimistic nor cynical, concludes that it is no good philosophising or worrying about what to do, we must just get on with what is in front of us; as he says at the end to the irrepressibly optimistic Pangloss, *il faut cultiver notre jardin*, 'we must go and dig the garden'.

Within this wonderfully-told tale, the absurdity of the pseudo-Leibnizian optimism and the uselessness of Martin's balancing pessimism is plainly and effectively satirised; but there is another level on which Voltaire is exploring a fundamental problem of religious belief: why should the innocent suffer? Voltaire himself, while he had been for many years an enemy of what he saw as the religious bigotry of the Church, had also been a Deist; that is, he had held a reasoned belief in the existence of a benevolent supreme being or creator who had set the world going according to Newtonian physics. His belief had undergone a crisis, however, as a result of the Lisbon earthquake of 1755 in which at least 20,000 people, selected apparently at random, had perished. How, he asked in a poem (*Sur le désastre de Lisbonne*, 1756), can a good and omnipotent God cause or allow such a holocaust to occur? Why did it happen in Lisbon rather than somewhere else? Does it mean that God lacks either goodness, or power, or both? The poet can find no satisfactory answer, but can only submit.

Now in *Candide* Voltaire continues to gnaw at the problem as the travellers meet rape, murder, disease, and numerous other evils visited on people who have done nothing to deserve them. A Panglossian belief that good will arise from evil will obviously not answer the question; neither is the Christian argument, that evil cannot be excluded from a world in which there is free will, a sufficient explanation for a natural disaster such as the Lisbon earthquake that cannot be said to have resulted from anybody's free will but God's. It is probably true that we are spiritually improved by suffering, but again that cannot apply to those who are killed in a natural disaster (although, as Pangloss might say, it may apply to the survivors). So Candide – who is unimpressed by the Manichean belief that God and Satan are in perpetual conflict and all is for the worst – searches for happiness in the form of Cunégonde; but, when he sees that she can no longer make him happy, he finds the strength in what his journey has taught him: to act pragmatically, to make the best of an imperfect world, and to get on with the job in hand.

Voltaire craftily arranged for his subversive fable to be published simultaneously in France, Switzerland, England, and the Low Countries, both to cause maximum sensation and to avoid immediate piracy before a ban could be imposed in France (and, eventually, by the Vatican). Tens of thousands of copies of *Candide* were printed in the first year; it was translated into English within six weeks, and into other major languages soon afterwards. As the editor and translator of the Oxford World's Classics version says, 'if ever a work deserved to be called a World's Classic, it is *Candide*'.

Translations

Of the several versions of *Candide* currently available, the Penguin Classics translation by John Butt (1947) and the Oxford World's Classics translation by Roger Pearson (1990) are both excellent. The World's Classics edition has the fuller introduction and notes, and has the further advantage of including translations of four more of Voltaire's philosophical fables (*Micromegas*, *Zadig*, *The Ingenu*, and *The White Bull*).

Jean-Jacques Rousseau, 1712–78

Rousseau is remembered today, as he was recognised in his own time, not so much as a creative writer as for his profound influence on the philosophical, sociological, and political thought of the later eighteenth century, and for his seminal role in evolving principles that were given practical effect in the French Revolution.

It is also true that his novels, while widely read at the time, have proved to have endured more for the ideas embodied in them than for their quality as works of art. But there was one great work, his autobiography, which did have high artistic quality, and which also had a great and lasting influence on the subsequent development of European literature.

Geneva, where Rousseau was born, was the principal city of French Switzerland; the home too of Calvin's grim Protestantism which held that all men are predestined either for Heaven or Hell, and – appropriately for this clockwork theology – the centre of watchmaking excellence. Rousseau's father was himself a watchmaker, but he left Geneva when the boy was ten and, his mother having died soon after he was born, Rousseau was brought up by friends and relations. At thirteen he was apprenticed to an engraver but, as was to happen again several times in his earlier life, Rousseau found ordinary work disagreeable – according to him, this master was a brute – and he ran away when he was sixteen.

Pausing at Annecy in Savoy, he met Madame de Warens, a woman twelve years his senior who was to be the major influence on the next ten years of his life; her piety set him on the path to Catholicism, and her maternal kindness was returned by Rousseau with a son's love, the motherless young man calling her *maman* ('mamma' or 'mummy'). He spent a year (1728–9) in Turin, where he was received into the Catholic Church and worked as an upper servant in two aristocratic households, from the second of which he was dismissed on account of a petty theft which he had in fact committed but would not admit to (see pp. 56–7 below). During the next winter with *maman* in Annecy, Rousseau became obsessed with the desire to learn music, an obsession that occupied him for the next few years (1729–36, when he was aged 17–24). During this period he visited Paris for the first time (1731), and worked as a music teacher, music copyist, and government land surveyor in Savoy; and it culminated in the temporary union of Rousseau and *maman* as lovers.

A turning point in Rousseau's life came in 1741 when, just short of thirty, he met Denis Diderot – leader of the *philosophes* in Paris – who befriended Rousseau and commissioned him to write articles on music and political economy for the *Encyclopédie*. Equally important to his development was a brief appointment as secretary to the French Ambassador to Venice (1743–4), which widened his horizons in music and led him to the conclusion – central to his later thinking – that people are what their governments make them.

The central belief of Enlightenment thinking was that human conduct would improve and human happiness would increase as ignorance and superstition were replaced by knowledge and understanding; and this rested on the assumptions that uncivilised man was naturally ignorant and superstitious, and that these characteristics were perpetuated in modern times by Church and State. Rousseau, in the extraordinary writings of the second half of his life, took virtually the opposite position, arguing that primitive man was, so to speak, without sin, and that it was civilisation and its instruments that corrupted him and caused his unhappiness; or, in a more basic formulation, all that God had made was good but everything made by man had debased this goodness. Aspects of this thinking underlay the two *Discourses* (1750, 1755); the novels *La Nouvelle Héloïse* (1761), and *Émile* (1762); and, greatest of all, *The Social Contract* (1762), which began 'Man is born free, and everywhere he is in chains',[3] and in which Rousseau's conclusions were to argue, not for an impractical utopia, but for the application now of the principles of liberty, equality, and fraternity that were to be appropriated after his death by the French revolutionaries. (They also led Rousseau to believe – without empirical evidence one way or the other – that savages must be noble.)

These beliefs and writings naturally led to controversy, and in his later life Rousseau was attacked because of them both by the likes of Voltaire and Diderot, who thought them perverse, and by the authorities, who thought them irreligious and dangerous. *The Social Contract* was banned in France, and was burned, along with *Émile*, in Geneva. There were also passionate followers all over Europe, but Rousseau was not a happy man. His relationship with *maman* came to an end in 1745 when he became the partner of a younger woman called Thérèse Levasseur, by whom he had five children (all consigned to the Foundling Hospital), and with whom he lived for the rest of his life. Settling down, however, was another matter. In 1754 he renounced Catholicism and regained his Genevan citizenship; with the publication of *Émile* in 1762 a warrant was issued in Paris for his arrest and he fled, eventually getting back to Switzerland; in

---

[3] The second *Discourse* (1755) had ended: 'it is manifestly against the Law of Nature, however we define it, that a child should command an old man, that an imbecile should direct a wise man, and that a handful of people should wallow in unnecessary luxuries while the starving multitude lacks the basic necessities of life' (trs. by Peter France, in *Rousseau: Confessions*, Cambridge University Press 1987, p.9).

1763 he became a citizen of Neuchâtel and renounced his Genevan citizenship; in 1765 his house in Neuchâtel was stoned, and he moved to, and was promptly expelled from, an island in the Bielersee, north of Neuchâtel; and so he continued to move on, first to Berlin, and then to England, where he was helped by the philosopher David Hume and where he wrote most of the *Confessions*. It is perhaps not surprising that his feelings of being persecuted by everyone developed towards the end of his life into full-blown paranoia.

Rousseau died in 1778, foreseeing but not welcoming the Revolution that was to come in 1789 – the Revolution that his ideas did so much to form and to encourage.

Confessions, written 1766–70, published posthumously

An autobiography is an account of someone's life written by the subject, and based both on his or her memories and on independent evidence such as documents and other people's recollections. As with all historical accounts, autobiographies cannot include everything that has happened, and autobiographers are obliged to select some things for inclusion and to leave others out, and they commonly use this process of selection to produce accounts that will conform to the manners of their time, and will also explain, interpret, and justify certain aspects of their lives. For this reason an autobiography is normally less reliable about some parts of the subject's life than a biography written by someone else; but, uniquely, an autobiography can include, at its author's discretion, things about the subject that cannot be known to anyone else.

There had been great autobiographies written before Rousseau's *Confessions*, but they were primarily intended to promote religious belief (St Augustine, 400; St Teresa of Avila, 1562+), to vindicate their subjects' careers (Benvenuto Cellini, 1558+), or to give an account of their times (Saint-Simon, 1752). What was new about Rousseau's autobiography (written mostly in the years 1766–70) was that he intended to give in it a true and uncensored account of his own feelings, thoughts, and actions as he saw them himself from the inside.[4] Rousseau believed that he was radically different from other people, and he felt that he was misunderstood. His purpose in

---

[4] Montaigne (see p. 30 above) certainly wrote a great deal about himself, but the *Essays*, on their multitude of different subjects, were not – and were not supposed to be – a coherent autobiography.

writing this unusual autobiography was therefore both to produce a
book that would be unique and worthwhile in itself – it would, for
instance, investigate the divergence between appearance and reality, between what people say and what they do and feel, as shown
by his own doings and feelings – and also one that would justify his
actions and beliefs. He would benefit, too, by increasing his own
self-knowledge, and by the pleasure of writing about himself; and
he wrote the book, lovingly and over a considerable period of time,
almost as if it were a novel about Jean-Jacques.

It begins:

> I have resolved on an enterprise which has no precedent, and which, once
> complete, will have no imitator. My purpose is to display to my kind a
> portrait in every way true to nature, and the man I shall portray will be
> myself.
>   Simply myself. I know my own heart and understand my fellow man. But I
> am made unlike any one I have ever met; I will even venture to say that I am
> like no one in the whole world. I may be no better, but at least I am
> different.[5]

And this is what Rousseau tries to do. He takes his life year by
year, episode by episode, and gives an account of what he felt and
how he behaved, however fatuous or disgraceful his feelings or
behaviour, with an unprecedented degree of frankness. He hopes
and believes, moreover, that he is telling us everything about
himself, recalling his whole life and leaving nothing out. He says:

> By relating to him [the reader] in simple detail all that has happened to me,
> all that I have done, all that I have felt, I cannot lead him into error, unless
> wilfully. [...] His task is to assemble these elements and to assess the being
> who is made up of them [...] It is not enough for my story to be truthful, it
> must be detailed as well. It is not for me to judge the relative importance of
> events; I must relate them all. [...] I have only one thing to fear in this
> enterprise; not that I may say too much or tell untruths, but that I may not
> tell everything and may conceal the truth. (Book IV, pp. 169–70.)

Of course Rousseau cannot really tell us *everything* about himself
and his life, however much he would like to; neither can he tell the
truth, for memory itself is selective and faulty. To recount in
complete detail everything, literally everything, that a person thinks
of and does in a single day – in one hour, even – would fill volumes,
for describing consciousness in greater and greater detail is like using
fractals to model a boundary: there is no end to the degree of detail

---

[5] *Confessions*, Bk I, trsl. by J. M. Cohen, Penguin Classics 1954, p. 17.

that is attainable. So, like every other autobiographer (or biographer, or historian) Rousseau does in fact select what he tells us from a larger body of evidence and experience; and he tells the truth about it as far as he can remember. What makes him different from his predecessors is that he selects aspects of his experience that it had not formerly been thought useful or proper to reveal. He tells us about the people he has loved, but he also tells us about his sexual experiences and fantasies; he tells us about his achievements as a thinker and writer, but he also tells us about his failures and about the mean and selfish things he has done – indeed, he tells us about the worst things he has done at length and with self-obsessed zeal.

Rousseau says that at least part of his purpose in writing this autobiography was 'confessional', that by confessing the worst things about himself he would to some extent purge himself of feeling guilty about them.[6] To take a notable example, he describes at the end of Book Two a crime he committed when he was in domestic service with kind and sympathetic employers in Italy. Rousseau, who at the age of nineteen has a fancy for pretty knick-knacks, steals from a lady of the family 'a little pink and silver ribbon, which was quite old'. It is seen in his possession, and he is asked how he came by it. Instead of admitting that he took it and asking his employers' forgiveness (which they might have afforded him), he claims that he was given the ribbon by one of the other servants, a pretty, innocent young cook called Marion, implying that she had stolen it; and he sticks to his story in the face of her tearful denial: 'Oh, Rousseau [Marion says], I thought you were a good fellow. You make me very sad, but I should not like to be in your place.' By this time Rousseau yearns to confess his sin, but his dread of being publicly shamed prevents him. In the end they are both sacked, their employer saying that 'the guilty one's conscience would amply avenge the innocent. His prediction,' Rousseau goes on, 'was not wide of the mark. Not a day passes on which it is not fulfilled.' And he dwells on the affair at gloomy, obsessive length:

> I may have ruined a nice, honest, and decent girl, who was certainly worth a great deal more than I, and doomed her to disgrace and misery. [...] I do not know what happened to the victim of my calumny, but she cannot possibly have found it easy to get a good situation after that. [...] Who can tell to

---

[6] 'Confession', in French as well as in English, can also mean making a declaration of religious belief, but it is unlikely that Rousseau intended this as a second meaning of his (plural) *Confessions*.

what extremes the depressed feeling of injured innocence might have carried her at her age? And if my remorse at perhaps having made her unhappy is unbearable, what can be said of my grief at perhaps having made her worse than myself?

This cruel memory troubles me at times and so disturbs me that in my sleepless hours I see this poor girl coming to reproach me for my crime, as if I had committed it only yesterday. [. . .] Nevertheless I have never been able to bring myself to relieve my heart by revealing this in private to a friend. [. . .] The burden therefore has rested till this day on my conscience without any relief; and I can affirm that the desire to some extent to rid myself of it has greatly contributed to my resolution of writing these *Confessions*. (Book II, pp. 86–8.)

His written confession, in fact, which was not to be published until after his death, is both less painful and more effective for his peace of mind than would be a private confession to the most sympathetic friend.

Similarly with his sexual desires and experiences: they are not all that startling to a modern reader: as a young man he wanted women to dominate and flog him, he masturbated frequently while believing the practice to be not only a vice but also dangerous to his health, he fended off homosexual advances, he eventually lost his virginity in what he felt was an incestuous seduction by the woman who for years had seemed like a mother to him and whom he called *maman*. But details of such desires and experiences had not hitherto been included in serious autobiography; and Rousseau is at least partly purging himself of the guilt he feels for them by writing what he cannot speak about.

Rousseau was right to say that his autobiography had no precedent, but wrong to suppose that it would have no imitators; for his book was followed by a numerous progeny of confessional autobiographies and autobiographical fictions which have continued down to our own day, including Goethe's *Wilhelm Meister* (1796–1829), Newman's *Apologia pro vita sua* (1864), Hamsun's *Hunger* (1890, see p. 157 below), Proust's *À la recherche du temps perdu* (1913–22, see p. 187 below), and Joyce's *A Portrait of the Artist as a Young Man* (1914–15).

In addition to its intrinsic merit, Rousseau's book helped to open the eyes of his successors to the fact that not only Rousseau, but each one of them was unique, unlike anyone else, better, perhaps, or worse than others, but at any rate different. They might learn too that self-analysis on the lines of the *Confessions* can be used, by the author and his or her readers, as a stepping-stone towards a better understanding of themselves, of other individuals, and of people generally.

Translations

The Penguin Classics translation by J. M. Cohen (1954) is pleasant to read and has a brief Introduction, but lacks the notes that the reader often needs; the *Confessions* is not included in the Oxford World's Classics. Translated by Christopher Kelly with full apparatus and Notes, the *Confessions*, takes up most of volume five of *The Collected Writings of Rousseau*, University Press of New England, Hanover and London 1995.

Further reading

For the general background, see Roger Price, *A Concise History of France*, Cambridge University Press 1993.

A. J. Ayer's *Voltaire*, Weidenfeld and Nicolson, London 1986, contains an excellent short biography, and chapters on the major works, including a summary of *Candide*.

The best biography of Rousseau is the *Confessions* itself, but Robert Wokler's *Rousseau*, Oxford University Press 1995, prefaces a brilliant short introduction to Rousseau's thought and work with a useful biographical summary. Peter France's *Rousseau: Confessions*, Cambridge University Press 1987, sets the work in its context in a challenging and informative study.

V Goethe and Schiller

German-speaking countries in the eighteenth century

Until nearly three-quarters of the way through the nineteenth century there was no single state which could be called Germany, only a number of areas in which German was spoken, some of which had political connections with each other. Since early medieval times there had been the Holy Roman Empire, a loose confederation of Catholic states allied to the Papacy which included much of what is now Germany; since the Reformation in the sixteenth century a number of these states had turned Protestant; and by the end of the seventeenth century, the principal German-speaking states – mostly poor, economically backward, ravaged by religious warfare, but ready for cultural development – were divided into three main regions. There were, first, Catholic Austria and (beyond Bohemia and Moravia) Silesia, all part of the Hapsburg Empire; secondly the Protestant Hohenzollern lands of Brandenburg (around Berlin), with Pomerania to the north and Prussia to the north-east, ruled by the Elector of Brandenburg who added the title of King of Prussia in 1701; and thirdly, in the west, hundreds of smaller principalities (including city-states, and states ruled by Prince-Bishops). These small states – some substantial, others minuscule, and mostly Protestant – were all under the nominal authority of the Holy Roman Emperor but were in practice largely autonomous, with forms of government varying from something like representative democracy to absolute autocracy. Some of the smallest of these states, indeed, could still seem like the countries in fairy-tales, where the forests were dark and dangerous, young princes set out to seek their fortunes, and the seventh son of a woodcutter might meet a lonely princess.

Warfare continued sporadically over the German-speaking lands during the eighteenth century, but economic conditions did gradually improve. The major political change was the enlargement and increasing power of Prussia, especially under Frederick II, the

Great, who reigned 1740–86, and whom we have already met in connection with Voltaire's visit to Berlin of 1750–3; elsewhere the Hapsburg Empire continued without much political change, as did most of the small German states in the west.

Court life – there were a great many courts – became more civilised, while intellectual life and the arts blossomed into an *Aufklärung*, a less iconoclastic German version of the French Enlightenment. To name the great German composers of the period is to tell its musical history – J. S. Bach, Händel, Haydn, Mozart, Beethoven, the first two from the Protestant north, the others from the Catholic south – while the philosophers included the polymath G. W. Leibniz (1646–1716, from Leipzig in Saxony), and one of the greatest of all thinkers, Immanuel Kant (1724–1804, from Königsberg in Prussia). German literature took a little longer to develop than did German music and philosophy, for – until Goethe and Schiller, the subjects of this chapter, began to exploit it – the German language was thought hardly suitable to serve as the medium for sophisticated fiction, poetry, or drama.

Johann Wolfgang von Goethe, 1749–1832

Johann Wolfgang Goethe – the 'von' was added later – was born to a bourgeois family in the Free City of Frankfurt-am-Main. His early life was unexceptional: good local schooling, followed by three years at Leipzig University; and, after an interval at home, two more years at Strassburg University where he was influenced by the poet and critic J. G. Herder (1744–1803). But only two years after leaving Strassburg, Goethe published two works of astonishing quality and originality which made him a celebrity in his midtwenties: the play *Götz von Berlichingen* (1773), and the epistolary novel *The Sorrows of Young Werther* (1774).

Götz, the story of a sixteenth-century German knight, the last survivor of an age of chivalry, opened the past to the modern imagination in a play that, like Shakespeare's histories, spoke in a language that all could understand and respond to, and which broke out of the restricting mould of Neo-classicism. *Werther*, even more extraordinarily, explored the inner life of its melancholy, suicidal hero in a completely new way, creating a mental world of turmoil, hopeless passion, and despair. *Götz* showed the way to the historical romances of Scott and his successors; *Werther* introduces the anguished quest for meaning in the apparent pointlessness and absurdity of life that was to be a major theme of literature from the Romantics onwards. From the moment of the book's publication, 'Wertherism' spread across Europe, a cultural phenomenon that reverberated in the self-consciously desolate hearts of young men disappointed in love, who would be discovered leaning pensively on gravestones, dressed in Werther's blue frock-coat and buff breeches. Fortunately the craze led to few actual suicides.

Weimar, to which Goethe moved as a handsome and celebrated young writer in 1775, was a small independent Duchy in Thuringia. The town of Weimar itself, walled and gated, had a mere 7,000 inhabitants living in tall-gabled old houses; and there was a court, an administration, and a five-hundred-man army. What made it attractive to a man of Goethe's wide-ranging abilities and warm personality was the ruling Duke himself, Karl August (1757–1828), who was then aged eighteen to Goethe's twenty-six, and whose youthful boisterousness was accompanied by a sharp but common-sensical mind, a desire to rule kindly and well, and a great gift for friendship which he lavished on Goethe. Their relationship quickly became as close and as frank as could be between ruler and subject; they called each other the familiar *du*, got drunk and played pranks together, and yet held each other in profound respect, a relationship very different from the competitive, often spiteful, association of Voltaire and Frederick the Great.

The Duke found that he wanted the talented Goethe to stay on with him in Weimar as something more than a genial friend: he wanted him to help to administer his Duchy, and Goethe allowed himself to be drafted into the administration of the little state, at first as a volunteer and then the following year with the official appointment of senior Privy Councillor. To the complaints of the career civil servants over whose indignant heads Goethe had been promoted, the Duke – having put benevolent autocracy into prac-tice – answered truthfully that the ablest man had got the job. So for the next ten years Goethe's energies were devoted to Weimar as controller of, at various times, roads, the army, and the treasury. He was very good at his work, and the Duke arranged for him to be ennobled as 'von Goethe' in 1782; but literature was for the moment subordinated to official duties and a growing interest in science. 'It is as if Byron', Professor Reed remarks, 'after publishing *Childe Harold*, had joined the civil service.'[1]

[1] T. J. Reed, *Goethe*, Oxford University Press [1997], p. 29.

By 1786 Goethe had had enough of it, and he fled to Italy. He stayed away from Weimar, mostly in Rome, for nearly two years, reawakening and enriching his aesthetic sensibility, and developing a view of the world in which nature, science, and art were seen together as parts of an endlessly developing creative process. In 1788 he returned to Weimar, which was now home to him, refreshed and keen to write again, and to pursue the scientific work which continued to fascinate him and to which he made major contributions in botany, chemistry, comparative morphology, and evolution. He was welcomed back by Karl August who generously agreed to Goethe's request that he should retire from full-time administrative work and act as adviser to the government only when it suited him to do so.

Goethe had had many love affairs, but soon after his return he took as his mistress (and eventually married) a beautiful, vivacious, but relatively ordinary and ignorant, young woman called Christiane Vulpius. Despite Christiane's lack of sophistication, she gave Goethe the love and emotional security that he needed, their relationship being something like that enjoyed between Joyce and his wife Nora. To this period belong the classical plays *Egmont* (1788), *Iphigenie* (1789), and *Tasso* (1790). It was also, of course, the period of the French Revolution.

In May 1794 Goethe made the most important artistic connection of his life, with the poet and critic Friedrich Schiller (whom we shall be meeting later in this chapter). Goethe was then forty-five, Schiller ten years younger. They were very different from each other in personality and outlook and might easily have become literary rivals and even enemies, but both men were outstandingly magnanimous and free of professional jealousy, and their differences – Schiller's passion for the idea of freedom from political tyranny, Goethe's for that of harmonious natural development – actually helped them (after a shaky start) to spur each other on in their common certainty of the value and importance of art. What Schiller did for Goethe was to encourage him to return from science to literature as his main pursuit, to complete a number of unfinished works and undertake new ones, most importantly the *Bildungsroman*, or novel of growing-up, *Wilhelm Meisters Lehrjahre* (1796), and the first part of *Faust* (1808).

Schiller died in 1805, and Goethe stayed on at Weimar, growing older in body but not in mind, still writing both prose and poetry, still falling in love. *Elective Affinities*, a strange novel of adultery, appeared in 1809; the continuation of *Wilhelm Meister*, the *Wanderjahre*, in 1821–9; and extracts from the second part of *Faust* in 1827–8 (the complete *Faust* Part II being published posthumously). Duke Karl August died in 1828, but his lifelong friend Goethe lingered a few years more, dying in 1832 at the age of eighty-three.

Goethe was a giant: lover, administrator, scientist, playwright, novelist, poet, who saw his own works as fragments of the grand confession of his life; the greatest writer in modern German, the language he did more than anyone to consolidate and perfect; a benevolent giant, eagerly living a full life that spanned a period of unprecedented change and development in the Europe that he helped to form.

Faust, Part One, 1775–1808

Goethe took as the scaffolding for *Faust* the early sixteenth-century legend of Dr Faustus, the German scholar who was believed to have sold his soul to the Devil in exchange for supernatural knowledge and power during the rest of his life on earth, a story familiar to him both from Marlowe's tragedy *Dr Faustus* (published 1604, 1611), and from a puppet-play that had long been shown in German-speaking areas, including Frankfurt in 1768 and 1770. In Marlowe's play Faustus, wearying of academic science, turns to magic and calls up Mephistophilis,[2] through whom he makes a fatal contract with the Devil: Faustus is to have twenty-four years on earth with Mephistophilis as his servant to do all he asks, at the end of which the Devil is to have Faustus's immortal soul. Faustus proceeds to get what he can from the bargain, with an ever-increasing lust for power, though predictably the Devil cheats him of any real benefit from it. He is encouraged by his good angel to repent and be saved, but is persuaded by his bad angel to believe that he is already damned, and to carry on with his futile self-indulgence. The play ends with Faustus's despairing monologue as he waits at the eleventh hour for the Devil to come and fetch his soul, when he realises the worthlessness of what he has had from the Devil's bargain, and cries out to his Saviour to let him repent even now. But by this time it really is too late, and the Devil's servants carry him away to hell.

In *Faust* Goethe keeps in touch with the main lines of this story – for example, Faust's bargain with the Devil, discussions with his

[2] So spelled in Marlowe's play; Goethe spells the name 'Mephistopheles'.

colleague Wagner, the raising of the spirit of Helen of Troy at the request of the Emperor – but changes it into something quite different, altering the terms of Faust's bargain with the Devil, adding numerous new characters, incidents, and episodes, and completely changing the ending.

The two Parts of *Faust* were composed over the extraordinarily long period of more than half a century, the first sketches dating from 1775 or earlier, and the work being completed only a short while before Goethe's death in 1832. There was, however, a gap in composition of nearly twenty years after the publication of Part I in 1808, and the second Part is so different in its approach from the first that it is difficult not to see them as separate works. Moreover, although the altered story was patched together as a play, the two parts are so long and diffuse that they are virtually impossible to perform in the theatre except in severely truncated forms; even Goethe seems to have thought them unsuitable for the stage. While composing Part I Goethe saw it as 'a loosely constructed commodious dramatic poem',[3] and that is what it is: a long closet drama[4] comparable in form to Ibsen's *Brand* and *Peer Gynt*.

The main changes to the traditional plot in Part I are the alteration of the terms of Faust's bargain with the Devil, and the introduction of Gretchen. In the old story, Faustus promises to surrender his soul unconditionally in return for present advantages; but now Faust agrees to forfeit his life only if he is ever deluded by enjoyment into asking for its prolongation:

> If ever to the moment I shall say:
> Beautiful moment, do not pass away!
> Then you may forge your chains to bind me
>   (lines 1699–1701, David Luke's translation) [. . .]

And, at the end of Part II, Faust, in his enthusiasm for freedom and at the moment of his death, does in effect ask for the prolongation of a beautiful moment:

> I long to see that multitude, and stand
> With a free people on a free land!
> Then to the moment I might say:
> Beautiful moment, do not pass away!
> Till many ages shall have passed

[3] Goethe, *Faust* Part I, trs. by David Luke, Oxford World's Classics 1987, p. xxvii.
[4] A play that is intended, or suitable, for reading rather than acting.

This record of my earthly life shall last,
And in anticipation of such bliss
What moment could give me greater joy than this?
(lines 11579–86, David Luke's translation)

Mephistopheles rejoices at the prospect of having Faust's soul, but he is cheated of it; distracted by his own lust for a chorus of enlightened angels, he fails to prevent them from bearing Faust's soul away to heaven.

The story of Gretchen is the second dramatic focus of Part I. She is a simple maiden whom Faust seduces, egged on by Mephistopheles. Faust is challenged by her brother, kills him, and flees the country. Abandoned by her lover, Gretchen bears his child, drowns it, and is condemned to death for infanticide. Faust returns with Mephistopheles on the night before her execution, and they attempt to spirit her away from prison, but she refuses the Devil's help and is left to her fate. There Part I ends, the ultimate cliffhanger.

Thus *Faust* is still a treatment of human temptation, the need that we experience over and over again in our lives to decide whether or not to compromise our principles in order to get something that we want. But it is much more than a simple story of salvation or damnation: Mephistopheles and Faust are types of despair and idealism, and the poem investigates their confrontation in depth, balancing evil against good, finally finding against the barren negativity of Mephistopheles in favour of Faust's conviction that the natural order inevitably moves towards the greater good, not only of mankind, but of the whole of creation.

The other great virtue of *Faust* is just that part of it which is most elusive: the quality of Goethe's poetry which is lost in translation. David Luke is a fine translator, but even he cannot always capture the incisive economy and the wide variety of Goethe's verse, which includes loose five- and six-stress lines, lyrics, songs of praise, folk verses, and – most characteristic of all – sharp, epigrammatic four-stress lines, a polished version of an old doggerel form called *Knittelvers*; all with glittering rhyme-schemes of masculine and feminine endings that simply do not translate into another language. Here is a key passage in which Faust first meets Mephistopheles in human form:

MEPHISTOPHELES [*stepping out from behind the stove as the mist disperses, dressed as a medieval wandering student*]
Why all this fuss? How can I serve you, sir?

FAUST   So that was the quintessence of the cur!
        A student tramp! How very comical.

MEPH.   Sir, I salute your learning and your wit!
        You made me sweat, I must admit.

FAUST   What is your name?

MEPH.   The question is absurd,
        Surely, in one who seeks to know
        The inmost essence, not the outward show,
        And has such deep contempt for the mere word.

FAUST   Ah, with such gentlemen as you
        The name often conveys the essence too,
        Clearly enough; we say Lord of the Flies,
        Destroyer, Liar – each most fittingly applies.
        Well then, who are you?

MEPH.   Part of that Power which would
        Do evil constantly, and constantly does good.

FAUST   This riddle has, no doubt, some explanation.

MEPH.   I am the spirit of perpetual negation;
        And rightly so, for all things that exist
        Deserve to perish, and would not be missed –
        Much better it would be if nothing were
        Brought into being. Thus, what you men call
        Destruction, sin, evil in short, is all
        My sphere, the element I most prefer.
           (lines 1322–44, David Luke's translation)[5]

In Mephistopheles's last speech Luke gives us a six-stress line followed by six five-stress lines, rhyming *abbcdcd*. The German original can be seen, even by those who know little of the language, to be have a sharper, more economical rhythm which English words cannot match, with one four-stress line, one five-stress line, and four four-stress lines, rhyming in couplets *abbccdd*:

MEPH. *Ich bin der Geist, der stets verneint!*
Und das mit Recht; denn alles, was entsteht,
Ist wert, dass es zugrunde geht;
Drum besser wär's, dass nichts entstünde.

[5] The German original of this passage is given on pp. 230–1 below. It is tautly spoken by Klaus Maria Brandauer in Istvan Szabo's film *Mephisto* (1981), in which an ambitious actor sells his soul to the Nazis in the 1930s. Brandauer plays the Faust-like actor who plays Mephistopheles.

So ist denn alles, was ihr Sünde,
Zerstörung, kurz das Böse nennt,
Mein eigentliches Element.
(*Faust*, Part I, lines 1322–44)

Translations

David Luke, the translator of the Oxford World's Classics version of *Faust* Part One (1987), estimates that between fifty and one hundred English translations of the poem have been made since it first appeared; and translators will no doubt go on trying for the unattainable, perfect version. The best recent translation is Luke's, which is both scholarly and racy, but the Penguin Classics version by Philip Wayne (1949) is still very readable. Both do their best to mimic Goethe's rather loose metre and his tightly-organised rhyming, in which they succeed pretty well, although there is a tendency to add stresses to the lines when the English unavoidably has more syllables than the German.

Friedrich Schiller, 1759–1805

The Duchy of Württemberg in Swabia, where Schiller was born and brought up, was larger and richer than Weimar; but, where Weimar's Duke Karl August was a benevolent autocrat, Duke Karl Eugen of Württemberg was the worst sort of absolute despot, profligate, selfish, and cruel; a Catholic monarch, moreover, in a Protestant state. The Estates (or parliament) of Württemberg theoretically controlled the privy purse, but in practice Karl Eugen got round their restrictions and did what he liked. Schiller's father was a lowly recruiting officer in the Duke's service and, when the Duke spotted talent in Friedrich and wanted him to be sent to the ducal Military Academy (the purpose of which was to turn out military and civil servants obedient to the Duke), the father had to submit, even though his son had been intended for a career in the Church.

Schiller had a hateful time under the severe military discipline of the Academy (1773–80) – the boys were constantly regimented, there were no school holidays, and they were not even allowed unsupervised visits from their parents – but what the teachers taught was not controlled by the military authorities, and the best of them followed a surprisingly liberal curriculum in philosophy and literature. Thus Schiller developed a loathing for the tyrannical limitation of individual freedom, while at the same time he was agreeably instructed in the liberal outlook of the Enlightenment and introduced to literary predecessors such as Shakespeare and Racine. In 1776, when he was seventeen, Schiller changed from the study of law to that of medicine, which led him to the consideration of one the key problems of the time, the relationship between the mind and the physical body. His first dissertation on this subject was rejected for being too unconventional, but he eventually produced one that was acceptable to the authorities, and he became a young and ill-paid army doctor in 1780.

With this background, it was inevitable that Schiller should revolt against the Duke's despotism; and this he did in 1781, when he was twenty-two, by writing a tragedy in prose, *The Robbers*. In this powerful melodrama (influenced by the *Sturm und Drang*, 'Storm and Stress', movement of young German writers) the hero, Karl Moor, a sort of Robin Hood with a tender conscience, is pitted against his wicked younger brother Franz, who has imprisoned their father, stolen the dukedom, and proceeded to rule cruelly and despotically after the manner of Karl Eugen. This version of traditional 'brother' stories such as Jacob and Esau and the Prodigal Son does not lead to the expected happy ending in which Karl rescues their father, defeats his brother, and eventually becomes a good duke himself, because Schiller rejects such simple antitheses of good and evil in favour of investigating a more complex underlying reality of tensions in characters and events. Here, robber Karl, following the suicide of his brother and the death of their father, cannot come to terms with his own lawless past and gives himself up to the authorities, with the certainty that he will be executed. There is a good deal of absurd theatricality in *The Robbers*, but it caused a sensation when it was published in 1781, and an even greater sensation when it was staged in a watered-down form the following year in Mannheim (just outside the state of Württemberg): 'the theatre was like a madhouse – rolling eyes, clenched fists, hoarse cries in the auditorium. Strangers fell sobbing into each other's arms, women on the point of fainting staggered towards the exit.'[6] These extreme reactions were no doubt caused chiefly by the theatrical power of Schiller's drama, even in its censored form; but the contemporary

---

[6] An eyewitness quoted by Lesley Sharpe in *Friedrich Schiller*, Cambridge University Press 1991, p. 29.

relevance of the character of the despotic ruler Franz will also have been obvious and exciting. Its influence both in Germany and abroad was great and lasting: 'My God! Southey!', wrote Coleridge when he read the play, 'Who is this Schiller? This convulser of the heart?'[7]

Duke Karl Eugen, predictably angry with Schiller, had him placed under arrest for a fortnight; and Schiller, seeing no future and much danger for himself if he remained in Württemberg, decided to escape. In September 1782 he fled across the border to Mannheim, where he hoped for success as playwright to the theatre there. In Mannheim, however, his style of dramatic writing was not appreciated, the salary was miserably small, and after two years his contract was not renewed. At this low point he was rescued by a small group of admirers led by C. G. Körner, who supported him for the next two years (1784–6) in Leipzig and Dresden. During this period he wrote much of his poetry (including his famous 'Ode to Joy'[8]), and the drama *Don Carlos* (published 1787); and at the end of it he moved to Weimar (where he had an unsuccessful first meeting with Goethe), and found employment writing reviews and history. On the strength of this post he was appointed Professor of History at Jena, a small town in the state of Weimar, in 1788. He married in 1790; in 1791 he almost died from a form of pneumonia; and in 1792 he published his *History of the Thirty Years' War*, the subject of his dramatic trilogy *Wallenstein*, discussed below.

Some of Schiller's most important works of criticism appeared in the early to mid-1790s: essays on tragedy and the sublime; the *Aesthetic Letters* of 1794 which associated beauty with freedom, prompted partly by his horror at the Terror following the French Revolution; and *On Naïve and Sentimental Poetry* (1795–6), in which he was concerned with the problem of overcoming the separation between the mind and the external world, and in which he equated naïve art with a classical directness of vision and sentimental art with romantic reflectiveness. These critical writings were widely influential in the coming Romantic revolution, not only in Germany but also in France and Britain.

---

[7] S. T. Coleridge, letter to Robert Southey, 3 November 1794.

[8] When '*An die Freude*' was sung in Berlin in the last movement of Beethoven's Ninth Symphony during the revolution in December 1989, the exclamation *Freude!* ('joy') was replaced by *Freiheit!* ('freedom'), a change that would surely have appealed to Schiller.

In June 1794 Schiller initiated further contact with Goethe. There was an exchange of letters, both men put aside any suspicions that they might have had of each other, and for the next decade, until Schiller's death, they formed one of the most genial and productive of all literary friendships from which emerged each one's masterpiece: *Faust* Part I and the *Wallenstein* trilogy (performed 1798–9). Now settled in Weimar, Schiller continued to write plays for the Weimar theatre: *Maria Stuart* (1800, about Mary Queen of Scots); *The Maid of Orleans* (1801, about Joan of Arc); *The Bride of Messina* (1803, in the classical manner); *William Tell* (1804, about the Swiss liberator, Schiller's only play without a tragic outcome); and *Demetrius*, left unfinished at his death.

Schiller's final illness began in February 1805, and he died, aged only forty-five, in May. By the middle of the century he was recognised, along with Goethe, as a German classic; a canonisation that was not altogether for the good of his reputation in Germany, where his work was forced on school-children with the result that appreciation of it tended to be defeated by its own celebrity. His influence on early French and British Romanticism has already been mentioned; and in the mid-nineteenth century German literature – and Schiller's work in particular – was widely known and admired by British readers. In nineteenth-century Russia it was Schiller's liberalism that was especially influential, inspiring radicals such as Alexánder Hérzen.

Wallenstein, 1798–9

The Thirty Years' War (1618–48) began as the reaction of the Archduke Ferdinand of Austria, shortly to become the Catholic Holy Roman Emperor Ferdinand II (reigned 1619–37), to a revolt in Protestant Bohemia. Some of the German states, Transylvania, and Sweden then became involved in what was turning into a larger conflict between Catholicism and Protestantism; and before it ended the war had drawn in most of the states of continental Europe, and had devastated much of Germany, where the greater part of the fighting had taken place. One of the warlords serving the Emperor was Albrecht von Wallenstein, Duke of Friedland in Bohemia (1583–1634), who raised an army largely at his own expense and proved to be a spectacularly successful general in the later 1620s. He was brusquely dismissed at the Diet of Regensburg in 1630 as a result of jealousies at the Viennese court, and he retired sullenly into private life, shorn of power but with his prestige intact. He was recalled as a leader when danger threatened the Empire in 1632, but now he was a discontented man, still aggrieved because of the insult he had received at Regensburg.

The action of Schiller's trilogy is set in 1634, when Wallenstein, encamped in Bohemia with a formidable Imperial army largely loyal to him personally, is tempted to pay the Emperor back by changing sides and throwing in his lot with the Emperor's enemies. Whether he really intends to betray his own side, or whether it is just a tempting idea, is never made clear, but he certainly thinks about it and does some preliminary plotting. Before he takes a final decision whether or not to act, however, he is discovered to be in communication with the enemy, and his old friend and fellow-general, Octavio Piccolómini, for reasons that are also morally ambiguous, decides to betray the plot and his friend to the Emperor; and so the betrayer is betrayed. When it comes to the point neither the unit commanders nor the troops of his army are as unconditionally loyal to Wallenstein as he hoped and believed they would be, but are all involved in complex webs of personal and political loyalties that admit of no simple solutions, and which draw them inexorably away from Wallenstein back to the cause of their Emperor. The rebellion has failed before it began, and Wallenstein is murdered by Butler, the Irish colonel who had formerly been his most loyal and dependable supporter.

Schiller first intended to use this story as the basis of a single tragedy, but he soon found that he had too much material. A prologue intended to show the spirit of the army when it was still loyal to Wallenstein was expanded into the eleven comic scenes of *Wallenstein's Camp*, in which ordinary soldiers and NCOs converse in four-stress rhymed doggerel (much less polished than Goethe's), expatiating on how much they admire and are devoted to their general before they know anything about the coming betrayals. This is the least successful part of the trilogy – at least in an English translation – partly because Schiller fails to follow Shakespeare's example of alternating comic scenes with serious ones but gathers them all together; partly because there is no action; and partly because the ordinary soldiers he portrays are not as convincing as his tragic characters.

With *The Piccolómini* and *Wallenstein's Death* the tragedy proper begins on a very different plane. These two five-act plays are really one long play in ten acts, written in flexible five-stress blank verse, but divided into two for the sake of theatrical practicality,[9] and they can be considered together. The three main characters are Wallenstein himself and the two Piccolóminis, Octavio the father and Max the son. Wallenstein does not appear until the third act of *The Piccolómini* (he was also absent in person from *Wallenstein's Camp*), but when he does appear it is as a troubled man, not at all the heroic figure acclaimed by the soldiers, but one unable, Hamlet-like, to make up his mind whether or not to act. He himself is convinced of the loyalty of his commanders, but Octavio Piccolómini has secretly taken sides against him, and is working to betray him to the Emperor. Towards the end of the play Wallenstein's greatness is more in evidence, but events force him into ever more impossible positions until he is finally murdered in his bed. Octavio Piccolómini, although he acts villainously in terms of friendship towards his old comrade and is to benefit personally by the betrayal, does so with real regret: he is aware that betraying Wallenstein is not a pretty thing to do, but his overriding loyalty is to the Emperor; and he reasons to Max:

> My son! It is not always possible
> In life to be as pure as little children,
> As we are bidden by the voice within us.
> In constant battle with despite and malice
> Even the upright spirit stays not true –
> This namely is the curse of evil deeds,
> That they will never cease to breed and bring forth evil.
> I split no hairs, I only do my duty,
> I carry out my Emperor's commands.
> Better indeed if we could always follow
> The promptings of our heart, but we must then
> Give up all hope in many a worthy purpose.
> Our place, my son, is here to serve the Emperor.
> Our hearts may say about it what they will.[10]

The ends, in short, if they are good enough, justify the means. Young Max Piccolómini, on the other hand, who is in love

---

[9] *Wallenstein's Camp* is very short, with only 1,107 four-stress lines; *The Piccolómini* has 2,651 five-stress lines, and *Wallenstein's Death* has 3,867 five-stress lines; the last two totalling 6,518 lines. For comparison, *The Comedy of Errors*, Shakespeare's shortest play, has 1,756 lines; and *Hamlet*, his longest, has 3,776 lines; the average length of all Shakespeare's plays is 2,700 lines, virtually the same as *The Piccolómini*.

[10] *The Piccolómini*, v, i, 3554–67, trs. by F. J. Lamport, Penguin Classics 1979.

with Wallenstein's daughter Thekla, is more straightforward. Max will continue to believe in Wallenstein, whom he reveres even more than he does his own father, until there is plain proof of his hero's desertion; but then he will fight Wallenstein openly, and if necessary give up Thekla, in order to remain true to his prior loyalty to the Emperor, however painful it is to do so. There are several important minor characters – among them Thekla herself, Wallenstein's sister-in-law the Countess Terzky, Colonel Butler the formerly-loyal Irishman who finally kills Wallenstein – and (except perhaps for Thekla) they are all well-realised and credible.

The action of the tragedy begins slowly, but picks up momentum as it goes along, until towards the end the clash of loyalties and the threat of violence – soon to be realised – generate an almost unbearable tension. Although there are large differences, there are also parallels with *Macbeth*: here again is a loyal soldier whose ambition gets the better of him, and who is eventually brought down by those who were once his comrades. Much of the dialogue and the imagery, and the blank verse in which they are cast, are also reminiscent of Shakespeare's tragedies, which of course Schiller knew well and admired (he actually translated *Macbeth* into German). But the *Wallenstein* trilogy is not just Shakespeare reworked in another time and place: it is the master work of one of the most original of European poets and dramatists, and is still a success in the theatre.

Translations

The only easily available translation is the Penguin Classics version of *The Robbers and Wallenstein* by F. J. Lamport (1979). Fortunately it is a good one, giving *The Piccolómini* and *Wallenstein's Death* in clear, fluent blank verse that is both easy to read and close to Schiller's German. S. T. Coleridge made a slightly freer blank-verse translation of *The Piccolómini* and *Wallenstein's Death* in 1800 which is wonderfully good; the arrangement of the acts and scenes differs from that of the standard text. Appendix B (pp. 231–3 below) gives the German text of the extract translated by Lamport above, together with Coleridge's translation of the same passage; and also a short extract in German from one of Wallenstein's soliloquies with three blank-verse translations by Coleridge (1800) and Lamport (1979), and from T. J. Reed's *Schiller* (1991).

Further reading

For the general background see Mary Fulbrook's admirable *A Concise History of Germany*, Cambridge University Press 1990, revised edn 1992.

The first biography of Goethe was written by an Englishman, George Eliot's consort G. H. Lewes, and it is still in many ways the best. Lewes's *The Life and Works of Goethe* appeared in 1855, when its author was still close in time to his subject, able to talk and correspond with many people who had known Goethe intimately; and the result is a thorough, clear-headed, and wonderfully readable classic of biography. Though now out of print, it was included in Everyman's Library from 1908, with many reprints, and can often be picked up second-hand. T. J. Reed's *Goethe*, Oxford University Press 1984, revised edn [1997], is an excellent introduction to Goethe's creativity. The lengthy Introductions and Notes included in David Luke's Oxford World's Classics versions of *Faust* Parts I and II give clear and scholarly guidance to the texts. It is also worth pointing out that there is a good Penguin Classics translation of *The Sorrows of Young Werther* by Michael Hulse (1989).

Lesley Sharpe's *Friedrich Schiller: Drama, Thought and Politics*, Cambridge University Press 1991, was the first general study of Schiller's work to appear for over forty years, and it is excellent: full, intelligent, and readable. Also strongly recommended is T. J. Reed's shorter monograph *Schiller*, Oxford University Press 1991. Both have good chapters on *Wallenstein*. Carlyle's *Life* of Schiller (1825) is a fine early account. F. J. Lamport's Penguin Classics translation of *The Robbers and Wallenstein* has a good short Introduction to all four plays, but no Notes or other apparatus.

VI Púshkin and Lérmontov

The Russian Empire in the nineteenth century

So far we have been considering landmarks in the literature of
Western Europe – of Italy, France, Spain, and Germany, with
Scandinavia to come – but Russia, straddling the boundary between
Eastern Europe and Asia, was (and is) a country yet more foreign to
British readers, and requires a more detailed preliminary survey.
Russian culture in general, moreover, and Russian literature in
particular, has always been powerfully affected by the extraordin-
ary nature of the country: its geography and climate, its demo-
graphy, and its political and social organisation.

Geography and climate

Russia is still very large, but in the nineteenth century it was enormous. Within its western borders were Ukraine, Belorussia, the Baltic
states, parts of present-day Poland (an unhappy subject state), and
the whole of Finland (which had a good deal of autonomy); in the
south were the Caucasian states, Kazakhstan, and other substantial
Muslim regions; and in the east were the wilds of Siberia and Alaska
(the latter sold to the United States in 1867). Even without Alaska,
the Russian Empire spread across 170 degrees of longitude and
almost 40 degrees of latitude, and encompassed twelve modern
time zones. Its area was approximately three times that of the
United States.

The land is generally flat, especially from Poland eastwards to the
Urals, except for the great range of the Caucasus mountains on the
southern frontier (which was Russia's equivalent of the American
Wild West). There are several huge lakes or inland seas, the Caspian
being the largest; and a number of great rivers that were vital for
transport before the coming of the railways: primarily the Don and
the Volga in the west, and the Ob, the Yenisei, and the Lena in

Siberia. Across European Russia the vegetation runs in five horizontal bands, from tundra in the extreme north, through coniferous forest, to mixed forest, to fertile grassland (steppe), and to arid grassland. The climate ranges from arctic in the north to subtropical on parts of the Black Sea coast; but everywhere in between it is continental and extreme, with very hot summers, and very cold winters with a lot of snow.

Railways

The first major Russian railway was the Petersburg – Moscow line completed in 1851; there was a railway boom in the 1860s and 1870s – about two decades after the West European railway boom – and another one between 1891 and 1905 which included the Trans-Siberian Railway. Russian railway building was mostly state-financed, and partly funded by the sale of Alaska to the United States. The trains were large (broad-gauge), comfortable, slow, and unpunctual.

Peoples

Most but not all of the inhabitants of the Empire were Russians: by the 1890s there were fifty-six million Great Russians (whom we now call simply Russians), twenty-two million Little Russians (Ukrainians), and six million White Russians[1] (Belorussians), all speaking related dialects of Russian: a total of eighty-four million Russians in a population of about 130 million (so the Great Russians were actually in a minority of the whole population). The rest of the population included a great variety of non-Russians: Finns, Balts, Poles, Germans, Jews, Tartars, Georgians and other Caucasian peoples, aboriginal Siberians, Turkic-speaking and other Muslim peoples, Mongolians, and many smaller groups. It was primarily an agricultural society: the number of town-dwellers was always dwarfed by the majority who lived in the countryside – 5 per cent were town-dwellers at the beginning of the nineteenth century, and still only 13 per cent at the end.

Constitution

The Russian Empire was an autocracy, under the absolute rule of the Tsar, or Emperor, from whom all power theoretically flowed,

---

[1] Not to be confused with the 'Whites', the anti-Bolsheviks who fought the Red Army in the Civil War of 1917–22.

and who was commander-in-chief of the armed forces. The Tsar was assisted in his rule by ministers of state (whom he appointed and dismissed at will), a civil service, and an officer corps. The nineteenth-century Tsars were alternately reformers and reactionaries (it being understood that 'reformer' is a strictly relative term, and that none of these Tsars willingly considered any limitation of their own ultimate autocratic power). They were:

Alexander I (reigned 1801–25) who succeeded when his unstable father Tsar Paul was murdered. He immediately instituted a wide range of reforms of the administration and became a key figure in the European war against Napoleon's France; towards the end of his reign he retreated into mystical reaction and undid much of the good he had earlier instigated. He was succeeded by his younger brother

Nicholas I (reigned 1825–55) who, following his accession, savagely repressed the attempted 'Decembrist' rising of liberal aristocratic officers, hanging five of them and banishing the rest to Siberia. He did reform the law and some of the worst aspects of serfdom, but he was essentially an illiberal despot. He was succeeded by his son

Alexander II (reigned 1855–81), the great liberalising event of whose reign was the emancipation of the serfs in 1861; but he also introduced reforms of, amongst other things, local government, the universities, military service, and the judicial system. Ironically he was assassinated by 'liberal' terrorists on the day he was to sign a decree instituting a consultative assembly. He was succeeded by his second son

Alexander III (reigned 1881–94), a convinced reactionary, who rejected the idea of a consultative assembly, and proceeded to undo as many of his father's social reforms as he could, to increase discrimination against the Jews, and to Russify national minorities. He was succeeded by his son

Nicholas II (reigned 1894–1917), the last Tsar: charming and not unintelligent, Nicholas was a rather weak man who was unable to see that absolute autocracy was not a viable system for ruling a Russia that was rapidly industrialising at the end of the nineteenth century. The revolution of 1905 forced his reluctant assent to the creation of a legislative assembly; and he abdicated following the February revolution of 1917. He and his whole family were shot by the Bolsheviks in 1918.

Nearly every citizen of the Russian Empire in the nineteenth century was obliged to be a member of one of five groups or 'Estates', each Estate having particular legal privileges, obligations, and restrictions. (The exceptions were the inhabitants of Finland, and certain people termed 'of other race', who included Jews and members of some primitive tribes.) The Estates were:

The hereditary *Gentry*[2] (including the aristocracy); in the later nineteenth century they comprised just over 1 per cent of the population of about 130 million. The Gentry were disproportionately important in Russian life and culture (just as the nobility had been in France under the *ancien régime*; see p. 46 above). They filled the higher offices, civilian and military; they owned most of the land; they were the best educated (most spoke French, and often other foreign languages as well); and they were relied on to maintain the status quo. They were exempt from military conscription, corporal punishment, and personal taxation. They were often eccentric and improvident.

The titles of the aristocracy were inherited by all the children of a titled father; hence the large number of Princes, Princesses, Counts, and Countesses in Russian fiction (there were also Barons and their Baronesses, but they could have come up as a result of merit rather than birth – or even of success in trade – and so were looked down on by Princes and Counts).

Since 1722 civil servants (who included not only government officials but also some of the upper ranks of other professions such as university and school teachers, tax collectors, lawyers, doctors, and so on) had been divided into fourteen (later twelve) 'classes', with their military equivalents, which are often mentioned in nineteenth-century Russian fiction (See the 'Table of Ranks' on p. 79).

The *Clergy*; just under 1 per cent of the population. The Clergy of the Russian (or Greek) Orthodox Church – the state religion that was descended from Byzantine Christianity – was itself divided into two classes: the black clergy of monks, who were celibate and who could be promoted to the upper ranks of the hierarchy; and the white clergy, or parish priests, who were compelled to marry, and could not rise above their station. The white clergy, who like the black actually dressed in dark clothes, were virtually a caste. Their sons often became priests in their turn and were likely to marry priests' daughters; and, unlike most English parish priests of the period, they were lowly members of society, ill-paid, sometimes ignorant, sometimes drunken, who did not necessarily enjoy the respect even of the peasants of their parish.

---

[2] Sometimes called the *Nobility*, although only a small minority of them had titles.

Class	Civilian Rank	Military Equivalent
1	Chancellor	Field Marshal
2	Actual Privy Councillor	General
3	Privy Councillor	Lieutenant-General
4	Actual State Councillor	Major-General
5	State Councillor	——
6	Collegiate Councillor	Colonel
7	Court Councillor	Lieutenant-Colonel
8	Collegiate Assessor	Major/Captain
9	Titular Councillor	Staff Captain
10	Collegiate Secretary	Lieutenant
11	(in abeyance)	——
12	Provincial Secretary	Sub-Lieutenant
13	(in abeyance)	Ensign
14	Collegiate Registrar	——

Table of Ranks

The *Military* Estate; 6.5 per cent of the population. This Estate consisted of the members of the armed forces, other than those officers – the majority – who belonged to the Gentry. The army was largely a conscript force, backward and cruel in its organisation and practices, in which peasants and lower town-dwellers were selectively but compulsorily enrolled for long periods – for twenty-five years before the Crimean War, and still for fifteen years after it. Discipline enforced by flogging was brutal, and to be called up as an ordinary soldier was widely believed to be a death sentence. For the officers it was quite otherwise, although there were obviously differences between the rather dreary service in provincial regiments, such as that performed by the artillery officers in Chékhov's *Three Sisters*, and a glittering career in a smart Guards regiment in Petersburg, such as that enjoyed by Vrónsky and his friends in *Ánna Karénina*.

The *Town-dwellers*, including hereditary Honorary Citizens; and, in descending order of rank, non-hereditary merchants and businessmen, small shopkeepers, artisans, and labourers; 9 per cent of the population. There was some mobility both ways between these groups. Rich merchants could if they wished buy their way into the hereditary gentry; while poor ones might be unable to pay the considerable fees of the occupational guilds and be obliged to move down a rank. The labourers were mostly displaced peasants from the countryside.

The *Peasants*, a massive 81.5 per cent of the population even at the end of the nineteenth century, lived in village communes under elected Village Elders. Until 1861 many (but not all) of them were serfs, 'souls' belonging to individual landowners and effectively slaves. After emancipation (coincidentally in the same decade that the black slaves were freed from their owners as a result of the Civil War in the United States) they were theoretically free, but were still restricted in what work they might do and in where they might travel, and they owed rent, or work in lieu of it, to their former owners. The communal land was farmed by a three-field strip system, as it had been in England in the Middle Ages. The farming was technically inefficient; and it was further hampered by the annual six-month lay-off caused by the severe winter, and by peasants' reluctance to change their traditional ways or to increase productivity.

The peasants' villages usually consisted of a single long, wide, unpaved street (of mud, dust, slush, or snow, depending on the season) with wooden huts situated in oblong plots along it. The huts were mostly crude thatched wooden structures with two or three rooms, housing people at one end and animals at the other. They were built by the peasants themselves around huge brick stoves in the principal room, on which some members of the family might sleep.

The peasants, who spoke an earthy, vivid Russian, were given to extremes of kindness and cruelty, and were always liable to violence and riot, in extreme cases burning down the manor house and murdering the landlord. They ate mostly cereals and potatoes, and drank tea and *kvass* (made from fermented black bread). When they could afford it, or could brew it themselves, many of the men drank vodka to excess, and beat their wives and children; the huts frequently caught fire. Two vivid but widely differing views of peasants and their lives are given in Tolstóy's *Anna Karénina* (1874) and Chékhov's short story 'Peasants' (1897).[3]

Alexánder Sergéevich Púshkin, 1799–1837

Alexánder Púshkin was born in Moscow to aristocratic parents[4] who neglected him, entrusting his upbringing and early education to French tutors and governesses; he learned Russian from the house serfs and from his nanny. From 1811 to 1817 he was a boarder at the Lycée for the gentry set up by Alexander II at

[3] It is instructive to compare these accounts with Hardy's *Far from the Madding Crowd* (1874) and Zola's *La Terre* (1887).

[4] One of Púshkin's great-grandfathers had been Abrám Hannibal, the Abyssinian 'moor' of Tsar Peter the Great, an ancestor of whom the poet was very proud.

Tsárskoe Seló near St Petersburg, where he already showed promise of becoming a major poet. From 1817 to 1820 he held an official sinecure in St Petersburg, where he spent his considerable spare time in dissipation and in writing poetry. From this period came his first major work, a mock epic called *Ruslán and Lyudmíla*, which appeared in 1820. In the same year he got into trouble with the authorities as a result of some privately-circulated poems that criticised the régime, and was exiled to the south of Russia, where he travelled in the Caucasus, the Crimea, and Bessarabia. In Bessarabia (the area that is now Moldova and part of southern Ukraine) Púshkin wrote three substantial narrative poems (*The Prisoner of the Caucasus*; *The Robber Brothers*; and *The Fountain of Bakhchísaray*; the verse drama *Borís Godunóv* followed in 1825); and there in 1823 he began his masterpiece, *Evgény* (or *Eugène* or *Eugene*) *Onégin*.[5] Later in 1823 he was allowed, while still in exile, to return to his parents' estate; and eventually, in 1825, he was called back to Moscow by the authoritarian Tsar Nicholas I, who – having successfully crushed the Decembrists – appointed himself Púshkin's censor. In 1831 Púshkin was married to the beautiful Natálya Goncharóva, and completed *Onégin*, eight years after it was begun. His later writings included the admirable short stories *The Queen of Spades* and *The Captain's Daughter* (1833–5), but he was increasingly unhappy in the early 1830s: leading a dissipated life, uncomfortable at Court, jealous of his wife's many admirers, and plagued by debt. In 1837 Púshkin was persuaded by rumours of an affair between his wife and Georges d'Anthès, a French royalist who was the adopted son of the Dutch Ambassador, to challenge the man. Púshkin was wounded in the duel that followed, and died two days later. He was aged thirty-eight.

This may not sound like a life of great achievement, but in its brief and not very happy course Púshkin wrote a body of poetry of such quality that he was quickly recognised as Russia's greatest poet, in the sort of way that Shakespeare is reckoned Britain's greatest poet, and Goethe Germany's; a position that he has occupied ever since. But of course the essence of his poetry, the special quality that makes him great, is exactly what cannot be translated into another language; and we have to make do with considering his greatest and hugely influential work in translation.

---

[5] Pronounced 'Onyégin' with a hard 'g'.

Eugene Onégin, 1831

Fortunately, reading this extraordinary verse-novel in translation is not a pointless exercise, both because it has much to offer even if it is read for its meaning alone, and because the two most easily available translations of it into English are very attractive ones. But, as A. D. P. Briggs argues in the first chapter of his forthright monograph on *Eugene Onégin*, the disadvantage of not being able to read it in Russian is a particularly severe one, for Púshkin explores the whole range of this expressive and beautiful tongue, and vitally develops it as a literary language. 'Whatever you do with it [Púshkin's poetic Russian] in English it will sound very different, and usually wrong', says Professor Briggs; and again, 'no translation [of *Eugene Onégin*] transmits anything to its reader beyond the basic story-line and a pallid afterglow of Pushkin's style. *Caveat lector*.'[6]

So, with this warning ringing in our ears, let us look first at Púshkin's versification. Each of *Eugene Onégin*'s eight chapters contains some forty to fifty-five stanzas of fourteen four-stress lines; and each stanza is in effect a sonnet with lines shorter than is usual in English or Italian verse. The rhyme-scheme is not the least brilliant part of Púshkin's invention, being *AbAbCCddEffEgg*, where the capital letters indicate double rhymes and the lower-case letters single ones (or, as we should say in English verse, feminine and masculine rhymes respectively; see the stanzas given below with the rhyme-scheme marked in the margin). This makes it possible for Púshkin to arrange the lines of the stanza either in the form of the 'English' sonnet (4 + 4 + 4 / 2), with the change of direction, or pause, after the twelfth line; or in the 'Italian' form (4 + 4 / 3 + 3), with the change between the octave and the sestet; or even to reverse the octave and the sestet (in an arrangement such as 4 + 2 / 4 + 4). He uses all these forms in *Eugene Onégin*, and other groupings as well. To show how this works in practice, here are two stanzas in Charles Johnston's translation, which follows Púshkin in his stressing and rhyming about as well as it can be done in English:

'My uncle – high ideals inspire him;	A
but when past joking he fell sick,	b
he really forced one to admire him –	A
and never played a shrewder trick.	b
Let others learn from his example!	C

[6] A. D. P. Briggs, *Eugene Onégin*, Cambridge University Press 1992, pp. 5, 115. *Caveat lector* means 'let the reader beware'.

But God, how deadly dull to sample   C
sickroom attendance night and day   d
and never stir a foot away!   d
And the sly baseness, fit to throttle,   E
of entertaining the half-dead: f
one smoothes the pillows down in bed,   f
and glumly serves the medicine bottle,   E
and sighs, and asks oneself all through: g
"When will the devil come for you?"'   g
(*Eugene Onégin*, One I, trs. by Charles Johnston)

This first stanza of the poem is basically an 'Italian' sonnet, with the lines grouped 4 + 4 / 3 + 3. Here is another one which is more like an 'English' sonnet, with the lines grouped 4 + 4 + 4 / 2:

He lay quite still, and strange as dreaming   A
was that calm brow of one who swooned.   b
Shot through below the chest – and streaming   A
the blood came smoking from the wound.   b
A moment earlier, inspiration   C
had filled this heart, and detestation   C
and hope and passion; life had glowed   d
and blood had bubbled as it flowed;   d
but now the mansion is forsaken;   E
shutters are up, and all is pale   f
and still within, behind the veil   f
of chalk the window-panes have taken.   E
The lady of the house has fled.   g
Where to, God knows. The trail is dead.   g
(*Eugene Onégin*, Six XXXII, trs. by Charles Johnston)

What is alluring about the 'Onégin' rhyme-scheme is both that it leads one on through the stanza, and that it has the strange and enduring quality of keeping the reader guessing about which rhyme is coming next, especially in lines 5–12.

The second of these stanzas (which is part of the description of the death of one of the characters in a duel) also gives an indication – surely something more than 'a pallid afterglow' – of the power and beauty of Púshkin's poetic language, in the marvellous image of the deserted house of the body, growing pale as life departs from it, to go who knows whither.

What then is *Eugene Onégin* about? The basic story is of a sophisticated, idle gentleman, Eugene, and a well-born but unsophisticated girl, Tatyána, who lives in the country. Tatyána falls in love with Eugene and confesses her love to him in a letter; Eugene meets her and tells her, not unkindly, that he cannot return her love. Some years later, when Tatyána is married to a prince and is a fashionable society hostess in Moscow, Eugene meets her again, and this time it is he who falls in love with her, and she who rejects him; she is still fond of him but chooses to remain faithful to her husband. These mirror-image attractions and rejections illustrate a perverse but very common human situation: the person who loves someone but is not loved in return, with a later exchange of roles, the disappointed lover becoming the uninterested loved one and vice versa. We are always liable to want what we cannot easily have, and to spurn what we easily can.

A secondary plot of almost equal importance concerns Eugene and his friend Lénsky, who is engaged to Tatyána's younger sister Ólga. Either because he is jealous of the others' happiness, or simply from a desire to cause trouble, Eugene flirts with Ólga at a dance, provoking Lénsky into challenging him to a duel. Eugene, the more experienced and the more ruthless of the two, fires first and kills – some say he murders – his young friend. Ólga soon marries someone else, and Lénsky's grave lies untended.

Looked at objectively, none of the characters in the novel is especially admirable, although none is uninteresting. Eugene's faults are plain to see: though intelligent, and attractive to some (including the narrator), he is in many respects an amoral and worthless young man. It is easy to sympathise with Tatyána – and Russians, particularly, find her adorable – but in truth she is not presented as being all that bright or charming. Her sister Ólga is a flighty miss; and Lénsky, the would-be poet, is Werther-like: immature and sentimental. Nevertheless the story and Eugene himself are consistently gripping, never losing tension or pace from the first stanza to the last. It is generally credible, too, including even (with some small suspension of disbelief) Tatyána's transformation in a mere two years from awkward country girl to assured society hostess.

An unusual feature of *Eugene Onégin* is the way the story is told. A novel has to have a narrator. Usually this is either an imaginary character who tells the tale from one point of view in the first person, or an equally imaginary narrator who has the godlike power of seeing events that no real person could see, including what the characters in the story are thinking, and who tells the story in the third person. Large and important parts of *Eugene Onégin* are told by just such an omniscient third-person narrator; but in other parts Púshkin himself appears, and he does so in two aspects.

In one of them he acts as a first-person narrator, an imaginary 'Púshkin' who is acquainted with the imaginary characters of the tale, the friend of the fictional Onégin, the acquaintance of Tatyá- na. In the other, Púshkin appears in his own person both to give us his metafictional[7] opinions about the story, and to tell us things about his own views and experiences outside the novel's frame.

Eugene Onégin is not only a riveting tale most skilfully told, but is also a major landmark in the development of European literature. It was not yet a fully-developed novel of psychological realism – for which we have to look to Lérmontov, our next subject – but it was a move in that direction; more importantly it was the first, enor- mously influential, stage on the road that was to lead to the great age of Russian fiction, the wonderful mid-century psychological investigations of Turgénev, Tolstóy, and Dostoévsky.

Translations

The examples given above are from the Penguin Classics version by Charles Johnston (1977), which (despite the misgivings of the Rus- sian specialists) is widely regarded as a very good translation indeed; certainly it reads engagingly from beginning to end, and it has a useful Introduction.[8] There is another, more recent but also very good translation in Onégin stanzas in Oxford World's Classics by James E. Falen (1990); some of his stanzas read slightly better than Johnston's, some slightly worse, but there is not much to choose between them (see Falen's translations on pp. 233–4 of the two Johnston stanzas given above); it has an excellent apparatus of Introduction and notes.

There is a literal translation, with an enormous commentary, by Vladímir Nabókov in four volumes (New York 1964), but this is chiefly of interest to Russian specialists.

Mikháil Iúrevich Lérmontov, 1814–41

Like Púshkin, his literary hero, Lérmontov was killed in a duel, in his case when he was barely twenty-seven; but, fortunately for Russian

---

[7] 'Metafiction' is fiction about itself; in its most obvious form (as happens occasionally in *Eugene Onégin*) the author dismisses the narrator and steps out of the frame to discuss the novel he is writing.
[8] It was the Johnston translation of *Eugene Onégin* that inspired Vikram Seth to write his witty Californian verse-novel *The Golden Gate* (1986), an absorbing story and a *tour de force* in Onégin stanzas (which Seth also uses for his Acknowl- edgements, Dedication, Table of Contents, and 'About the Author').

literature, and for us, the literary output of his last four years, when he was in his mid-twenties, was copious and of the highest quality. Lérmontov was born in Moscow to ill-matched parents, his mother being well born but sickly and his father a retired officer of no social or other distinction. Lérmontov's mother died when he was four, and he was passed to his aristocratic maternal grandmother by his ne'er-do-well father for a consideration of 50,000 roubles and the promise that the boy would be the old lady's sole heir. As a result of this unusual transaction Lérmontov was brought up by his grandmother and hardly ever saw his father again.

After a pampered but unhappy childhood and adolescence, Lérmontov was standoffish at Moscow University, where he failed to make contact with his fellow-students the novelist Iván Goncharóv, the critic Belínsky, and the political thinker Alexánder Hérzen. He then transferred to the Cavalry Training School in St Petersburg, and was commissioned into the aristocratic Life Guard Hussars in 1834 at the age of twenty. His life in the Guards was at first frivolous and dissipated, but he was pulled up short by the death of Púshkin in 1837. His poem 'Death of a Poet', which not only attacked Georges d'Anthès, Púshkin's killer, but also implied blame to the Imperial court for exacerbating the scandal which led to Púshkin's death, predictably got Lérmontov into trouble with the authorities and resulted in his posting to a regiment in the Caucasus, the wild southern frontier – that is to say, into exile.

He was allowed to return after a few months, but in 1840 he was again sent to the Caucasus for being involved in a duel with the son of the French Minister in St Petersburg. The cause of this second exile was not so much the duel as that Lérmontov was perceived as being prickly and proud; that he made light of military orders; and that he did not trouble to hide his contempt for the Court and society. In Piatigórsk the following year he persisted in insulting a Major Nikolái Martýnov – someone Lérmontov had known and annoyed for several years – until, irritated beyond endurance, Martýnov challenged him. In the pistol duel that followed in a mountain valley, Lérmontov intentionally fired into the air, but Martýnov carried on and shot through the heart. It was suggested that, if Martýnov had not killed Lérmontov, someone else was sure to have done so before long. A few months before this second early death of a great Russian poet in a futile duel, Lérmontov had virtually foretold his own end in an extraordinary untitled poem describing the death of the poet in a duel, 'in a dale of Dagestán', his lifeblood draining from a wound in his chest.

Lérmontov had begun writing – poems, drama, prose – from an early age, but it was not until 1837 and 'Death of a Poet' that he moved from a Byronic narcissism to the skilled maturity of his later work. There were a number of fine narrative poems, notably the historical *Song of Tsar Iván Vasílevich* (1837), a coded commentary on the death of Púshkin; the satirical *The Tambóv Treasurer's Wife* (1837–8); *The Demon* (completed 1840, about the love of a fallen angel for a mortal); and *The Novice* (1840, the trials of a novice monk on short leave from his monastery). These poems, and his lyrics, gave Lérmontov his place as Russia's leading romantic poet, and indeed her greatest poet after Púshkin; but it was Lérmontov's novel, *A Hero of Our Time* (1840), that made him a writer of world importance.

A Hero of Our Time 1840

The novel is made up of five stories or chapters and an editorial interpolation, all concerning Grigóry Pechórin, a Russian army officer in the Caucasus, but narrated in different ways. The basic story is that Pechórin, on his way from St Petersburg to the Caucasus in 1830 is stranded at the village of Tamán, where he has an adventure with some smugglers (chapter 3, 'Tamán'). After two years of active service, Pechórin becomes involved with two women and kills a fellow-officer in a duel (chapter 4, 'Princess Mary', the longest and most elaborate of the chapters). In the same year he is posted to a fort in Chechénya, where he meets Captain Maxím Maxímich, a good-natured old soldier who has the touching simplicity of Tolstóy's Captain Túshin (chapter 1, 'Bela'). Still in 1832 Pechórin spends a fortnight in a Cossack settlement and has an uncanny experience with an officer of the unit stationed there (chapter 5, 'The Fatalist'). In 1833 he captures a Circassian girl as a common-law wife, but she is then assassinated (chapter 1, 'Bela'). In 1837, on his way to Persia, he meets the narrator and Maxím Maxímich in Vladikavkáz and hurts the old man's feelings by his coldness towards him (chapter 2, 'Maxím Maxímich'). Finally it is heard that in 1838 or 1839 Pechórin dies on his way back from Persia, and the narrator publishes Pechórin's self-analytical journal (containing 'Tamán', 'Princess Mary', and 'The Fatalist') with an editorial introduction.

The novel has three narrators, who all tell their stories in the first person. The first of them is 'Lérmontov', the first-person narrator who appears at the beginning of 'Bela'; the second is Maxím Maxímich telling the story to the first narrator; and the third is Pechórin himself writing in his journal, which is itself introduced by the first narrator. (All this may sound complicated, but the story is quite easily followed in the reading of it.)

A Hero of Our Time thus has two main threads: the individual adventures and episodes related in each of the separate short stories or chapters; and, more fundamentally, the character of the hero of our time, Grigóry Pechórin, as it is developed through the book. He is, to quote Vladímir Nabókov,

> a fictional person whose romantic dash to cynicism, tigerlike suppleness and eagle eye, hot blood and cool head, tenderness and taciturnity, elegance and brutality, delicacy of perception and harsh passion to dominate, ruthlessness and awareness of it, are of lasting appeal to readers of all countries and all centuries – especially to young readers. (*A Hero of Our Time*, Foreword, Oxford World's Classics p. xvii)

He is indeed a man of contradictions, a man often at war with himself; more a Byronic hero than a 'superfluous man', that nineteenth-century Russian gentleman or intellectual who had enough to live on but not enough to do. 'Contradiction is, with me', Pechórin says at one point, 'an innate passion; my entire life has been nothing but a chain of sad and frustrating contradictions to heart or reason.'[9] This is clarified in another passage of self-analysis:

> For a long time now, I have been living not with the heart, but with the head. I weigh and analyse my own passions and actions with stern curiosity, but without participation. Within me there are two persons: one of them lives in the full sense of the word, the other cogitates and judges him. (*A Hero of Our Time*, ch. 4, Oxford World's Classics pp. 133–4)

One of the results of this is that his every pleasure is blighted by disillusionment and boredom:

> In my early youth, from the minute I emerged from under my family's supervision, I began madly to enjoy every pleasure that money could buy, and, naturally, those pleasures became repulsive to me. Then I ventured out into the *grand monde*, and, soon, I became likewise fed up with society: I have been in love with fashionable belles, and have been loved, but their love only irritated my imagination and vanity, while my heart remained empty ... I began to read, to study – I got just as sick of studies – I saw that neither fame nor happiness depended on them in the least, since the happiest people

---

[9] *A Hero of Our Time*, ch. 4, trs. by Vladímir Nabókov Oxford World's Classics p. 75.

are dunces, while fame is a question of luck, and in order to obtain it, you only have to be nimble. Then I began to be bored ...' (*A Hero of Our Time*, ch. 1, Oxford World's Classics p. 33)

Questions present themselves. In the first place, is Pechórin a portrait of an individual? Lérmontov himself said in the Author's Introduction that *A Hero of Our Time* 'is indeed a portrait, but not of a single individual; it is a portrait composed of all the vices of our generation in the fullness of their development'. But this is to avoid the question; Pechórin is a rounded, realistic character, not a mere collection of vices; and besides, it may be doubted whether these 'vices' of disillusionment and ennui could be caused chiefly by the nature of 'our time' – Russia under the despotism of Tsar Nicholas I – even though it may be that some of those who lived in it were deprived of opportunities for personal fulfilment. In any case, it is the character of Pechórin, rather than his environment or even what happens to him, that is the focus and prime interest of the novel.

So we go on to ask how far the character of Pechórin is a self-portrait by Lérmontov. The biographical parallels are obvious – it is not hard to see characteristics of the arrogant Lérmontov in the arrogant Pechórin – and to some extent, certainly, it must be so; but fictional self-portraits notoriously stray from their originals, and it is likely that Lérmontov's relationship to Pechórin is no closer than – and perhaps not so close as – that of Joyce to Stephen Dedalus.

For all its strange originality as a work of fiction, and for its oddities of construction and narration, *A Hero of Our Time* is a vividly readable and engrossing novel; and it followed *Eugene Onégin* as the first fully-developed Russian novel of psychological realism, the direct ancestor of the great mid-century novels of Turgénev, Tolstóy, and Dostoévsky.

Translations

Vladímir Nabókov claimed that his 1958 version, now in Oxford World's Classics, was the only actual 'translation' into English of *A Hero of Our Time* (see p. 5 above), all the others being so poor as not to deserve the name. Whether this is true or not, his version is a good and readable one, with an idiosyncratic Introduction and Notes. Another of Nabókov's contrary pronouncements was that Lérmontov's Russian prose was 'inelegant', 'dry', and 'drab', a view that is not shared by most other commentators. The Penguin Classics version by Paul Foote (1966) also reads well, and was checked by several distinguished Russian specialists; it has a good Introduction but no notes.

Further reading

For the general background see Richard Pipes's *Russia under the Old Régime*, Weidenfeld and Nicolson 1974 (now in Penguin Books); for the literary background, Ronald Hingley's *Russian Writers and Society in the Nineteenth Century*, 2nd revised edn., Weidenfeld and Nicolson, London 1977, is an excellent guide. *The Cambridge History of Russian Literature*, ed. Charles A. Moser, rev. edn. Cambridge University Press 1992, has useful sections on the authors and novels discussed here.

A. D. P. Briggs's *Alexánder Púshkin: Eugene Onégin*, Cambridge University Press 1992, is a first-rate analytical introduction by a Russian specialist, which challenges commonly-held but, he believes, over-indulgent views of the novel's characters. Briggs also emphasises the importance of knowing something about the Russian language (for some of us, alas, too late); and includes a good chronology of Púshkin's life. The latest biography of Púshkin is by Elaine Feinstein: *Pushkin*, Weidenfeld Nicolson Orion, 1998.

John Garrard's *Mikháil Lérmontov*, Twayne, Boston 1982, is a lively and perceptive study of Lérmontov's life and work.

France: Restoration and the July Monarchy, 1815–48

The history of modern France – that is, from the start of the Revolution in 1789 – began with some eighty years of frequent political upheaval; followed by a further seventy years of relative political stability (the Third Republic, 1871–1940[1]). The degree and frequency of the constitutional changes in the earlier period can be seen from the table of French Governments, 1789–1940, on p. 92. Thus, between 1789 and 1871 there were some ten régimes (not counting other constitutional changes that took place in 1789–99); the shortest lasted for a mere five days, and the two longest (the July Monarchy and the Second Empire) for only eighteen years each.

After Waterloo and Napoleon I's final exile to St Helena, the Bourbon monarchy was restored in France in the person of Louis XVIII, younger brother of Louis XVI (who had been guillotined in 1793). He proved to be a feeble king, unable to prevent the 'White Terror' that followed his accession, when hundreds of Revolutionaries and Protestants were massacred, or later to curb the reactionary tendencies of the nobility, who had the greatest influence on government policy during his reign. His brother, the elderly Charles X who succeeded him in 1824, was no better, and his repressive policies precipitated the July Revolution in 1830. The Restoration had been a dismal time for France: humiliated by defeat in battle, with Paris recently occupied by foreign troops and the economy stagnating, the political left and centre watched in dismay as the crude reaction of the monarchy and its right-wing administrations seemed to be leading the country back to the *ancien régime*. And to some extent this was true, for the economic and social structures

[1] Technically the Third Republic was not superseded by the Fourth until 1945, following the Liberation of France from German occupation the year before; but it came to an end in all but name in 1940 with the establishment of the collaborationist government of Marshal Pétain.

1789–99	French Revolution; First Republic
1793	Louis XVI executed [2]
1799	Napoleon Bonaparte First Consul
1804	Napoleon I Emperor
1804–14	First Empire
1814–15	Napoleon I deposed and exiled; First Restoration of Louis XVIII
1815	Napoleon I escapes from exile; Waterloo and final exile; Napoleon II Emperor (for five days)
1815–30	Second Restoration of Louis XVIII; succeeded by Charles X, 1824
1830	July Revolution; Louis-Philippe King
1830–48	July Monarchy
1848	Revolution of 1848; Louis-Philippe overthrown
1848–52	Second Republic
1852	Napoleon II! Emperor
1852–70	Second Empire
1870	Napoleon III overthrown
1871	Paris Commune
1871–1940	Third Republic (Monarchist 1871–9; Opportunist 1879–99; Radical 1899–1940)

French Governments, 1789–1940

did not undergo any great change until the 1840s. Meanwhile the nobility flourished, republicanism simmered underground in the cities, and the peasants were as badly off as ever.

Louis-Philippe, who became king after the July Revolution of 1830 and who believed that political control should remain firmly in the hands of the rich, did initiate some measures of constitutional reform: he doubled the size of the electorate (though it was still very small), allowed Parliament to initiate legislation, and disestablished the Church. But the July Monarchy became increasingly unpopular with the middle classes and the urban masses, who saw power still concentrated in the hands of a tiny élite; and it came to an end with the huge popular uprising of 1848. Louis-Philippe fled to England and a new Republic, the Second, was proclaimed.[3]

Honoré de Balzac (1799–1850) lived nearly all his life in this

[2] The second son of Louis XVI became titular King of France as Louis XVII when his father was executed in 1793, but he never reigned; he died, possibly from poisoning, in 1795.

[3] For France under the Second Republic and the Second Empire, see pp. 107–8 below.

early period of political instability, and was for most of it at the centre of things in Paris. Gustave Flaubert (1821–80), who grew up in the later part of the period, was also affected by the political turmoil even in his provincial home city of Rouen. It was a very different world from that of their British near-contemporaries Mrs Gaskell, Thackeray, Dickens, Trollope, and George Eliot, who lived in the period 1810 to 1882.

Honoré de Balzac, 1799–1850

Honoré Balzac – like Goethe's 'von', the 'de' came later – was born at Tours of lower-middle-class parents who paid him little attention during his childhood. He was put out to nurse until he was four, then sent for a further three years to a *pension*, and thence to a boarding school at Vendôme until he was fourteen; his warmest family relationship was not with his parents but with a sibling, his younger sister Laure. At seventeen he became an impecunious law student in Paris, where he was to live for the rest of his life, but he soon determined to make his fortune as a writer rather than as a lawyer. He first wrote an unsuccessful tragedy, *Cromwell* (published posthumously), and then a number of second-rate, derivative novels (1820–5), anonymously and mostly in collaboration with other writers. He tried to become a businessman as well as a writer in 1825–8, when he set up in partnership with professionals as printer, publisher, and typefounder, but he lacked commercial sense, and was obliged to sell out to his partners at a loss, enabling them to get on better without him. It was not until 1829, when he was thirty, that his first mature novel, *Le Dernier Chouan*, was published under his own name. From then on, for the next (and last) twenty years of his life, Balzac wrote furiously, producing the amazing total of some ninety novels, most of which were to be incorporated in the great interlinked series with reappearing characters which he was to call (in 1841) *La Comédie humaine*. His first resounding success was with *La Peau de chagrin* (1831–2); and the series included, besides *Le Père Goriot* (1834–5), *Eugénie Grandet* (1833), *Les Illusions perdues* (1837), and *La Cousine Bette* (1848).

We know a great deal about Balzac's later life, but he was so bound up in his writing that there is not much to say about it. He was a man of extremes and contradictions: personally charming and attractive to women – there were a number of love affairs, the most important of them beginning when he was twenty-two, with a woman of his mother's age – but egotistical and physically something of a slob[4]; socially aware but snobbish; self-indulgent but capable of punishing and sustained hard work. He died of heart disease, exacerbated by overwork, at the age of fifty-one.

Le Père Goriot [5], 1834–5

By the time Balzac started to write *Le Père Goriot*, he already knew that he wanted his fiction to contain a realistic[6] description of French society at all levels, and of its various environments, to an extent and in a degree of detail never achieved before. The setting of the novel, Paris in 1819, is itself one of its major features;[7] and the narrative revolves around physical objects as much as it does about its other main material interest: money. In this environment three human stories are linked together: those of Eugène de Rastignac, a young law student who reflects Balzac's own days of sporadically reading law in Paris (though Rastignac is both better looking and of nobler birth than Balzac had been); of an arch-criminal called Jacques Collin who has escaped from prison and is lying low under the name of Vautrin; and Jean-Joachim Goriot himself, a retired vermicelli merchant[8] in his sixties who dotes on his two married daughters.

---

[4] A surviving daguerrotype of Balzac by an anonymous photographer (well reproduced in Nigel Gosling's *Nadar*, London 1976, p. 2, and badly reproduced in several books about Balzac, heavily touched-up and sometimes reversed) shows a rather handsome, fleshy man of about forty, with floppy dark hair and a drooping moustache.

[5] There is no need to translate the title as *Old Goriot*, or even to leave it in French; '*le père* so-and-so' can indeed mean 'old so-and-so', but Goriot's fatherhood is at the core of the novel, and 'father' must be retained in the title somehow. In fact old codgers can be called 'Father' in English – Father Time, Father Christmas, the organ builder Father Smith, and so on – just as they can be called *le père* in French; and the clerical connotation of 'Father' is no more an obstacle in English than is that of '*le père*' in French. However, Balzac's novel is not usually called *Father Goriot* in English, so I have used the French title.

[6] The terms 'realism' and 'naturalism' in literary criticism are easily confused. 'Realism' refers both to detailed accuracy of description and to the rejection of romantic escapism (Balzac, Flaubert, George Eliot); while 'naturalism' refers to a special type of realism in which human beings are seen as victims of natural forces and their social environment (Ibsen, Zola, Gissing, Hardy); see p. 176 below.

[7] There is a parallel here with James Joyce's *Ulysses* (1922), in which the Dublin of 1904 is similarly anatomised. Another parallel between Balzac and Joyce is that they both liked to write considerable parts of their books by making additions to the printed proofs (a practice that would scandalise a modern publisher).

[8] This is the term that Balzac uses, but it is clear from the text that Goriot had been a dealer on a large scale in all sorts of products made from flour, including starch.

The initial setting is the boarding house of Madame Vauquer, a seedy establishment where all three main characters are lodging at very modest rents. It is described in obsessive detail, as if Balzac were attempting to categorise each item scientifically: the shabby furniture, the gimcrack ornaments, the faded wallpaper, the peeling paintwork, the all-pervading smells of dirt, drains, and cooking. Similarly with its inhabitants: the grasping, stupid proprietress, her two slipshod servants, and the group of threadbare lodgers who try to hide the poverty of their lives beneath a façade of jolly communal jokes, gossip, and intrigue. In parallel with this squalid lodging house we are shown the life and environment both of the aristocracy and of the very rich. Rastignac, although his family at home in the south have lost most of their money, has the entrée to the fashionable salon of Madame de Beauséant because he is her cousin; while Goriot's daughters have married respectively a great name and a wealthy financier; and we see in some detail how they all live.

None of the three main characters behaves well, but each has positive characteristics. Rastignac cadges money from his poverty-stricken family, and pursues women for what he can get out of them, but he has charm and a genuine moral sense; Vautrin is a criminal without pity for those he preys on, but is able to look at the world and his own amorality without fear; while Père Goriot himself made his fortune by rigging the cereals market during the famines of the early 1790s, and now nurtures a blind passion for his worthless daughters, but he is attractively modest and kind to those about him.

The outcome of the three main stories is that Rastignac finds a balance between his moral and emotional sensitivity and his ruthless pursuit of wealth and status; that Vautrin is betrayed and captured by the authorities, but has the self-control not to give them the excuse they want for killing him during his arrest; and that Goriot, having given away literally all his great wealth to his ungrateful, grasping daughters whom he both loves and hates, dies Lear-like in want, supported not by them but by two students (one of them Rastignac) who are almost as impoverished as himself. These stories may sound melodramatic, and indeed Balzac was always ready to plunge into melodrama (as he does here in dealing with the background and fate of the arch-criminal Vautrin, who is presented as an improbable Napoleon of crime). For the most part, however, the interlinked tales are balanced and adequately convincing.

Although the characters in *Le Père Goriot* are fascinating and on the whole credible, they are not presented realistically in all respects; in particular, the dialogue, though usually natural-sounding between the lodgers in the boarding house, stretches out into impossibly long speeches when Balzac has some sociological or moral point to make. The dying monologue of Goriot in particular, though magnificent, goes on for page after improbable page.

Balzac uses an omniscient third-person narrator, linked mostly to the point of view of the student Rastignac; the narrative focus is not aimed only at Rastignac, however, but sometimes at Vautrin, and sometimes at Goriot, suggesting the complex interaction of their lives. The Parisian maze is indicated by a series of major metaphors that are spread through the narrative – metaphors of the open sea, the cave, the jungle, battle, and mud – all showing how hard it is to find one's way and keep one's balance in the strangeness and danger of the great city.

Two features were especially remarkable and new in Balzac's technique in writing *Le Père Goriot*: the high degree of material realism; and the device, used for the first time here, of reappearing characters. The realistic description of the Maison Vauquer has already been mentioned, and the same treatment is applied, though more lightly, to the environment of the rich and aristocratic characters. The idea of introducing characters that would reappear in other novels seems to have struck Balzac while he was actually writing *Le Père Goriot*, when he decided to use as the Rastignac character someone who had already appeared (at a later fictional date) in an earlier novel. From now on Balzac would amass a cast of some two thousand characters, great and small, who would step in and out of the huge series that became the *Comédie humaine*, giving the novels a sense of being – like life itself – open-ended rather than having beginnings, middles, and ends. It remains true, however, that most of the novels in the series – and especially *Le Père Goriot* – do not depend vitally on their relationship with the others, but can be read perfectly well by themselves.

Translations

Balzac wrote fast, and his French was not polished; but the Oxford World's Classics version, with Introduction, apparatus, and notes, by A. J. Krailsheimer (*Père Goriot*, 1991), makes the best of it, and must be the first choice. The Penguin Classics translation by Marion

Ayton Crawford (*Old Goriot*, 1951) is perfectly readable and has an Introduction but no notes.

Gustave Flaubert, 1821–80

Gustave Flaubert was born in Rouen, not far from the Channel coast of Normandy, to a successful, professional, middle-class family, his father being the head surgeon at the local hospital. The family environment remained one of the most important influences on Flaubert's development: especially close were his father and his sister Caroline, who both died when he was in his mid-twenties; his mother, who died when he was just over fifty; and his nanny, who survived him. And, although he travelled widely and lived for part of his life in Paris, the Rouen area was always his home.

Flaubert was at first an impressive student at the Collège de Rouen, but was eventually expelled for bad behaviour. Nevertheless he passed his *baccalauréat* in 1840, and went on to study law in Paris; there he did less well, failing his exams in 1843. Meanwhile other forces were at work in him. In 1836, when he was fifteen, Flaubert conceived an obsessive and, as it turned out, a hopeless passion for Elisa Schlesinger, the wife of a German music publisher; a passion so overwhelming that it prevented him from ever fully loving another woman – not that it was to interfere with the active erotic life that he subsequently pursued. At about the time that he fell in love with Madame Schlesinger he went to bed with one of his mother's maids, and for most of the rest of his life he had a succession of love affairs, and other sexual contacts in and out of brothels, without ever succumbing to deep emotional involvement. Then in 1844 Flaubert suffered his first attack of epilepsy, a shattering event by which he was persuaded – without much difficulty – to abandon the law, and to retire for most of the time to the country near Rouen and the solicitous care of his mother. Here he could withdraw from the world, avoiding the strong feelings that lead to pain but retaining the curiosity with which he could attain the objectivity he sought as a writer.

In 1846 Flaubert was much distressed by the death of his father. Later in the same year he began a lengthy, fraught love affair with the poet Louise Colet, a woman as immoderate in her needs and emotions as Flaubert was himself, a near-impossible relationship in which they spent most of their time apart over a period of eight years, writing superlative letters to each other.[9]

What Flaubert really needed was the leisure to think and work on his own, and in 1851–7 he wrote and published his masterpiece, *Madame Bovary*. He wrote it with obsessive care, crafting and recrafting each paragraph, each sentence, never completely satisfied with what he achieved. The resulting novel caused a sensation, and Flaubert (then aged thirty-six) was frightened and distressed by the prosecution for irreligion and immorality that followed its publication. He was triumphantly acquitted, however, and became a celebrity, admired by his fellow-writers, and lionised by Parisian society.

The historical novel *Salammbô* followed in 1862 – another huge success – and Flaubert frequented society salons in the intervals of his work; he was presented to Napoleon III in 1864, and appointed *chevalier* of the Legion of Honour the following year. Other books followed: *L'Éducation sentimentale* (1869, Flaubert's own favourite); *The Temptation of Saint Anthony* (1874, a grotesque prose work set out in dramatic form); and the fine *Three Stories* (1877). His last novel, unfinished at his death, was a bitter social comedy, *Bouvard et Pécuchet*.

Although his work was greatly admired and he himself was fêted, the last years of Flaubert's life were not happy ones. In 1870, when his home was occupied by German troops, he felt deeply ashamed of being French and stopped wearing the insignia of the Legion of Honour. In 1872 he was devastated by the death of his mother; and then hurt again by his niece (his sister Caroline's daughter) who, with the connivance of her husband, fleeced him of practically all his money and by 1873 was threatening to turn him out of his own house. Poor, lonely, and worn out by his relentless work on *Bouvard et Pécuchet*, Flaubert died in 1880, aged fifty-eight.

Women and adultery in the nineteenth century

Before going on to look at *Madame Bovary*, the first of the three great nineteenth-century bourgeois novels of adultery included here – the other two being Tolstóy's *Ánna Karénina* (1874, p. 130) and

[9] A selection of Flaubert's letters of 1830–57, edited and translated by Francis Steegmuller, was published by Harvard University Press (1980).

Fontane's *Effi Briest* (1895, p. 183)[10] – it is worth digressing to consider the social and legal position of respectable married women in the nineteenth century, and the consequences of their committing adultery during this period.

Sexual morality, marriage, and adultery

Sexual morality has traditionally been centred on marriage, the lifelong union of a man and a woman from which a family would grow. The greatest threat to this union – and therefore the gravest sexual transgression – was perceived to be adultery, voluntary sexual intercourse between a married person and a person (married or not) other than his or her spouse. The form of adultery most feared and abhorred was that committed by a wife and mother.

Sexual morality and Old Testament law

The laws, both private and public, governing sexual activity in and out of marriage in the nineteenth century were derived from biblical teaching. Having recorded the commandment that 'Thou shalt not commit adultery', the Old Testament gave unambiguous instructions for dealing with sexual transgressions (in Deuteronomy, 22:22–9). It was laid down here that the sin of adultery is committed by both parties only if the woman is married; and it appears that a man's sexual relations with an unmarried woman (whether she is willing or not) are especially culpable only if she is a virgin. An important implication of the whole was that a man does not sin if he has sexual relations with unmarried non-virgins, whether or not he himself is married.

---

[10] None of the major English novelists of the mid-nineteenth century – Mrs Gaskell, Thackeray, Dickens, Trollope, George Eliot – were prepared to tackle this subject head-on. They included seduction and fallen women in their stories, but none of them wrote a novel which had as its main theme adultery committed willingly by a previously-respectable middle-class wife.

One work by a major English novelist which did include an adulteress as a leading character is *Jude the Obscure* (1895) by Thomas Hardy (born 1840), but its setting is lower-class, not middle-class, and Sue Bridehead's adultery with Jude is committed, with the greatest reluctance and sense of guilt, only after she has been legally separated from her husband. Even then *Jude* was considered to be grossly immoral when it first appeared. (More in tune with the times were the fantastic scruples of Grace Fitzpiers and Giles Winterbourne in Hardy's *The Woodlanders*, 1887.)

Perhaps the most outspoken nineteenth-century novel of bourgeois adultery committed by wives as well as husbands, and of the hypocrisy surrounding it, is Zola's *Pot-bouille* (1882).

Jesus on adultery

Jesus's teaching on the subject of adultery in the New Testament went beyond the Old Testament law in proposing, first, 'what, therefore, God hath joined together [in marriage], let no man put asunder' (Matthew 19:6); secondly, 'Whosoever shall put away his wife, except it be for fornication [by the wife], committeth adultery' (Matthew 19:9); thirdly, 'Whosoever looketh after a woman to lust after her hath committed adultery with her already in his heart' (Matthew 5:28); and, finally, that a woman taken in adultery might be condemned only by judges who had not themselves sinned: 'he that is without sin among you, let him first cast a stone at her' (John 8:7).[11]

The first two of these propositions (which forbade divorce, except the divorce of an adulterous wife) were accepted as the basis of Christian marriage until the mid-twentieth century. The other two were never taken very seriously; the third (committing adultery by experiencing lust for a woman) because it referred to a 'sin' committed by virtually every heterosexual male; and the last (requiring male judges of adultery by a woman to be without sin themselves) because to accept it would have limited the sexual licence and control customarily exercised by men.

Women's opportunities and limitations

By the mid-nineteenth century women were beginning to move from a position of servitude in the patriarchal family to one of relative freedom as an individual. So far this movement affected chiefly unmarried women from the end of adolescence to marriage, and – to a lesser extent – older women who remained unmarried. Women – at least in Protestant countries – might (usually) choose between such mates as offered themselves; alternatively they might choose not to marry, even if they were asked to. Nevertheless, middle-class women in most nineteenth-century European societies remained under greater authority – of their parents, of their spouses, of society – than did their brothers, their freedom to enter into relationships and to direct their own lives being strictly circumscribed.

Marriage was understood to involve the principle of 'separate spheres' as an unwritten subtext of the marriage contract. In

---

[11] Biblical scholarship suggests that the story of the woman taken in adultery is an apocryphal addition to the gospel of St John, but in the nineteenth century it was generally believed to be authentic.

marrying, a woman agreed to keep out of the public sphere, including politics, business, and most active pursuits, on the understanding that she would be suitably maintained and that her moral and practical influence would be respected in the sphere of the family. Thus the married woman conceived, bore, and brought up the children, ran the household, engaged and controlled the servants, and so on; and her influence in the domestic, emotional, educational, and spiritual affairs of the family might be considerable. But she seldom had control even of her own property; in France the wife's property rights depended on the marriage contract, and in England the first law giving property rights to wives was not enacted until 1870. The unmarried middle-class woman did not have much more real freedom than the wife, the careers available to her normally being limited to such things as employment as a governess, a schoolteacher, a companion, or a helpful maiden daughter or aunt within a family; and in all of these positions she would be expected to know her subordinate place.

Double standards in sexual morality

Both sex before marriage and adultery were considered to be absolutely forbidden to middle-class nineteenth-century women; it was just possible for a respectable married woman to commit adultery provided that no one else at all – husband, family, friends, servants – found out about it; but if the adultery were discovered, or if an unmarried girl allowed herself to be seduced, she could neither be forgiven nor keep her social position. There were a few married women whose adultery was known or suspected and who were prepared to brazen it out; upper-class, or cosmopolitan, or bohemian women such as Bezúkov's shameless wife Princess Hélène in *War and Peace*; the sophisticated Varvára Pávlovna in Turgénev's *A Nest of Gentlefolk*; or G. H. Lewes's wife Agnes who openly lived with – and had four children by – another man. But in general a woman known to have 'sinned' was shunned by good society.

For men, on the other hand, while sexual licence might not be openly encouraged, much greater freedom was possible. A middle-class man might have sexual relations with socially inferior women, both before and after marriage, provided that he was reasonably discreet about it; he need not be socially ostracised for adultery with another man's wife; he might keep a mistress, or go to a

brothel;[12] and the only heterosexual relationship that was absolutely forbidden to him was one with an unmarried girl of his own
class.

Women perceived to be inferior to men

Central to women's limitations and men's licence was the belief,
very widely held by women as well as men, that men were not only
stronger physically than women but that they were also intellectually and morally superior to them. Indeed, there had been a
theological argument going back to the early Fathers of the Church
about whether women even had souls – whether, in fact, women
were not human beings at all but a higher form of animal.[13] This
was no longer an issue, but to most Europeans in the nineteenth
century – as to most Muslims, and many Jews today – it still seemed
perfectly natural that men, especially as fathers or husbands, should
lead the way and make the decisions, and that women should accept
their rule in all matters of substance, and should be willingly
subservient to them. Ibsen's play *A Doll's House* (1879, p. 146)
caused a huge sensation in Europe precisely because its heroine,
Nora Helmer, comes to believe that her position as a respectable
middle-class wife and mother is restricted, degraded, and false, and
because she determines to escape from it even though it means
leaving her husband and children.

There were not many Noras, however; and it could seem reasonable to most people that men should require their women to be
chaste before marriage and faithful during it, without necessarily
being chaste or faithful themselves. At the same time this rationa-
lised the biological urge of the male to fertilise as many females as
possible, and to keep jealous guard on at least one of them.

Separation, divorce, and remarriage

If a marriage went wrong, separation might be available, but
divorce and remarriage ranged during the nineteenth century from
impossible to very difficult. Until the passage of the Matrimonial
Causes Act of 1857 – which was controversial, and resisted by the
Church of England – married couples in the United Kingdom could

---

[12] Prostitution, either freelance or institutionalised in a brothel, offered sex for
money rather than sex for fun, and was seen by many men – and by some women
too if they cared to face it – as a useful safeguard, protecting society against more
threatening forms of male fornication and adultery.

[13] See p. 31 n. 15 above.

be divorced only by a private Act of Parliament, which meant that in practice divorce was unavailable to nearly everyone. In France, where divorce had been legalised during the Revolution, it was abolished again between 1816 and 1884. In most Roman Catholic and Greek Orthodox societies, indeed, divorce continued to be unavailable to everyone except the very rich throughout the century. But even after 1857 divorce could be granted in the United Kingdom only on the grounds of adultery by the wife, or of adultery *in addition to* cruelty or desertion by the husband; and divorced people were not received in good society for the rest of the century.[14] Attitudes towards divorce in the rest of Protestant Europe were generally somewhat less restrictive, especially in Scandinavia.

Adultery committed by nineteenth-century wives

What is especially notable about nineteenth-century bourgeois (and sometimes aristocratic) wives who committed adultery is that they did so knowing that they risked doing terrible damage to their families and to their positions in society, and even being sent away from home without means of support. Of course a woman could get tired of her spouse, just as much as a man could, and, finding herself admired and valued by someone else, could fall in love, or begin a flirtation that she could not control, with adultery as the outcome. The urge to commit adultery could be strengthened by her own sexual desire; or she could be tempted to sin precisely because the fruit of adultery was forbidden, because of the excitement offered by secretly defying convention and the law. But the price she might have to pay in loss of family, status, and livelihood could be enormous.

Madame Bovary, 1856–7

At first glance *Madame Bovary* can seem to be a commonplace story with a simple, unoriginal plot, featuring characters who are without exception flawed or downright unpleasant; and to some extent this is true. To take the plot first, a mediocre country health officer – he is not even a real doctor – marries a young woman who

---

[14] Indeed divorce continued to be discreditable in English society well into the twentieth century; Evelyn Waugh wrote of the mid-1930s, 'some people were shy of divorce because of their love of society; they did not want there to be any occasion when their presence might be an embarrassment, they wanted to keep their tickets for the Ascot enclosure' (*Put Out More Flags*, 1942, pt. 3, ch. 4).

wallows in worldly and romantic longings that cannot be supplied by her husband or mitigated by their officiously meddlesome neighbour; she gives herself to a lover who deserts her; she takes another lover and they get tired of each other; she allows herself to be put hopelessly into debt by a local shopkeeper; and, seeing no way out of the resulting emotional and financial mess, she takes poison and kills herself, abandoning her husband and her daughter. As to the characters, the husband is a dull fool, the wife is both self-deluding and egocentric (though also a sad and convincing character with whom Flaubert himself was inclined to identify), her lovers are selfish and inadequate (she finds that adultery with them is no better than marriage), the shopkeeper is a swindler, and the neighbour is a pompous busybody.

Needless to say, all this was intentional on Flaubert's part. Although he was himself thoroughly bourgeois in his background and way of life, valuing comfort, stability, and wealth, he nevertheless detested bourgeois ways and bourgeois values; and *Madame Bovary* – with its subtitle *Mœurs de province*, 'Provincial Manners' – was at one level an attack on the bourgeois culture of Normandy in the 1830s and 1840s. But besides this it was Flaubert's conscious intention to write an experimental novel, experimental not so much in its plot or characterisation as in its style and its handling of the details of everyday life; a novel, even, in which style was the essential quality, a work of art that was therefore largely concerned with itself.

He laboured heavily over the language, writing sometimes no more than a page or two in a whole week of hard work, looking for the right sound, the right balance, the right word. 'Whatever the thing you wish to say', Flaubert wrote, 'there is but one word to express it, but one word to give it movement, but one adjective to qualify it; you must seek until you find this noun, this verb, this adjective.' (This is good advice for any writer.)

Then, in describing dryly and realistically the facts and objects of daily life in a country town, he sought to transform the ordinary by bringing together its beauty and ugliness and finding aesthetic value in their combination. The result is a realism more positive and interconnected than Balzac's obsessive cataloguing of every last detail of the Maison Vauquer in *Le Père Goriot*. This aspect of Flaubert's style was revolutionary, showing up the unreality and melodramatic modes of other contemporary fiction; and it accorded perfectly with the subdued irony he displayed towards his characters, raising them from being merely ridiculous or despicable to being figures of pathos or tragedy.[15]

Other technical innovations in *Madame Bovary* included a minimum of authorial comment, the third-person narrator rarely appearing in his own person, but often looking through Emma's eyes; the avoidance of extensive dialogue, and of long speeches within dialogue passages; and the unsensational but still powerfully affecting presentation of sex. It may be remarked that in two of our three novels of adultery (*Madame Bovary* and *Ánna Karénina*) the sexual encounters of the heroines with their lovers, which are obviously central to the stories, are presented in allusive, indirect ways which, while avoiding straightforward descriptions of the sexual act (which would in any case have been unacceptable in novels of their period), convey its intensity and passion as effectively as any explicit depiction of sex in a modern novel or film.[16]

Translations

Three translations of *Madame Bovary* are currently available as Penguin and Oxford World's Classics paperbacks, and a fourth as an Everyman Classic hardback. They are sampled and discussed in Appendix A, pp. 217–22 below; and the reader is invited to consider the evidence and make his or her own choice of which one to read. The most stimulating Introduction is that by Terence Cave in the Oxford World's Classics version (1994), which also has apparatus and notes.

Further reading

For the general background, see Roger Price, *A Concise History of France*, Cambridge University Press 1993.

Herbert J. Hunt, *Honoré de Balzac: a Biography*, University of London Press 1957, is sensible and down to earth; see also Diana Festa-McCormick, *Honoré de Balzac*, Twayne, Boston 1979. David Bellos's *Honoré de Balzac: Old Goriot*, Cambridge

---

[15] Authorial irony towards fictional characters was not of course new; it was used, for instance, in *Don Quixote* (see p. 38), a novel which Flaubert knew well and much admired.

[16] The main sexual encounters are between Emma and Rodolphe in *Madame Bovary*, pt II, ch. 11. Effi Briest's affair with Major von Crampas is hinted at rather than described, and it is never made clear what did take place between them.

University Press 1987, is an admirable, fact-filled introduction to the novel by an expert.

There are various satisfactory biographies of Flaubert, such as Enid Starkie's two-volume *Flaubert*, Weidenfeld and Nicolson, London 1967, 1971, and H. R. Lottman's *Flaubert: a Biography*, Methuen, London 1989. But perhaps the most intimate, and certainly the most entertaining, book about Flaubert is not an academic biography but a novel: *Flaubert's Parrot*, Cape, London 1984 and later reprints, a witty and graceful investigation of the Master by Julian Barnes (himself a novelist); it even includes a useful chronology of Flaubert's life and work from three points of view in chapter 2. Strongly recommended on the academic side is Stephen Heath's *Flaubert: Madame Bovary*, Cambridge University Press 1992, an intelligent and illuminating analysis of the book and its author, full of factual information as well as clear-headed criticism.

France: Second Republic and
Second Empire, 1848–71

The Second Republic that was proclaimed in the course of the 1848 Revolution got off to a bad start and never really recovered. The Chamber of Deputies, intimidated by the Parisian revolutionaries, introduced manhood suffrage (the first major state ever to do so), and National Workshops to occupy the urban unemployed. To pay for these they also increased the Land Tax (which was levied chiefly from the peasants) by nearly a half. The peasants expressed their displeasure in the April elections by returning a large number of extreme reactionaries; the National Workshops were shut down; and a worker's rising in Paris (the 'June Days') was brutally put down by the authorities. A new Constitution was introduced in November which gave executive power to a President, a post to which Louis-Napoleon Bonaparte (a nephew of Napoleon I) was soon elected by an overwhelming majority.

In May 1850 the conservative government legislated to disfranchise a third of the new electorate. The President tried to stop this happening, but he failed. Worse, he also failed to obtain the required majority for a second term as president, so in December 1851 he staged a violent *coup*, reinstated universal manhood suffrage, and was elected president for a further ten years. A year later he proposed the replacement of the Second Republic with the Second Empire, offering himself as hereditary Emperor, Napoleon III; and a national referendum in November 1852 approved the change by 7.8 million votes to 250,000 (more than 30 to 1).

Napoleon III proved to be an intelligent, crafty monarch, who was determined that France should have the stability, prosperity, and political development that she needed, despite the opposition of the conservative political élite. In domestic policy he promoted economic prosperity by means of *laissez-faire* economics; rail-way construction, which both opened up domestic agricultural markets and connected northern France to the Mediterranean and North Africa; and the expansion of the coal and steel industries – all of which helped to reduce unemployment. Then there was the building of the Suez Canal by Ferdinand de Lesseps (1859–69, financed jointly by France and Egypt), and the rebuilding of Paris by Baron Haussman (1853–70). In politics he granted trade union rights (1864–8), and greater parliamentary powers and re-sponsibilities in a new Constitution approved by referendum in 1870.

Napoleon's weakness proved to be in foreign policy. After a good start in the Crimean War (1854–6), and with the annexation of Savoy and Nice (1860), over-confidence led him into a disas-trous confrontation with Prussia in 1870. Misjudging Prussia's intentions and strength, Napoleon was manoeuvred by Bismarck into the Franco-Prussian War of 1870–1, in which the French army was decisively defeated by the Prussians in battle, and he himself was captured and overthrown as Emperor, at Sedan in September 1870.

Paris was beseiged from September 1870 and fell to the Prussians in January 1871, when there were peace talks and elec-tions for a new government. From March 1871 a workers' Com-mune took power in Paris but was savagely put down by government troops in May, who systematically shot *communard* prisoners while the *communards* shot government hostages; after which the Monarchist phase (1871–9) of the Third Republic was established. Baudelaire was already dead by the time of the Commune, but Rimbaud was much influenced by its revolution-ary fervour.[1]

French culture and art were not much unsettled by the distur-bances of the Second Republic, and were positively encouraged by the relative peace, the self-confidence, and the economic expansion of the Second Empire. Paris considered itself, with some reason, to be the cultural capital of Europe, and its style and vivacity affected not only Flaubert and Baudelaire, but also the poets Gautier, Leconte de Lisle, Sully-Prudhomme, and Verlaine; the critics Sainte-Beuve and Taine; and the beginnings (in the 1860s) of the Impressionist school of painters.

[1] For the later history of the Third Republic, see pp. 173–5 and 206–7.

Charles Baudelaire, 1821–67

When he was born in Paris in November 1821, Charles-Pierre (later shortened to Charles) Baudelaire's father was aged sixty-two and his mother was twenty-seven. His father died in 1827, and less than two years later his mother married again, this time to a forceful and ambitious army officer, Major Aupick, who eventually rose to become a general and an ambassador. This loss of both parents (as it must have seemed to the child) was a severe blow to Baudelaire, made worse by his stepfather's rigid notions about the need for discipline in the home. The family moved about as Aupick was posted to Lyons in 1831, where Baudelaire attended the Collège Royale, and then back to Paris in 1836, where he became a boarder at Voltaire's old school, the Collège Louis-le-Grand. By this time he was a rebellious fifteen and, although his academic work was outstanding, he was eventually expelled from the Collège in April 1839, ostensibly for refusing to hand over a note that had been passed to him by a classmate, but really because the school thought that he was a bad influence on the other pupils; he was nevertheless allowed to take his *baccalauréat* later that year.

From then on it was downhill as far as Baudelaire's respectability was concerned. He knew that he wanted to be a writer, and a bohemian way of life attracted him. He lived away from home, quickly drifted into dissolute pleasures – sex, alcohol, and hashish – and as early as the autumn of 1839 he had got into debt and contracted syphilis. In June 1841 his stepfather tried to discipline him by packing him off to India, but Baudelaire jumped ship at Mauritius and was back in France by February 1842. At this point, when he was twenty-one, he came into his inheritance from his father, 100,000 francs, the income from which (1,800 francs a year) could have given him a comfortable living if he had stayed at home with his mother and stepfather; but he set up on his own, started spending his capital, dressed himself as a dandy, and became involved with a young black woman, Jeanne Duval, with whom he lived on and off for the next twenty years.

In 1844 his mother and Aupick, now a brigadier-general, appalled by Baudelaire's decadent irresponsibility, had his affairs put in the hands of a legal guardian; and from this time he lived on a monthly allowance, occasional gifts from his mother, and whatever he could borrow. It was not much of a life – he attempted suicide in 1845, and became addicted to opium in 1847 – but it was probably the life he had to lead if he was to become the poet he believed he could be. For by now Baudelaire was writing seriously, early drafts of the poems that were to be published years later, and occasional pieces of prose. In 1845 he had published a review of the annual Paris art exhibition and a single poem in a magazine (a collection of poems, *Les Lesbiennes*, was also announced but was never published); in 1846, another and abler exhibition review; and in 1847, a semi-autobiographical novella, *La Fanfarlo*. In 1848, the year of the Revolution, he edited a short-lived radical journal, and started a long series of translations from Edgar Alan Poe. Another collection of poems, *Les Limbes* ('Limbo'), was announced but again never appeared. And so he went on, having love affairs, translating, writing unpublished verse, until 1855 when eighteen poems came out with the title 'Les Fleurs du mal'[2] in the prestigious *Revue des deux mondes*.

The crucial year was 1857 – the year incidentally when *Madame Bovary* was published in book form – when Baudelaire was aged thirty-six. General Aupick died in April, and Flaubert's mother moved to their summer residence in Honfleur. In June *Les Fleurs du mal*, now comprising one hundred poems plus 'Au Lecteur', was finally published as a book. Obviously it was wonderful; equally obviously its descriptions of nudity, sex, homosexuality, necrophilia and so on offended against the taste of the time. The edition was confiscated, and in August author, publisher, and printer were tried, convicted, and fined for offences against morality and public decency.[3] Amazingly only six of the poems were banned from future editions of the book, most of them concerning nudity. In 1861 these six poems were duly dropped from the next edition, and a further thirty-two were added; in the same year Baudelaire thought of putting himself forward for election to the Académie Française, but changed his mind when he found that he had no supporters.

Physically Baudelaire continued to deteriorate, though he went on writing, mostly essays and reviews, but including *Les Épaves*,[4] a collection of twenty-three poems including the six banned ones,

---

[2] Usually translated as 'The Flowers of Evil', but Baudelaire saw a pun in '*Fleurs*', implying that his poems were both the *product* of evil (in the sense of flowering from it), and, like flowers, the *adornment* of evil. *Mal*, moreover, can mean 'illness' as well as 'evil'; and even in the latter sense it is a weaker word than is 'evil' in English, for it can also mean no more than 'a wrong' or 'a bad thing' (see F. W. Leakey, *Baudelaire: Les Fleurs du mal*, Cambridge University Press 1992, pp. 47–50).

[3] The conviction was not officially overturned on appeal until 1949.

[4] Variously translated as 'wrecks', 'derelicts', 'relics', and 'waifs'.

which was published in Belgium in 1866. He had a minor cerebral haemorrhage in 1860; by 1865 he was obviously very ill; in June 1866 he lost his power of speech and became semi-paralysed; and in August 1867 he died aged forty-six. He was certainly France's greatest nineteenth-century poet; some say her greatest poet of all.

Les Fleurs du mal, 1857, 1861, 1868

Like *The Divine Comedy, Don Quixote* and *Faust, Les Fleurs du mal* is a major landmark in European Literature: the first, impassioned flowering of the Modernist poetry that has developed – in English as well as French – since it appeared in 1857. And here is the usual difficulty, for a great part of the value and importance of the poems included in it lies not in their literal meaning but in their metre and sound and language; and once more these are qualities which cannot be translated.

Still, we must do the best we can. The hundred poems in the first edition are grouped in five unequal parts: *Spleen et idéal* ('Spleen and the Ideal', seventy-seven poems); *Les Fleurs du mal* (twelve poems); *Révolte* (three poems); *Le Vin* ('Wine', five poems); and *La Mort* ('Death', three poems). The poems in the first and longest part concern the creative artist, love, 'spleen',[5] the urban setting, and other miscellaneous subjects. The *Fleurs du mal* section concerns sexual rebellion and humiliation; the poems in *Révolte* are religious – or, rather, blasphemous; while those in 'Wine' and 'Death' concern particular social groups to which they are addressed. Among the best of them – and certainly among the best known – are the introductory 'Au Lecteur' ('To the Reader'), with its much-quoted last line *'Hypocrite lecteur – mon semblable – mon frère!'* ('Hypocritical reader – my fellow-creature – my brother!'); the sonnet 'Correspondances'; and the longer 'Un Voyage à Cythère' ('A Voyage to Cythera'). We will look at the second and third of these wonderful poems.

It is worth first of all trying to say 'Correspondances' aloud in French (even if one knows little of the language), in order to get some idea of its supple metre, its rich sound, and its ornate vocabulary.[6] Here the *e*s that would normally be mute are marked '*ё*' where they are sounded in the poem, so giving the lines their twelve syllables

---

[5] That is, bad temper and boredom – Baudelaire uses the English word.
[6] For the technicalities of French versification, see pp. 20–1 above.

each. The rhyme-scheme of the sonnet is *aBBa CddC dEd Eff*, where the capital letters indicate feminine rhymes (ending with mute *e*), and the lower-case letters masculine rhymes. Following the French text with its opulent, lingering vowels and diphthongs is a fairly literal prose translation by Francis Scarfe, which gives the meanings – not so heady in English – of the French words:

> *La Nature est un temple où de vivants piliers*
> *Laissënt parfois sortir de confusës paroles;*
> *L'homme y passe à travers des forêts de symboles*
> *Qui l'observënt avec des regards familiers.*
>
> *Commë de longs échos qui de loin se confondent*
> *Dans unë ténébreuse et profonde unité,*
> *Vastë commë la nuit et commë la clarté,*
> *Les parfums, les couleurs et les sons se répondent.*
>
> *Il est des parfums frais commë des chairs d'enfants,*
> *Doux commë les hautbois, verts commë les prairies,*
> *– Et d'autrës, corrompus, richës et triomphants,*
>
> *Ayant l'expansion des chosës infinies,*
> *Commë l'ambrë, le musc, le benjoin et l'encens,*
> *Qui chantënt les transports de l'esprit et des sens.*

Nature is a temple in which living pillars sometimes utter a babel of words; man traverses it through forests of symbols, that watch him with knowing eyes.

Like prolonged echoes which merge far away in an opaque, deep oneness, as vast as darkness, as vast as light, perfumes, sounds, and colours answer each to each.

There are perfumes fresh and cool as the bodies of children, mellow as oboes, green as fields; and others that are perverse, rich, and triumphant, that have the infinite expansion of infinite things – such as amber, musk, benjamin, and incense, which chant the ecstasies of the mind and senses.

(*Baudelaire*, Penguin Poets 1961, pp. 36–7)

The natural world, Baudelaire says, is like a vast temple which sends mankind confusing signals, challenging him to interpret them. The scents, colours, and sounds that he senses correspond with each other so that a transcending unity can be inferred from them. Taking scents as an example, they can correspond with touch (the flesh of children), sound (of oboes), and colour (the green of fields); or can (as scents of amber, musk, benjamin, incense) be themselves the keys to infinite worlds, corrupt, rich, and triumphant.

'Correspondances' is a poem of historic importance as well as being an extraordinary work of art, for it became the inspiration of the Symbolist movement: a group of French poets – notably Verlaine, Rimbaud (see below), and Mallarmé – who, in the 1870s and 1880s, further developed what became the Modernist tradition in European poetry. They were reacting against the objectivity and technical conservatism in much contemporary verse, and aiming instead for a poetry of spiritual suggestion by the use of private symbols, describing 'not the thing itself but the effect that it produces' (Mallarmé); their influence on their successors – in English literature through Joyce, Virginia Woolf, and T. S. Eliot – was widespread.

'Un Voyage à Cythère' is very different: a savage account in fifteen quatrains of the poet's visit to the island of love, where he finds that it is not what he expects it to be.[7] The voyage begins promisingly:

> My heart was soaring gaily as a bird and hovering untrammelled round the rigging; the ship sailed on beneath a cloudless sky, like an angel enraptured by the cloudless sun.
>
> 'But what can that drab dark island be?' – 'It's Cythera,' they told us, 'a place much famed in song, the tame Eldorado of all old bachelors – as you see, after all, it's not much of a place!'

Hitherto the poet has known of Cythera only as the enchanted and enchanting isle of Venus:

> – But Cythera was now but the barrenest of lands, a rocky desert haunted by piercing cries. However, I glimpsed a strange thing there.
>
> It was not a temple with shady groves wherein the flower-loving young priestess walked, her body aflame with secret desires, loosening her robes to catch the passing breeze.
>
> No: as we passed close enough to the shore for our white sails to disturb the birds, we saw it was a three-branched gibbet looming black against the sky, like a cypress tree.
>
> Fierce birds, perched on their prey, were savagely rending the ripened corpse of a hanged man, each plunging its filthy beak like a scalpel into the carcass's bleeding wounds.
>
> His eyes were already two empty sockets, and from his caved-in belly the heavy intestines were rolling down his thighs, and his torturers, gorged on hideous tit-bits, had thoroughly castrated him with their beaks.
>
> At his feet a pack of jealous beasts were circling and prowling to and fro with uplifted maws, while one bigger than the rest was leaping high in their midst, like the executioner surrounded by his henchmen.

'O grotesque gallows-bird', cries the poet, now understanding what it means, 'your sufferings are mine!' For the poet himself is being

---

[7] The French text of the extracts quoted in translation here is given on pp. 234–5 below.

punished by disgust and by mortal disease for the harm he has done as a lover. The poem ends in the same ironically fine weather in which it began:

> – The sky was entrancing, the sea was calm, but for me all was now dark and smeared with blood. Alas, my heart lay buried in this allegory as in a winding-sheet.
>
> O Venus, in your isle I found nothing standing but a symbolic gallows, with my own image hanged upon it. – O heavenly Father, give me strength and courage to contemplate my heart and body without disgust![8]

Thus the poet says goodbye to romantic love with a prayer asking for the strength and courage simply to look at himself – the only place in all his poetry where Baudelaire cries out directly to God.

This is a small enough sample of the the astonishing quality and authority of *Les Fleurs du mal*; and it is well worth going to the book itself – preferably in a parallel-text version – to explore its riches in all their wonderful variety.

Translations

The translated quotations given here are from Francis Scarfe's prose versions which appear as footnotes to the French texts in the Penguin Poets selections from *Baudelaire* (1961; this book is no longer in print, but Scarfe's translation of Baudelaire's complete poems and prose poems is published by Anvil Press Poetry). As can be seen by comparing them with the originals given above and in Appendix B (pp. 234–5), they are sufficiently literal without being wooden. The Oxford World's Classics *Charles Baudelaire: The Flowers of Evil* (1993) is a parallel-text verse translation by the American poet James McGowan. There have been many verse-translations of Baudelaire, and McGowan's is not a bad one; but the requirements of English metre and rhyme inevitably cause the translator to make changes to the meaning of the original. The current Penguin Classics *Baudelaire in English* (1997), edited by Carol Clark and Robert Sykes, is a selection of Baudelaire's work without the French text.

Arthur Rimbaud, 1854–91

Children and adolescents with prodigious gifts as musical composers or executants – Mozart is the obvious example – are a well-known phenomenon; but young writers with similarly prodigious

---

[8] From *Baudelaire*, trs. by Francis Scarfe, Penguin Poets 1961, pp. 97–100.

gifts are a rarity. Keats and Baudelaire wrote wonderful poetry in their early twenties, but on the whole writers need to grow up before they can be at their best. Arthur Rimbaud is the great exception: he started writing French verse of extraordinary quality (although at first somewhat derivative) when he was fifteen; wrote great poems in his own style when he was sixteen; and stopped writing poetry when he was seventeen. He continued to write prose poems for two years more, then finally lost interest in literature and gave up writing altogether when he was nineteen (though he was to live for nearly as long again).

Rimbaud was born at Charleville in the Ardennes, a provincial town on the Meuse near the Belgian border. His father was an army officer who left his wife and family when Rimbaud was six. His mother, who inherited farm property from her family, was an excessively strict single parent, a representative of the restrictive adult world against which turbulent children and adolescents commonly rebel. Certainly Rimbaud did so inside himself, though at first he was obliged to obey his mother and go to school; at the Collège de Charleville he did very well academically from the ages of ten to fifteen, becoming skilled in writing Latin verse, and carrying off all the school prizes. But at fifteen he had had enough of school. Encouraged by Georges Izambard, a young schoolmaster of revolutionary views, Rimbaud had begun to write poetry of high quality. In August 1870 he took a train to Paris, hoping to be in at the end of the Second Empire but, having no money to pay his fare, he was locked up on arrival, rescued by Izambard, and eventually sent back to his mother. Ten days later he ran away again, this time to wander in Belgium for a fortnight, looking for work as a journalist (the poem 'Ma Bohème' refers to this brief period of freedom); again he was sent home with Izambard's help, in time to watch the bombardment of his home town by the Prussians. Now he refused to go back to school, and did his best to embarrass his family by wandering about Charleville ragged and unwashed, blaspheming in cafés and smoking a foul clay pipe.

Now just sixteen, Rimbaud wrote poems, and read 'unsuitable' books (on such subjects as socialism and the occult) in the Charleville public library; the poem 'Les Assis' ('The Seated Ones') is his ferocious attack on the librarians who unwillingly brought them to him. His chief literary influence became, inevitably, Baudelaire, both as poet and as seer; but where Baudelaire always retained an underlying sense of moral purpose even in his wildest explorations of sensuality, Rimbaud was eager to give up all morality – he was only in his mid-teens – to indulge in any debauch, to find shortcuts in the occult, all for the sake of experience and sensation.

In February 1871 he ran away for a third time, to Paris again, where for a fortnight he ate from dustbins, slept rough, and was probably assaulted sexually by soldiers in a barracks. Finding nothing in Paris but poverty, he walked back to Charleville (a trek of 120 miles, passing through the lines of the Prussian army), where he stayed until the autumn, writing assiduously. He sent some of his poems (a few of which had been published in periodicals in 1870–1) to the poet Paul Verlaine (1844–96), who invited Rimbaud to stay with his wife's family in Paris, whither he went in September 1871, still not quite seventeen, and having written, just before leaving, his longest poem, *Le Bateau ivre* ('The Drunken Boat'). The arrival at the bourgeois, 'arty' home of Verlaine's Parisian in-laws of this unexpectedly young, filthy, and ill-mannered provincial was an absurd disaster, as much for Rimbaud as for his hosts, and he soon left to camp wherever he could find someone's studio or attic in which to lay his verminous head. He was not a success in Parisian literary society, which found him personally irresponsible, immoral, and antisocial, and his poetry grotesque in its vocabulary and imagery.

For most of the next two years Rimbaud and Verlaine lived together in Paris and London (to the further disgust of Verlaine's wife and parents, who thought – perhaps rightly – that they were having a homosexual affair), making what little money they could from writing and giving French lessons, drinking absinthe, smoking (probably opium and certainly hashish as well as tobacco), and getting on each other's nerves. Verlaine, although the older by ten years, was dominated by the younger man, and eagerly joined Rimbaud in his debauches (though without losing his own great talent as a poet). In June 1872, Rimbaud – not yet eighteen – wrote his last poems in verse, although he continued to write prose poems for a while longer; and this may have been the period when he wrote his collection of prose poems, published later as *Les Illuminations*.

After several brief partings, the end of his association with Verlaine came in the summer of 1873 – Rimbaud was now nearly nineteen – when Verlaine, intoxicated, acquired a pistol in Brussels and tried to shoot Rimbaud, wounding him slightly in the wrist. Verlaine went to prison for two years for assault and Rimbaud returned home to Charleville, where he completed a book of prose poems and verse, *Une Saison en enfer* ('A Season in Hell').

This brings us to the end of Rimbaud's extraordinarily brief and brilliant career as a poet. In the summer of 1874, before his twentieth birthday, he finally lost interest in literature, deciding that his 'illuminations' had been 'hallucinations', and abandoning *Une Saison en enfer* which he had had printed but which he never paid for or published (beyond giving away a few author's copies to his friends). He spent most of the rest of his life abroad, travelling in Europe and the Middle East, and finally working as a buyer for a French firm at a trading post in Abyssinia – a colonial heart of darkness – exploring, gun-running, and slave-trafficking on the side. In 1886 Verlaine published *Les Illuminations* 'by the late Arthur Rimbaud' (he really didn't know whether his old friend was alive or not). The book was a sensation, which Rimbaud chose to ignore, describing his teenage poetry to anyone who asked about it as absurd, ridiculous, and disgusting. In February 1891 he developed a tumour on his knee; he returned to France where the leg was amputated, but his condition continued to deteriorate. After a few months at home with his family he travelled to Marseilles, where he died in November, just after his thirty-seventh birthday, neither knowing nor caring whether the bulk of his poetry would ever be published.

Poems, 1870–3

Rimbaud's poetry divides into three groups of unequal size. The largest of them contains the poems of 1870–2; then come the poems (mostly in prose) of *Les Illuminations*, 1872; and finally the prose poems with a small amount of verse of *Une Saison en enfer*, 1872–3. Here we shall look at two of the poems written at different stages of his development, and a short prose poem.

The sonnet 'Ma Bohème' ('My Bohemian Life') was written around the time of his sixteenth birthday in October 1870, and lyrically recalls Rimbaud's magic fortnight of freedom wandering in southern Belgium. This is Oliver Bernard's fairly literal prose translation:[9]

---

[9] Along with the French text, there is a good verse translation by Norman Cameron of this poem in Appendix B, p. 235 below.

My Bohemian Existence (A Fantasy)

I went off with my hands in my torn coat pockets; my overcoat too was becoming ideal; I travelled beneath the sky, Muse! and I was your vassal; oh dear me! what marvelous loves I dreamed of!

My only pair of breeches had a big hole in them. – Stargazing Tom Thumb, I sowed rhymes along the way. My tavern was at the Sign of the Great Bear. – My stars in the sky rustled softly.

And I listened to them, sitting on the road-sides on those pleasant September evenings while I felt drops of dew on my forehead like vigorous wine;

and while, rhyming among the fantastical shadows, I plucked like the strings of a lyre the elastics of my tattered boots, one foot close to my heart! (*'Ma Bohème'*)

On the two occasions in 1870 when Rimbaud was rescued by Georges Izambard he was briefly cared for by the schoolmaster's three maiden aunts in Douai; and 'Les Chercheuses de poux' ('The Lice-seekers'), written about a year after 'Ma Bohème' in the autumn of 1871, just before his seventeenth birthday, is probably a memory of two of these kindly ladies picking nits from Rimbaud's head. This time we have Norman Cameron's verse translation:[10]

The Lice-pickers

When the child's forehead, racked by torments hot and red,
Begs the white benison of some vague, swarming dream,
Two tall and charming sisters come close to his bed,
Their fragile hands with silver finger-nails agleam.

Beside a widely open window, where the blue
Air bathes a tangled bunch of flowers, they set the child,
And in his heavy hair besprinkled with the dew
Their delicate fingers travel, terrible and mild.

He hears the singing of their breaths sharp with suspense,
Flower-sweet with herbal, rosy honeys, that a kiss
Interrupts now and then, saliva on the tense
Lip suddenly caught back, or longing for a kiss.

Amid the perfumed silence he can hear their black
Eyelashes beat; he lolls in drunken paradise,
While 'neath their royal nails, with soft, electric crack,
Their gentle fingers spell death to the little lice.

[10] For the French, and a prose translation, see p. 236.

And now there mounts in him the wine of idleness,
A concertina-sighing that is close to raving;
And, while he palpitates beneath each slow caress,
There falls and rises endlessly a tearful craving.

('Les Chercheuses de poux')

In this poem Rimbaud's choice of words is especially vivid: the ladies' delicate fingers *'promènent'*, 'walk' in his heavy hair; their breaths are *'craintives'*, 'timorous'; and their finger-nails *'font crépiter ... la mort des petits poux*, 'make the death of the little lice crackle'. The whole poem evokes an inescapable thrill, a shuddering tingle up the spine.

Finally, here is a short prose-poem from *Les Illuminations*: it is the first part of 'Veillées' ('Vigils'), probably written in the summer of 1872, given both in French and in a prose translation:

Veillées

C'est le repos éclairé, ni fièvre ni langueur, sur le lit ou sur le pré.
C'est l'ami ni ardent ni faible. L'ami.
C'est l'aimée ni tourmentante ni tourmentée. L'aimée.
L'air et le monde point cherchés. La vie.
– Était-ce donc ceci?
– Et le rêve fraîchit.

('Veillées, I')

Vigils, I

It is rest in the light, neither fever nor languor, on the bed or on the meadow.
It is the friend neither ardent nor weak. The friend.
It is the beloved neither tormenting nor tormented. The beloved.
The atmosphere and world unsought. Life.
– Was it this, then?
– And the dream is growing cold.

(Trs. by Oliver Bernard)

In the first of three 'vigils' over the dead (actual or symbolic), Rimbaud strips his prose poem of all narrative and descriptive elements, and concentrates on the essence of the watcher's perceptions and feelings until there is literally no more to be said.

Translations

Rimbaud's *Collected Poems* in French, plus a few letters, etc., (Penguin Classics, 1962, 1997) has an excellent footnote translation in prose by Oliver Bernard. Rimbaud's *A Season in Hell and Other Poems* (Anvil Press Poetry 1994) is a parallel-text selection with the verse and prose translations of Norman Cameron (1901–53). Both versions (which are quoted above and in Appendix B) are thoroughly worth while.

Further reading

For the general background, see Roger Price, *A Concise History of France*, Cambridge University Press 1993.

The standard French biography of Baudelaire is *Baudelaire* by Claude Pichois, trsl. by Graham Robb, London, Hamish Hamilton, 1988. *Baudelaire* by Joanna Richardson, London, John Murray 1994, is a more recent and fuller critical biography (though it lacks English translations of some of the poems quoted in French). F. W. Leakey, *Baudelaire: Les Fleurs du mal*, Cambridge University Press 1992, is an excellent introduction, and has a useful chapter on Baudelaire's versification and poetic technique.

For Rimbaud there is still nothing better in English than Enid Starkie's fascinating and detailed *Rimbaud*, originally published in 1961 and still in print in paperback (1982). Oliver Bernard's Introduction to the Penguin Classics Rimbaud: *Collected Poems* (1962, 1997) does well in the limited space available to it.

IX Turgénev, Tolstóy, and Dostoévsky

The great age of the Russian novel, 1856–80[1]

A mere two-and-a-half decades, which coincided with the reign of
the relatively liberal Tsar Alexander II, saw the publication of
thirteen great novels by Turgénev, Goncharóv, Tolstóy, and Dostoévsky that are the glory of nineteenth-century Russian fiction.
These novels were:

Turgénev	*Rúdin*, 1856
	A Nest of Gentlefolk, 1859
	On the Eve, 1860
	Fathers and Children, 1862
	Smoke, 1867
	Virgin Soil, 1877
Goncharóv	*Oblómov*, 1857
Tolstóy	*War and Peace*, 1863–9
	Ánna Karénina, 1875–7
Dostoévsky	*Crime and Punishment*, 1866
	The Idiot, 1868
	Devils (The Possessed), 1872
	The Brothers Karamázov, 1880

There were predecessors of comparable quality – we have already
looked at Púshkin's *Eugene Onégin*, 1828, and Lérmontov's *A
Hero of Our Time*, 1839; and there was also Part I of Gógol's *Dead
Souls*, 1842 – but this extraordinary concentration of superlative
fiction was, and has remained, unparalleled in the history of
Russian or any other literature.

The fact that this great age of fiction was also the time of
Alexander II (ruled 1855–81) was not merely coincidental. The
Russian Empire under Alexander was still an absolute autocracy,

---

[1] For a general account of the Russian Empire in the nineteenth century, see pp. 75–
80; and for the liberal and radical movements that brought it to an end, pp. 160–2.

still a police state in which active opposition to the régime was punishable by imprisonment or exile, and in which all publications were censored; but Alexander II was a less actively repressive autocrat than were either his father Nicholas I or his son Alexander III. Besides permitting the emancipation of the serfs (1861), Alexander's régime tolerated a greater degree of liberal opinion and a slackening of the censorship. All novels were indeed subject to censorship, but the censors were not interested in the art of fiction as such, or in mildly liberal opinions, but only in anything that was considered obscene, or that might be politically unacceptable to the authorities, such as criticism of the monarchy or support for revolutionary change. Turgénev, Tolstóy, and Dostoévsky, were therefore able to discuss in their novels liberal or otherwise unorthodox ideas that might have been censored at other times. Even so, Turgénev (who had been banished to his country estate in 1852) and Dostoévsky (who had been exiled to Siberia in 1849) both found it convenient to live abroad for much of this period.

A long-standing disagreement between educated Russians, going back to the reforms of Peter the Great, gave rise to renewed controversy from the 1840s. This was the dispute between the 'Westernists' and the 'Slavophiles'. The question was, were Russians Europeans, like the English, the French and the Germans, or were they primarily Slavs, people of a different culture with roots further east? Should Russians be prepared to absorb Western ideas and democratic institutions, or should they foster their Russian-ness, their xenophobia and anti-Semitism, and support the autocracy and the Orthodox Church? Of the three novelists discussed in this chapter, Turgénev was a convinced Westernist, while Dostoévsky was, in his later years, a passionate Slavophile. Tolstóy, although he disliked Western morals and materialism, wrote in *Ánna Karénina* a thoroughly European novel.

The major works of the great age of Russian fiction were normally published serially in periodicals – the so-called 'thick journals' such as *The Contemporary* (founded by Púshkin and shut down in 1866) and *The Russian Herald* (1856–1906) – that were widely read by the educated and landowning classes. (It has been said that nineteenth-century Russian novels were written by landowners about landowners for landowners.) A single journal, M. N. Katkóv's *The Russian Herald*, actually serialised all four of Dostoévsky's greatest novels, three of Turgénev's four last novels, and parts of both *War and Peace* and *Ánna Karénina*, some of them running together in the same issues – quite a bargain for the subscriber.

Iván Sergéevich Turgénev, 1818–83

Turgénev was born in Orël province, half-way between Moscow and Khárkov. His mother, a wealthy and tyrannical landowner, dominated his childhood and adolescence until he was able to escape to the universities of, successively, Moscow, St Petersburg, and Berlin (1833–41), where he did well academically but was considered to be an intellectual lightweight; and he met a number of émigré radicals, including the exiled political philosopher Alexánder Hérzen, and the radical – later anarchist – Mikháil Bakúnin, who became his close friend. He was already inclined towards Westernism but – as is evident throughout his fiction – he retained a love, a yearning even, for the beauties of the Russian countryside, and an affection for all sorts of Russian country people.

Turgénev never married, but in 1843 he became closely attached to a married opera singer, Pauline Viardot, though in what precise capacity has never been certain, and he remained her admirer for the rest of his life. In 1845 he quarrelled with his mother about his devotion to Pauline, and he left Russia two years later to join the Viardot family, returning in 1850 when his mother fell ill and died. Turgénev now became a fairly rich man who could afford to travel and live abroad, which he did, on and off, for the rest of his life.

A kind, gentle, and generous person, who had no vanity or pomposity about him, Turgénev was also timid to the point of cowardice, indecisive, and lacking (to some extent) in strength of character. His susceptibility to women resulted in a number of amorous friendships and at least one, and probably more than one, illegitimate child; yet he never shirked what he saw as his duty, and he firmly believed that it was endeavour, not results, that counted in a man's life.

Turgénev began writing as a poet under the influence of Púshkin and Lérmontov; his verse was more competent than inspired, but in composing it he acquired a mastery of the Russian language that he was to put to use in his fiction, and in his one notable play, *A Month in the Country* (1848–50). His first important work in prose was the sequence of short stories that were published in *The*

Contemporary from 1847, and were collected in 1852 under a title that has been variously translated as *A Sportsman's Sketches*, *Sketches from a Hunter's Album*, etc. These evocative tales had less to do with sport and hunting than with the Russian countryside, its provincial society, and its peasants; they made his reputation, but annoyed the authorities, who saw them as an attack on serfdom; and indeed they had some influence on the future Tsar Alexander II's decision to emancipate the serfs. A further annoyance of the authorities in 1852 – a laudatory obituary of Gógol when Gógol was not to be mentioned – resulted in Turgénev being imprisoned for a month, and then being banished for over a year to his country estate at Spásskoie (1852–3). After this he lived much abroad, mostly in Germany and France, and from 1863 to 1870 in Baden-Baden, a spa in the Black Forest where émigré Russians congregated, writing novels that nostalgically evoked his beloved Russian countryside. He also stayed several times in England, where he was much admired, and became acquainted with the Carlyles, Thackeray, George Eliot, Tennyson, Browning, and Swinburne.

Taken together, the six novels named at the beginning of this chapter, although not on the heroic scale of Dostoévsky or Tolstóy's work of the same period (all six of them add up to less than the length of *War and Peace*[2]), are an achievement of very high quality. In all of them social analysis is subordinate to the study of human relations, and their dominant feature is the exploration of character. The first four (from *Rúdin*, 1856, to *Fathers and Children*, 1862) were outstanding studies of various aspects of Russian liberalism, and secured Turgénev's European reputation as a novelist of world standing; *Smoke* (1867), set in the émigré world of Baden-Baden, was less well received in Russia; while *Virgin Soil* (1877) his last and longest novel, had a proletarian hero who is less convincing than his earlier protagonists. Turgénev's great talent was still evident, however, in such shorter works as his novellas *King Lear of the Steppes* (1870) and the extraordinary love story *Spring Torrents* (1872).

Despite the relative weakness of *Virgin Soil*, Turgénev's reputation remained high throughout Europe as well as in Russia; and in

---

[2] Of the novels dealt with in this chapter, *Fathers and Children*, at 82,000 words, is much the same length as the average mid-twentieth-century novel; *Ánna Karénina*, at 346,000 words, and *The Brothers Karamázov*, at 358,000 words, are each more than four times as long.

1879 he was the first Russian writer – and indeed the first novelist – to be awarded an honorary degree by Oxford University. In 1880–1 he was in love one last time with Sávina, a young Russian actress; and he died, surrounded by his beloved Viardots, in 1883, aged sixty-five.

Fathers and Children, 1862

Turgénev's elegantly-constructed masterpiece (also known as *Fathers and Sons*[3]) is a study of the 'nihilist'[4] intellectual Evgény Vasílyich Bazárov, a medical student aged twenty-nine, who moves through the various settings of the novel, changing as he goes. This prickly idealist – the 'tragic' hero, and Turgénev's most fully-realised fictional character – goes on holiday in the spring of 1859 with his university friend Arkády Kirsánov, a lad of twenty-two who hero-worships Bazárov, and who may be seen as the story's 'comic' hero. They arrive at the rundown country estate of Arkády's father and uncle, Nikolái and Pável Kirsánov, aged forty-four and forty-eight respectively. Here Arkády learns, with patronising approval, that his father, a widower, has taken a young peasant girl as his common-law wife, and that they have a baby son; and here Bazárov upsets these two gentlemen of the previous generation with his eccentricities (addressing the servants as equals, wearing odd clothes, collecting frogs for dissection), and especially infuriates the old Petersburg dandy, uncle Pável, with his nihilist arguments. 'How is it possible', Pavel exclaims, 'not to recognise principles and rules!'

> 'We are acting on the strength of what we consider useful,' said Bazárov. 'At the present time condemnation is more useful than anything else, so we condemn.'
> 'Everything?'
> 'Everything.'
> 'What? – not only art and poetry but . . . It's terrible to think what else . . .'
> 'Everything,' Bazárov repeated with inexpressible calmness.

---

[3] 'Fathers and Children' is the literal translation of the Russian *Ottsy y deti,* but some translators have preferred 'Fathers and Sons' as being a more accurate reference to the plot.

[4] 'The features of a typical nihilist were: being a student; wearing unconventional dress; long hair (for men), short hair (for women); the preaching and practice of free love; devotion to the rights of women; also, on the theoretical side, materialism, utilitarianism, atheism, and a belief in science and human welfare.' (Ronald Hingley, *Russian Writers and Society in the Nineteenth Century,* London 1977, p. 172.) The unconventional dress, the long (or short) hair, the free love, and the devotion to women's rights tend to recur among revolutionary students, and were prominent features of the 1960s as well as of the 1860s.

Pável Petróvich stared at him. He hadn't anticipated this, but Arkády had even gone red with pleasure.

'However, permit me to say this,' Nikolái Petróvich started saying. 'You're condemning everything or, to be more precise, you're pulling everything down, but surely you've got to build something as well.'

'That's not for us to do. First we've got to clear the ground.' (*Fathers and Children*, ch. 10, tr. by Richard Freeborn.)

Bazárov and Kirsánov go next to the local town where they meet a hollow politician and two would-be 'bohemians', the lightweight Sítnikov and the 'emancipated' woman Evdóksia Kúkshina, whom they use and snub. At a ball they are introduced by Sítnikov to the beautiful widow Odíntsova (a few months younger than Bazárov); she is charming, clever, and rich, and she immediately attracts both the young men. At her invitation they go for a fortnight's visit to Nikólskoe, her country estate, where she lives with an old aristocratic aunt and her younger sister Kátia, aged twenty.

Here Kirsánov immediately falls boyishly in love with Odíntsova; but Odíntsova and Bazárov are more seriously attracted by each other – across a class barrier – though neither of them will admit it at first, Odíntsova because she does not want to upset her comfortable, orderly life, and Bazárov because to fall in love would be a weakness that would imply a belief in something and so offend against his nihilist principles. Eventually Bazárov is manoeuvred by Odíntsova into admitting his 'weakness' and declaring his love for her, but she refuses to accept it, and the two young men leave Nikólskoe for the unpretentious home of Bazárov's father – a retired army doctor – and mother, who both dote on him excessively.

Bored by his parents' pathetic devotion, Bazárov leaves home only three days later with Arkády to return to the Kirsánovs' estate, making an unwelcome call at Nikólskoe on the way. Arkády, however, has begun to fall in love with Odíntsova's younger sister, Kátia, and he soon returns to stay at Nikólskoe leaving Bazárov with his father and uncle. Bazárov thoughtlessly flirts with father Nikolái's young peasant mistress; this is observed by uncle Pável (who is attracted to the girl himself), and Bazárov is challenged by Pável to a duel. This duly, and absurdly, takes place. Pável is lightly wounded, and Bazárov returns for the last time to Nikólskoe, where he says goodbye both to Odíntsova and to Arkády, who – prepared at last to give up his devotion to Bazárov and nihilism – becomes engaged to Kátia. Arkády and Kátia are married at the same time as

Arkády's father marries his young mistress, and uncle Pável retires to Dresden.

Bazárov returns home to his parents, this time for good as he realises how unimportant and temporary his life is compared with the immensity of nature and time. He decides to remain at home and devote his life to doctoring the peasantry. Ironically – for he is strong in his idealism – he contracts blood-poisoning during a post-mortem which quickly results in his futile death.

This complex and cleverly-constructed story has an omniscient third-person narrator who keeps out of sight for most of the time, an ironically humorous storyteller who pauses occasionally to relate the histories of some of the characters. Of all of them, Bazárov is most fully brought to life, and comes across as both maddening and admirable: there is nobility in the purity of his political philosophy, however mistaken it may be, and there is humanity and decency beneath his arrogance and bad manners. The character who most resembles him is, paradoxically, uncle Pável, equally certain of his own rightness, and equally quixotic in his behaviour. The four main settings – the town and the three very different country estates – offer other parallels and contrasts; and it is instructive to compare Turgénev's severe descriptions of land-lord-peasant relations at the time of Emancipation with Tolstóy's more optimistic approach in *Ánna Karénina* (1875–7 see below), and Chékhov's bitter short story 'Peasants' (1897).[5]

Fathers and Children, along with Turgénev's other major novels, has as subtext the author's Westernism: his fundamental, if pessimistic, belief that what was wrong with Russian society and institutions could only be set right if the educated classes would (however improbably) take lessons from the way things were done in liberal Europe; and that there was no solution to be found in the autocracy, in the conservative peasantry, or in violent revolution.

Translations

As with the other novels of the great age, there is much to be said for the translation by Constance Garnett, which in this case appeared in 1895. Although this was more than thirty years after Turgénev's novel appeared, Mrs Garnett (a skilled and experienced translator from Russian to English who happened to have been born in year of its publication, 1862) was still much nearer to it than we can be

[5] See also p. 80 n. 3 above.

another century on. Richard Freeborn's translation (Oxford World's Classics, 1991) is a satisfactory modern version which draws on Turgénev's working papers, including the manuscript discovered in 1988, and which has a good Introduction and notes. The Penguin Classics translation by Rosemary Edmonds (1965) now includes Isaiah Berlin's Romanes lecture on *Fathers and Children* (1970).

Lév Nikoláevich Tolstóy, 1828–1910

It is possible to look at most nineteenth-century novelists, including Turgénev and Dostoévsky, and see them as people we can understand; extraordinary people, indeed, great, perceptive artists with wonderful talents, but still vulnerable, still people. Tolstóy, on the other hand, seems in some ways to have been something more than a mere man, a phenomenon on a different scale altogether: a very great artist, certainly, and sometimes spectacularly wrong in his opinions, but beyond this a natural force – intellectual, moral, and spiritual – that affected everything that he touched, and was uncontrollable by society or the state.

Tolstóy was an aristocrat, the fourth son of Count Nikolái Tolstóy of Yásnaia Poliána in Túla province, 120 miles south of Moscow; his mother died when he was two, his father when he was nine. His early life was not remarkable. He was educated first at home, then at the University of Kazán (where he dropped out after three years of Oriental Languages and Law). He made an adventurous journey to the Caucasus – Russia's 'Wild West' of the south – with one of his brothers in 1851; he was commissioned as an artillery officer in 1854, when he was twenty-six, and he saw active service in the Crimean War in 1854–5.

When he left the army in 1856 he was already acclaimed as a writer for the semi-autobiographical sequence *Childhood, Boyhood,* and *Youth* (1852–6), and for the forthright war-reporting of *Sevastópol*[6] *Sketches* (1855). During the next five years, 1857–61, he wrote a few short stories, but was more concerned with making two visits to Western Europe, and with busying himself farming and founding a school for the peasants at Yásnaia Poliána. The year 1862, however, was different: he was devastated by the

---

[6] In Russian 'Sevastopol' has the stress on the third syllable, but the English pronunciation puts the stress on the second syllable.

death of two of his brothers, and he married Sófia Andréevna Behrs, the daughter of a socially-ambitious Moscow doctor (who, as it happened, had once had an affair with Turgénev's mother).

Marriage was a turning-point for Tolstóy. It not only provided him with an outlet for his powerful sex-drive – though he went on tumbling peasant girls when it got too much for him – it also brought him a strong partner who believed in his genius and who would help him with his work as critic and copyist. The following year, having published *The Cossacks*, he began to write *War and Peace*, and Sófia's practical and moral support was essential to its progress. Not that their married life was easy; Tolstóy was demanding and difficult, Sófia bore thirteen children, and they quarrelled and fought without cease, as strong partners who love and depend on each other sometimes do.

With the publication of *War and Peace* (1865–9), the sprawling, unprecedented work of history and fiction set in the time of the Napoleonic Wars, which turned out to be a heroic national epic to which all sorts of Russians could respond, Tolstóy became a national icon. But, before he moved on to more controversial matters, he had one great novel of adultery[7] to write: *Ánna Karénina*, the overwhelming love story that is the central work of nineteenth-century fiction (1875–7), and is discussed in the next section.

With the completion of *Ánna Karénina* Tolstóy came to the second turning point in his life: a spiritual crisis which he described in *A Confession* (begun in 1879, published in 1882), a short work of overpowering emotional force in which he condemns the sensuality and materialism of his earlier life, and turns instead, not to the worldly Orthodox Church, but to the pure teaching of the Sermon on the Mount, mediated by the simple piety of the Russian peasant. There was some self-deception in this, for his life hitherto had not been wholly bad, the virtues of Russian peasants were at least equalled by their vices, and the primitive Christianity which Tolstóy wanted to practice was not a real possibility for the passionate artist that he actually was. Nevertheless this change of direction was to prove permanent, and much of the rest of his writing and teaching was to be affected by his 'conversion'. There was the novella *The Death of Iván Ilých* (1886), about a man's attitude to his own mortality; splendid fables such as *How Much*

---

[7] See pp. 98–103 and p. 99 n. 10.

Land Does a Man Need? (1886); *The Kreutzer Sonata* (1889), a moral tract about sex (Tolstóy came to think that married couples should remain chaste except for the purpose of begetting children, though he found himself unable to live up to this ideal); and a number of essays and short books on religious and moral topics, such as *The Kingdom of God Is Within You* (1893).

He did not give up writing fiction entirely. There was one more substantial novel, *Resurrection* (1899), a half-successful story about a servant girl who, after being seduced, becomes a prostitute, and whose titled seducer, finding himself a member of the jury at her trial for murder, is morally reborn; he follows her to Siberia and offers to marry her. More successful was a wonderful Caucasian novella, *Hádji Murát* (written 1897–1904, published posthumously) in which Tolstóy returned in imagination to his adventures on the southern frontier of half a century before, and wrote again simply for the pleasure of telling a good story supremely well.

How Tolstóy got away with works in this last period which, coming from anyone else, would have been condemned and punished as seditious, is something of a wonder; but the fact was that he was so famous and so revered in Russia that the government dared not touch him. So he lived on at Yásnaia Polyiána, excommunicated by the Orthodox Church, annoying the authorities, quarrelling with his wife, and finally running away from home and dying at a railway station in 1910 at the age of eighty-two.[8]

Ánna Karénina, 1875–7

Ánna Karénina is the result of the last upsurge of creative imagination in the unreconstructed Tolstóy: a vast, many-coloured novel teeming with rounded characters (including himself), beautiful and complex in its structure and exposition, and deeply satisfying in its psychological perception and moral teaching.

Tolstóy greatly admired contemporary English novels – especially those of Dickens, Trollope, and George Eliot – and it is very likely that he read *Middlemarch* when it appeared a year before he

---

[8] 'At once insanely proud and filled with hatred, omniscient and doubting everything, cold and violently passionate, contemptuous and self-abasing, tormented and detached, surrounded by an adoring family, by devoted followers, by the admiration of the entire civilised world, and yet almost wholly isolated, he is the most tragic of the great writers, a desperate old man, beyond human aid, wandering self-blinded at Colonus.' (Isaiah Berlin, quoted in Michael Ignatieff, *Isaiah Berlin, a Life*, Chatto and Windus 1998, p. 213).

started writing *Ánna Karénina,* and that he would have appreciated not only its moral seriousness but also its multiple, interrelated themes, and its presentation of lives that were being lived before the first page and that would continue to be lived after the last; for these are features of the structure of his own, morally serious book.

There are two main stories in *Ánna Karénina* that run in parallel, with connections between them at their margins. There is the story of Ánna, married to Karénin, her upright, boring husband, with a little boy whom she adores. She meets Captain Count Vrónsky, they fall desperately in love with each other and she becomes pregnant with Vrónsky's child. Karénin knows but will not divorce her. Ánna nearly dies in childbirth, Karénin forgives her, and Vrónsky tries unsuccessfully to kill himself. None of this solves anything, Ánna leaves Karénin for Vrónsky, but Karénin keeps their son. Ostracised by society for living in sin, and longing desperately for her elder child – the new baby does not much interest her – she allows the relationship with Vrónsky to deteriorate; and eventually, feeling that she has lost everything, she kills herself by throwing herself under a train.

The other story is about Konstantín Lévin, who – like Pierre Bezúkov and Prince Andrew in *War and Peace* – is an aspect of Tolstóy himself, and who – as farmer and country gentleman – shares many of Tolstóy's circumstances, interests, and tastes. He woos and marries Princess Kitty Shcherbátskaia (a connection by marriage of Ánna's) in much the same way as Tolstóy had won Sófia Behrs; likewise he farms his country estate, helps to mow the hay, concerns himself with agricultural improvements and the rural council, worries about his peasants, is devastated by the death of his brother, entertains his guests, goes hunting, bickers with his wife, and brings up their children, all much as Tolstóy did at Yásnaia Poliána. The Lévins' story ends happily, with Konstantín still puzzling about the meaning of life and Kitty content with simply living it.

The two parts of this dual structure of successful and unsuccessful families are connected by the Oblónskys, for the Oblónskys have connections with both Ánna and the Lévins – Stíva is Ánna's brother, Dolly is Kitty's sister – and the continuing account of their troubled doings ensures that the two parallel but contrasted main stories are kept in contact with each other. The Oblónskys serve as the keystone of the great arch of which the pillars are on the one hand Ánna, Karénin, and Vrónsky, and on the other the Lévins.

In Turgénev's *Fathers and Children* we had a conventional mid-nineteenth-century novel, with a fascinating central character and supporting cast, and with a third-person narrator who stands back and tells the cleverly-structured story, even beginning with a description of the appearance of the characters as they come on stage. In *Ánna Karénina* Tolstóy modifies and develops Turgénev's technique on a much larger scale, plunging straight in with his famous first sentence: 'All happy families resemble one another, each unhappy family is unhappy in its own way'. As an impersonal, reliable third-person narrator, he takes us immediately into the action, and tells us incidentally what the novel is about: 'families'; and specifically families that succeed in being happy (because, we are to learn, they are morally sound), and families that do not.[9] This is a novel not just about individuals (Ánna, Lévin) but about the relationships of husbands and wives, parents and children, siblings and friends: Oblónsky, Dolly, and their children; Oblónsky and his sister Ánna; Ánna, Karénin, and Seriózha; Vrónsky and his mother; Vrónsky and his fellow-officers; Ánna, Vrónsky, and little Ánna; Lévin and each of his two brothers; Lévin, Kitty, and their children.

First to appear is the Oblónsky family, which hovers between success and failure; and Tolstóy introduces Stíva Oblónsky not with a set-piece description of his appearance and personality, but obliquely, his comfortable physical characteristics becoming apparent as we learn about his self-indulgent moral character and the awkward situation he is in. Then in the rest of Part One of the novel (there are eight parts altogether, this one consisting of thirty-four short sections) all the other main characters and their inter-relationships are introduced and set going in a structural *tour de force*:

> Sections 1–4: Oblónsky tries to explain his adultery to his wife; she refuses to be reconciled.
>
> 5: Oblónsky goes to the office; Lévin arrives, they agree to dine together.
>
> 6–9: Lévin's reason for coming to Moscow is to propose to Kitty Scher-bátskaia, Dolly Oblónskaia's sister; he meets his half-brother Kozny-shév, then goes to a skating lake to find Kitty; they have a stilted conversation.

[9] *Fathers and Children* also considers the Kirsánov and Bazárov families, and *The Brothers Karamázov* is about the members of the dysfunctional Karamázov family; but in neither of these cases are family relationships as central as they are in *Ánna Karénina*.

10–11: Oblónsky and Lévin dine together; Oblónsky tells Lévin that Vrónsky is courting Kitty.

12–15: reception at the Shcherbátskys; Lévin proposes to Kitty and is refused because (with her mother's encouragment) she thinks she prefers Vrónsky.

16–18: Vrónsky goes to the railway station to meet his mother who is arriving from Petersburg; while waiting for the train he meets Oblónsky, who has come to meet his sister Ánna Karénina who is travelling to Moscow by the same train, and they find that Countess Vrónskaia and Ánna have been travelling together; at the station a railway worker is ominously run over by a train.

19–21: Ánna has been summoned to Moscow by her brother to help him patch things up with Dolly; she skilfully procures a reconciliation between them.

22–3: at a society ball Kitty, who had hoped that Vrónsky would propose to her, is dismayed to find that Vrónsky has eyes only for Ánna, and she for him.

24–5: Lévin visits his other brother Nikolái Lévin, a consumptive living with his lower-class common-law wife.

26–7: Lévin, unhappy because he has failed to win Kitty, returns to his country estate, where his only companion is his housekeeper.

28–31: Ánna, disturbed by her emotional reaction to Vrónsky, decides to return immediately to Petersburg; Vrónsky takes the same train in order to be where she is, and they meet in a snow-storm at a halt on the way and tacitly admit their love for each other; at Petersburg she is met by Karénin, who now seems absurd to her.

32–3: Ánna reunited with her son Seriózha; the meddling Countess Lýdia Ivánovna calls; the new falsity of Anna's life at home with Karénin.

34: Vrónsky at home with his fellow-officers and other smart friends in Petersburg.

Although many other interesting characters appear later in the novel, by this point we have met all the principal ones and know something about them and their relationships with each other. This supplies a solid base from which the rest of the narrative can grow, and to which it can be related by the reader.

A central feature of Tolstóy's technique in *Ánna Karénina* is the concentration here and there on a number of special events, which are described with particular intensity. The best known of these is the exhilarating description of Lévin mowing a hayfield with his peasants (Part III, sections 4–6), but there are others that are scarcely less powerful. For instance: Kitty, Ánna, and Vrónsky at the ball (I,22–3); the steeplechase and the death of Frou-frou (II,25); Ánna's confinement and Karénin's change of heart (IV,17); Lévin and Kitty's wedding (V,3–6); expatriate life at a

German spa[10] (II,30–5) and at the painter Mikháilov's studio in Italy (V,10–13); Nikolái's death (V,17–20); Lévin's shoot with Oblónsky and Vásenka Veslóvsky (one of Tolstóy's few comic characters), and Lévin's subsequent dismissal of Veslóvsky (VI,8–14); and Kitty's confinement (VII,13–15). Not all of these intensely-described incidents are central to the plot of *Ánna Karénina*, but all are high points in the text, adding new dimensions to the novel's moral stance, characters, and happenings.

Ánna Karénina is not better or worse than *War and Peace* (which Tolstóy did not consider to be a novel at all): it is simply a different sort of book, the nineteenth-century European novel carried to its ultimate stage of development.

Translations

Once again, Constance Garnett's translation (originally published in 1901) is a good one, and was made only twenty-five years after *Ánna Karénina* originally appeared; but another early translation of great importance is that of Louise and Aylmer Maude (1918, revised 1939), for the Maudes had known Tolstóy and had discussed with him the problems of translating his Russian into English. The Maudes' translation has been reprinted, with Introduction, Notes, etc. by W. Gareth Jones (Oxford World's Classics 1995), and is perhaps the best choice for the reader coming to the book for the first time. The Rosemary Edmonds translation, *Ánna Karénin* (1954), in Penguin Classics lacks the period authenticity of the earlier versions, and leaves the female proper names in their male forms.

Fiódor Mikháilovich Dostoévsky, 1821–81

Unlike Turgénev and Tolstóy, Dostoévsky was town-bred, and his background was considerably less affluent. The second son of a doctor's seven children, he was born in Moscow where he was brought up and educated locally as a weekly boarder. His mother died in 1837; the next year he went to St Petersburg for a five-year course at the Military Engineering School, graduating as an officer in 1843. While he was away his father, who had bought a small

---

[10] It is interesting to compare Tolstóy's description in *Ánna Karénina* of the Shcherbátskys' stay at Bad Soden with Turgénev's different approach in his account in *Smoke* (1867) of Russian expatriate life in Baden–Baden.

country estate, died in suspicious circumstances – he was probably murdered by his peasants – causing Dostoévsky a severe emotional shock. Receiving a small inheritance, which he squandered, Dostoévsky retired from the army in 1844 to set up as a writer. While lodging with a slightly younger contemporary, the novelist Dmítri Grigoróvich, Dostoévsky wrote his first short novel, *Poor Folk*, a grimly realistic story of urban poverty that already displayed the powerful psychological perception, and ability to see the fantastic in the normal, of which Dostoévsky was master. Grigoróvich, stunned, took the manuscript to the poet Nekrásov, who took it to the influential critic Belínsky (who was to be the dedicatee of Turgénev's *Fathers and Children*). 'A new Gógol' was proclaimed, the book was published in 1845, and Dostoévsky was an instant celebrity.

Things did not continue smoothly for him, however. In 1849 he was arrested, partly because of his participation in the liberal discussion groups of the 'Petrashévsky circle', but more because of a conspiratorial association with Nikolái Speshnëv, an aristocratic atheist and revolutionary who was to be the original of Stavrógin in *Devils*. Dostoévsky was tried, imprisoned for eight months in the Peter and Paul Fortress, and sentenced to death. Having been led out to execution, hooded, and tied to a post to be shot – the Tsar's little joke, described in detail by Price Mýshkin in *The Idiot* (pt 1, ch. 5) – he was reprieved and sent to Siberia as a convict until 1854; his *Memoirs from the House of the Dead*, 1860–2, is a lightly-fictionalised description of his penal servitude in Omsk. It was from this time that Dostoévsky became subject to severe epileptic fits (though he was to value the fits for the moments of transcendent vision that immediately preceded them). He was then compulsorily posted to the army as a private soldier, where he rose through the ranks to become an officer again in 1856. The following year he married Mária Isáeva, a widow (it was not a happy marriage); and in 1859 he was allowed to resign his commission and go home to resume his career as a writer after a traumatic gap of ten years.

Dostoévsky was now purged of his rational idealism and possessed instead of a sense of religious mission, believing that humanity – and Russian humanity especially – could be saved only through love and suffering in the name of Christ. In 1861 he began a periodical *Vrémia* ('Time'), with his brother Mikháil, but it closed in 1863. He also travelled abroad, running into debt and gambling at roulette in unsuccessful attempts to escape from it, and being infatuated with a vamp called Polína Súslova (1861–3). In 1864 his brother and his wife both died.

The following year, desperate for money, Dostoévsky signed an outrageous contract with F. T. Stellóvsky, an unscrupulous book-dealer: for 3,000 roubles he sold the rights in all he had written and committed himself to producing a new novel in little over a year; failing which all his *future* work would also become Stellóvsky's property. To overcome this last, monstrous condition Dostoévsky set to work on what was to become his first great novel, *Crime and Punishment*; but, seeing that he would not be able to finish it in time to avoid the penalty clause in his contract with Stellóvsky, he produced in less than a month a short novel called *The Gambler*, dictating it to a young stenographer, Ánna Grigórievna Snítkina. *Crime and Punishment* (a psychological study of a murderer who believes himself to be above any law, but who learns that a purely utilitarian morality leads only to despair) and *The Gambler* (based on Dostoévsky's own experiences at roulette) were both published in 1866. He married Snítkina the following year, and they went abroad and settled in Dresden.

Crime and Punishment is the first great modern psychodrama, a form of storytelling that Dostoévsky was to use again in his last three novels, and one that was to have a profound influence on Modernist fiction in the twentieth century. In its depiction of physical squalor and in its psychological penetration it is plainly a descendant of *Poor Folk*, but now Dostoévsky is able to go much further into the inner selves of his characters, and to produce a work of art that is at once convincing, satisfying, and inspiring.

The Idiot (about a positively good man, a nineteenth-century Russian Christ) followed in 1868, and then Dostoévsky returned to Russia to edit *Grazhdanín* ('The Citizen') in 1871, to which he contributed his outstanding *Writer's Diary* (1873–81, containing both short stories and a wonderful variety of political and literary criticism). During his travels abroad he had become increasingly contemptuous of European ways and values, and he now pro-claimed himself a confirmed xenophobe, anti-Semite, monarchist, and Slavophile. *Devils* (also known as *The Possessed*, a study of the emptiness at the nihilistic heart of the Russian intelligentsia) appeared in 1872; and his last and perhaps greatest novel, *The Brothers Karamázov*, in 1879–80. He died, widely admired in Russia, in 1881, aged fifty-nine; his funeral was attended by more than 30,000 people.

The Brothers Karamázov[11] 1879–80

Fathers and Children is a well-made and perceptive study of character and ideas in an established fictional form; and *Ánna Karénina* carries this form of the nineteenth-century European novel virtually to its limit; but *The Brothers Karamázov* expands the form itself. Like the other two it takes the idea of the family as part of its foundation, and like them it is a gripping study of character, ideas, and beliefs; but it is also an extraordinary psychological investigation of a number of different personalities in conditions of extreme stress.

Perhaps the least complex thing about this amazing book is its plot – which would do very well for a modern murder mystery set in California – neatly summarised by W. J. Leatherbarrow in his excellent monograph on *The Brothers*:

> Fyódor[12] Pávlovich Karamázov, a corrupt and lascivious provincial landowner, is the father of three legitimate sons: Dmítry, a retired army officer; Iván, a brilliant intellectual; and Alyósha, a novice monk under the tutelage of the local monastic elder, Father Zosíma. Dmítry is the child of Fyódor Pávlovich's first marriage, Iván and Alyósha the sons of his second. Fyódor is also the suspected father of an illegitimate son, Smerdyakóv, the result of a liaison with a local idiot girl, Líza Smerdyáshchaya. Smerdyakóv now works as a servant in the Karamázov household.
>
> When Fyódor Pávlovich is found murdered, suspicion falls on Dmítry, although we later learn that the crime was committed by Smerdyakóv. Dmítry's violent nature and his conviction that he has been cheated out of his inheritance have already led to furious scenes between him and his father. What is more, father and son are locked in dangerous sexual rivalry over a local seductress, Grúshenka, whose charms have already enticed Dmítry away from his betrothed, Katerína. All this points to Dmítry's guilt, and he is arrested. At his trial things go badly for him and he is sentenced to Siberia. Grúshenka, now reformed, decides to accompany him and Katerína remains to look after Iván, whose mental breakdown follows recognition of Smerdyakóv's guilt and the role played in his father's murder by his own conversations with the lackey. But nothing can be proved. Dmítry goes to serve his sentence, Smerdyakóv commits suicide, Iván succumbs to his

---

[11] In the Translator's Note to his Oxford World's Classics translation, Ignat Avsey points out that, while *The Brothers Karamázov* mimics the word-order that is required in Russian, in English we normally say 'The Wright Brothers', 'The Marx Brothers', 'Warner Brothers', 'Moss Bros', and so on; and he therefore calls his translation *The Karamázov Brothers*. However, because the form *The Brothers Karamázov* is so familiar, and because this word-order does occasionally appear in English (in 'The Brothers Grimm', for instance), it seems best to retain it.

[12] Dostoévsky gives his own Christian name to this most scandalous of his major characters.

illness, and the novel ends with Alyósha leaving the monastery and following Zosíma's advice to go out into the world. (W. J. Leatherbarrow,
Dostoyévsky: The Brothers Karamázov, Cambridge University Press
1992, pp. 1–2.)

Two points may be added. The first is that this melodramatic
plot, while it is enticing in itself, says nothing about the compelling
religious and political controversies that share the heart of *The
Brothers Karamázov* with its psychological investigations. The
other point is that Dostoévsky intended the work which we know
as *The Brothers Karamázov*, and which he completed only two
months before his death, to be the first part of a huge two-part
work of fiction. In the unwritten second part, Aliósha Karamázov
– whom Dostoévsky nominates as the hero of *The Brothers
Karamázov* in its very first sentence, but who is if anything rather
less interesting than most of the other leading characters – was to
have been developed as the main character as he went out into the
world.

The eight chapters of Part I, Book II, of *The Brothers Karamázov*
('An Unseemly Encounter') show Dostoévsky's skill, at the height of
his powers as a novelist, in getting under the skins of his characters.
Fiódor Karamázov, together with his two elder sons Dmítri and
Iván, and Miúsov (a distant relative), go to the local monastery to
visit Father Zosíma – the *stárets* who is Aliósha's teacher and
guide[13] and who.is reputed to be a saint – and to have lunch with
the abbot. Old Karamázov deliberately and insultingly plays the
buffoon throughout both disastrous encounters, the visitors are
provoked into exposing themselves in absurd and inappropriate
behaviour, and the visit ends with a wild scene of mutual recrimi-
nations in the abbot's refectory. Although Dostoévsky's approach is
superficially realistic, the effect – especially of father Karamázov's
antics – is surreal, and the boundaries between the rational and the
irrational become increasingly blurred.

The dysfunctional Karamázov family in *The Brothers Karamázov*, overshadowed by the crime of parricide, serves as a symbol of
what Dostoévsky saw as the disintegration of Russian society and
the Russian state; sons rise against father as subjects rise against the
monarch, and all is moral confusion. The father is corrupt; and the
four brothers represent four different forms of evil: Dmítri is

---

[13] The relationship between a *stárets* (which means 'elder') and a novice monk was
that of master and disciple.

physically and emotionally violent (a parricide in the making if not in fact), Iván the intellectual rebels against the divine order, Aliósha is guilty of the failure of his faith, and Smerdiakóv – the actual murderer – mirrors the dark side of all their natures.

Besides Dostoévsky's psychological explorations, *The Brothers Karamázov* investigates the relationship between the State and the Church and its implications for religious belief. Against Father Zosíma, who represents a mystical approach to God's love, is pitted Iván, who argues that the State and the Church have each taken on some of the other's characteristics. The State, he says, has become a sort of Church, demanding inappropriate reverence and obedience, while the Church has assumed some of the authority of a State; and he illustrates this proposition with a paradoxical fable, his unwritten 'poem' (V, 5), which describes how Christ, returned to earth in sixteenth-century Spain, is recognised by the people but imprisoned by the Grand Inquisitor, a sinister forerunner of Lenin. But the monks – even the saintly Zosíma – are ambiguous figures, tainted by a whiff of corruption, and Dostoévsky's point is that no man-made structures, whether religious or political, can be anything but imperfect; that paradise cannot be regained through the reform of the state or Church by means of socialism or institutionalised Christianity; and that nothing can replace the brotherhood of man attained through the love of God.

It has been argued that in Dostoévsky's novels the third-person narrator tells the story in a more fragmented way than had hitherto been normal, that the narrator is 'polyphonic', speaking in the different voices of the several characters. There is some truth in this, though it is not obvious when actually reading the novels, and certainly 'Dostoévsky' himself as narrator is not entirely absent. What is true is that Dostoévsky foreshadows the psychological, Modernist approach to fictional narration, which becomes more obvious in the novels of Hamsun, Conrad, Mann, Joyce, and others, for the influence of *The Brothers Karamázov* on twentieth-century fiction has been enormous. The central themes of the novel – its concern with human alienation and exposure of the inadequacy of reason, its depiction of a fragmented unstable world, and its attempts to rediscover a core of permanent values – have all become the common currency of twentieth-century fiction.' (W. J. Leatherbarrow, *Dostoyevsky: The Brothers Karamazov*, Cambridge University Press 1992, p. 106.)

Translations

Again, Constance Garnett was the first major translator of Dostoévsky, and her version of *The Brothers Karamázov*, originally published in 1912 and frequently reprinted, was well translated; it also had an important influence on British and American writers of the early twentieth century. Ignat Avsey's Oxford World's Classics version (1994) reads easily and has a valuable apparatus and notes. David Magarshak's translation has now been superseded in Penguin Classics by David McDuff's version (1993), which also has an Introduction and notes. Personally I slightly prefer the World's Classics translation to the Penguin, but there is not much to choose between them.

Further reading

As was suggested in chapter VI, for the general background see Richard Pipes's *Russia under the Old Régime*, Weidenfeld and Nicolson 1974 (now in Penguin Books); while for the literary background, Ronald Hingley's *Russian Writers and Society in the Nineteenth Century*, 2nd rev. edn, Weidenfeld and Nicolson, London 1977, is an excellent guide. *The Cambridge History of Russian Literature*, ed. Charles A. Moser, rev. edn Cambridge University Press 1992, has useful sections on the three authors and novels discussed here.

For Turgénev, the best biography is Leonard Schapiro's elegant *Turgénev: His Life and Times*, Oxford University Press 1978. Richard Freeborn's *Turgénev: the Novelist's Novelist*, London 1960, is a useful introduction; and David Lowe's *Turgénev's 'Fathers and Sons'*, Ann Arbor 1983, is a stimulating detailed study. See also Jane T. Costlow, *Worlds within Worlds: the novels of Iván Turgénev*, Princeton 1990, ch. 5.

A. N. Wilson's *Tolstóy*, Hamish Hamilton, London 1988 and Penguin Books, is a readable and perceptive biography by a fellow-novelist; *Tolstóy and the Novel* by John Bayley, London 1966 is also recommended. Anthony Thorlby's *Tolstóy: Ánna Karénina* (Cambridge University Press 1987) deals with various aspects of the novel's themes and techniques. *Tolstóy: The Critical Heritage*, trs. and ed. by A. V. Knowles, London 1978, collects the early criticism.

Konstantín Mochúlsky's *Dostoévsky: His Life and Work*, trs.

Michael Minihan, Princeton University Press 1967, is a fascinating critical biography by a Russian. Also recommended is Richard Peace, *Dostoiévsky: an Examination of the Major Novels*, Cambridge University Press 1971. W. J. Leatherbarrow, *Dostoyévsky: The Brothers Karamázov* (Cambridge University Press 1992) is a particularly good monograph on the novel.

X   Ibsen, Strindberg, and Hamsun

Scandinavia[1] in the nineteenth century

Although they had been states of some international importance in the past – Sweden had been a notable contender in Europe as recently as the seventeenth century – the three Scandinavian countries were peripheral and small in population, and did not carry much weight in nineteenth-century Europe. At the beginning of the century Sweden ruled over Finland, and Norway was a semi-autonomous dependency of Denmark. In 1805 Russia annexed Finland; and at the Congress of Vienna of 1815 Norway was transferred from the Danish to the Swedish Crown, but was allowed to keep its own parliament in Christiania,[2] the Storting. This new two-state arrangement – the monarchies of Sweden-plus-Norway, and Denmark – lasted until 1905, when Norway became an independent monarchy.

The three continental Scandinavian languages – Danish, Norwegian, and Swedish – were mutually intelligible to their speakers in the nineteenth century (as they still are), but the language of Sweden (used by Strindberg), both spoken and written, differed more from those of Denmark and Norway than Danish and Norwegian did from each other; until the later nineteenth century written Danish was in fact identical to written Norwegian. Ibsen wrote in 'Dano-Norwegian'; and, while his plays could be staged in Copenhagen without alteration, it was customary to translate them into Swedish for staging in Stockholm. From the 1840s the Norwegian language, written as well as spoken, was deliberately 'nationalised' in some of its features, and was developed in two forms: the *Riksmål* (now *Bokmål* or 'book language') of the south-east which is closer to

---

[1] Meaning here Denmark, Norway, and Sweden.
[2] Christiania had been called Oslo until 1624, the name that it was to be given again in 1925.

Danish, and the *Landsmål* (now *Nynorsk*, or 'neo-Norwegian') of the west and north which is more 'Norwegian'. Hamsun, although he was brought up in the north of Norway, wrote chiefly in *Riksmål* because it was the form most easily understood in Scandinavia as a whole.

Only one international event disturbed the course of Scandinavian development in the mid-nineteenth century: this was the matter of Schleswig-Holstein, which had a powerful effect in promoting Scandinavian nationalism and cultural consciousness. In 1800 Schleswig and Holstein were two contiguous, semi-autonomous duchies owing allegiance to the Danish Crown, located in the neck of land joining Denmark to Germany, mostly Danish-speaking in Schleswig to the north and entirely German-speaking in Holstein to the south. At the Congress of Vienna in 1815 Holstein (but not Schleswig) was incorporated in the German Confederation. In 1848 Denmark annexed Schleswig (which was partly German-speaking); in response Prussia invaded Denmark but, at a settlement in 1852 imposed by the other major European powers, both duchies once more became semi-autonomous and allied to Denmark. Then in 1864 Denmark annexed Schleswig again, to the fury of the Prussians, who invaded Denmark for the second time. As a result the whole of Schleswig-Holstein became part of Prussia in 1866 and, from 1871, of the German Empire.[3] The Scandinavians were outraged, though Sweden and Norway did not go so far as to intervene militarily on Denmark's behalf.

The Scandinavians were few in number – the population of Norway at the end of the nineteenth century was 2,221,000; of Denmark 2,450,000; and of Sweden 5,136,000 – and their countries were, by European standards, economically backward. The towns were very small. Skien, where Ibsen was born, had only 3,000 inhabitants in 1829, and Christiania, the capital, had less than 30,000. Stockholm, where Strindberg was born, was larger with a population of 90,000 in 1849 (which is still less than that of present-day Cambridge), but the streets were unpaved and unlit, and there was no sewage system or piped water supply.

On the other hand the educated classes were interested in cultural affairs both in and out of Scandinavia, they commonly read one or two foreign languages, and they appeared to be more broadminded

---

[3] Northern Schleswig reverted to Denmark as the result of a plebiscite after the First World War; the rest of Schleswig-Holstein is now a German *Land*, or province.

– especially in Denmark – and more widely educated than people in most other European cultural centres. There were also ancient and distinguished Scandinavian universities; and in the arts, as well as in learning, the Scandinavians could hold their own with their European contemporaries, as we shall now see.

Henrik Ibsen, 1828–1906

It would be difficult to exaggerate the importance of the theatrical revolution initiated by Henrik Ibsen, whose plays from *Catiline* (1849–50) to *When We Dead Awaken* (1899) exactly spanned the second half of the nineteenth century; rather as Wordsworth invented modern poetry, so Ibsen invented modern drama. Coming from a provincial, middle-class background in southern Norway, Ibsen had a difficult childhood and youth. His father's business failed, and it was rumoured that Ibsen was the son of another man who had had an affair with his mother; so that he was not only extremely poor but also felt himself despised and rejected. Writing in such spare time as he had from being an apothecary's assistant, Ibsen developed as a poet with great facility and technical skill; and he also showed talent as a draughtsman and painter. In 1846 he had a brief love affair and fathered an illegitimate son.

He wrote his first play in 1849–50, and had a second play performed in 1850. From 1851 to 1857 he was employed as stage-manager, playwright, and general dogsbody to a new and unskilled but enthusiastic company of players in Bergen, which often put on a new show every *week*. This was followed (1857–62) by a theatrical appointment in Christiania, a better paid but, Ibsen found, less satisfying position than before. During this period he continued to write plays, mostly in verse; he married in 1858, and had a legitimate son in 1859; and he became progressively disenchanted with his country and its people, which he found pusilanimous, narrow and inhibiting. From 1864 – the year in which Prussia invaded Denmark, and Norway did not join in – the Ibsens left home for voluntary exile in Rome, then Dresden, then Munich, remaining abroad until 1891, when they returned to live near Christiania. Here Ibsen died in 1906 after a series of strokes.

Ibsen's first two masterpieces, the great verse dramas *Brand* and *Peer Gynt*, appeared in 1866 and 1867, and were a sensation in Scandinavia. Intended to be read rather than performed, they argued that the individual conscience, however much impeded by personal weakness and self-indulgence, was the only battleground for a man's victory over the difficulties of life. Two prose works followed – *The League of Youth* (1869), a political farce, and *Emperor and Galilean* (1873), an immensely long closet drama concerning the Emperor Julian's apostasy and tyranny – but it took another four years for Ibsen to make up his mind to abandon verse completely and to write social dramas in prose. The first of them was *Pillars of the Community* (1877, a study of a hypocritical leader), which was followed at approximately two-year intervals by a further eleven plays, culminating in his last work, *When We Dead Awaken* in 1899.

It was these twelve plays that forced the revolution in European drama. They concerned ordinary people such as might be met with every day, not the great men and women of classical tragedy; their dialogue was written in ordinary, everyday language, not heightened by verse or artificial rhetoric; and they addressed problems that recognisably affected every thinking man and woman in late nineteenth-century European society. The real breakthrough came with *A Doll's House* (1879), a study of nineteenth-century marriage, which we shall be looking at in a moment.

Ibsen's remaining ten social dramas continued to evolve and develop, breaking new ground, addressing old but hitherto ignored or suppressed social, moral, artistic, and spiritual problems: *Ghosts* (1881, extra-marital sex, incest, syphilis); *An Enemy of the People* (1882, profit preferred to public safety, and the whistle-blower defeated); *The Wild Duck* (1884, idealism, and whether the truth should be told). The last six plays deal with the trolls within rather than the trolls without: *Rosmersholm* (1886, the desire to live up to radical ideals frustrated by inner weakness); *The Lady from the Sea* (1888, infatuation for a demon lover defeated by a deeper love); *Hedda Gabler* (1890, arrogance compensating for self-contempt); *The Master Builder* (1892, talented youth comes knocking at the door of declining age), *Little Eyolf* (1894, sensual man cannot live up to his own ideals); *John Gabriel Borkman* (1896, the quest for material success may lead to emotional bankruptcy); and *When We Dead Awaken* (1899, Ibsen's epilogue: fame achieved at the expense of personal happiness, the only way out being upwards to the spiritual heights beyond life).

In his own life, Ibsen always put art first, and humanity second. His creed was to be true and faithful to oneself, and to develop the will to do what one must. Ibsen saw himself as supporting 'the revolution of the spirit'; and understood, as Shaw remarked in connection with *The Wild Duck*, that 'people cannot be freed from their failings from without. They must free themselves.'[4] Truth to oneself mattered more to Ibsen than social questions, even matters of importance to him such as women's rights. He was intuitively perceptive but not widely educated; he read newspapers in preference to books, and there were large gaps in his general knowledge (for instance in science). As a person he was a loner, an egocentric introvert, and determinedly private. He could be kind and charming, and he could be malicious and cruel; he ruthlessly cast off the girl who bore his illegitimate son, and refused as far as possible to acknowledge the child. Living parsimoniously, he loved, supported and worked hard for his wife and legitimate son. He was timid physically but not in print; he dressed smartly, enjoyed medals and decorations, and was jealous of protocol. He could drink too much, but did not allow drink to affect his work, which he put before everything else, and which he performed with meticulous regularity.

Ibsen's plays, with their ordinary people apparently carrying on their ordinary lives, required new standards of realism in dramatic production, which they duly received. Increasingly from the 1880s, scenery, mostly of interiors, reproduced as closely as possible the rooms and other environments in which ordinary people lived, while furniture and other properties were the real thing; costumes were simply the clothes that people wore every day; and the style of acting gave the impression of people conversing naturally, speaking to each other rather than out into the auditorium.

Ibsen's influence on Western drama was widespread and profound. As *A Doll's House* advanced through the theatres of Europe, it changed the intellectual climate as it went. Some countries – England among them – resisted it for longer than others, but in the end Western theatre was irreversibly changed.

A Doll's House, 1879

'*A Doll's House* exploded like a bomb into contemporary life', an observer recalled later; and this was for two reasons. The obvious one, and the one for which the play is chiefly remembered, is that, in attacking reigning social conventions, it 'knew no mercy; ending not in reconciliation, but in [in]exorable calamity, it pronounced a

---

[4] Bernard Shaw, *The Quintessence of Ibsenism*, 1913, p. 98.

death sentence on accepted social ethics.'[5] The less obvious one is that it was a work both of theatrical genius and of astonishing technical originality, which all at once demonstrated the exhaustion of the stage conventions of the past by replacing them with tight, economical dialogue, a small cast of credible characters, gripping development in three acts, and an uncompromising outcome. These new methods were realistic, hard-hitting but simple in form, and they related the action of the play to the life its audience actually lived; methods which revolutionised European drama and which affect it still.

The social convention that *A Doll's House* attacked was the submission of a wife to her husband. As I have said in connection with the subject of women and adultery in the nineteenth century (p. 102 above), it then seemed perfectly natural that men, especially as fathers or husbands, should lead the way and make the decisions, and that women should accept their rule in all matters of substance, and should be willingly subservient to them (a belief that has not entirely disappeared in the West even today). But in Ibsen's play the heroine, a simple housewife, comprehends with horror her abject place in marriage and society; and, in finding herself, rejects it.

The plot turns on a misdemeanour that Nora Helmer committed years before when her husband Torvald was ill: in borrowing money for his treatment (without his knowledge) from a man called Krogstad, she forged her father's signature as security for the loan. Krogstad, now her husband's employee, has been dismissed because of his own murky past, and he comes to Nora to blackmail her, threatening to expose her crime if she does not persuade Torvald to reinstate him in his job. The climax comes when Torvald refuses to keep Krogstad on, and Krogstad sends him a letter revealing what Nora has done. Torvald's reaction to the letter is one of abject fear and rejection of Nora; and he only recovers his self-possession when a second letter from Krogstad withdraws the threat of exposure. (Krogstad changes his mind at the instance of Nora's old friend Mrs Linde, one of the two other principal characters in the play; the other one being Dr Rank, who would have been glad to rescue Nora, but whose help she rejected when she learned that he was in love with her.)

All is now revealed to Nora: she had hoped (but perhaps not quite believed) that her husband would stand by her and defy Krogstad even when he found out what she had done, that there

---

[5] Michael Meyer, *Ibsen*, Sphere 1992, p. 476.

might even be a miracle, and he would take the blame on himself. He has cravenly failed her in every respect, she sees that her marriage has been a sham, and she cannot forgive him:

NORA   [...] I must take steps to educate myself. You are not the man to help me there. That's why I'm leaving you.

HELMER   (*jumps up*) What did you say?

NORA   If I'm ever to reach any understanding of myself and the things around me, I must learn to stand alone. That's why I can't stay here with you any longer.

HELMER   Nora! Nora!

NORA   I'm leaving here at once. I dare say Kristine will put me up for the night ...

HELMER   You are out of your mind! I won't let you! I forbid you!

NORA   It's no use forbidding me anything now. I'm taking with me my own personal belongings. I don't want anything of yours, either now or later. [...]

HELMER   And leave your home, your husband and your children? Don't you care what people will say?

NORA   That's no concern of mine. All I know is that this is necessary for *me*.

HELMER   This is outrageous! You are betraying your most sacred duty.

NORA   And what do you consider to be my most sacred duty?

HELMER   Does it take me to tell you that? Isn't it your duty to your husband and your children?

NORA   I have another duty equally sacred.

HELMER   You have not. What duty might *that* be?

NORA   My duty to myself.
     (*A Doll's House*, Act III, trs. by James McFarlane and Jens Arup)

The argument continues as Torvald moves from outrage to pleading and self-pity, but Nora's determination is unbending. ('I would gladly toil night and day for you, Nora, enduring all manner of sorrow and distress. But nobody sacrifices his *honour* for the one he loves.' – 'Hundreds and thousands of women have.') In the end she does leave – husband, children and all – banging the door behind her. This is where the play hit its audience where it hurt, and where it can still hurt; for, as Michael Meyer says,

There is hardly a married woman in the [modern] audience who does not want (or has not at some time wanted) to leave her husband. The unspoken thoughts in the cars and taxis returning from a modern performance cannot vary much from those in the returning carriages of a century ago.[6]

The ending was so painful and unwelcome, indeed, that Ibsen reluctantly, and under severe pressure, wrote an alternative 'happy' ending for a prima donna of the German theatre, in which Nora stays for sake of the children; but it was soon abandoned.

A Doll's House was an instant and enormous success in Scandinavia. Published in book form in December 1879, it was staged in Stockholm, Christiania, and Bergen in January 1880; and in Germany in February 1880, initially with the happy ending. It took some years to have its full effect elsewhere; no full version of the play was produced in England until 1885, or in France until 1894; but since then very few years have passed without a production somewhere in the world.

Translations

Peter Watts's translation of *A Doll's House* is included in the Penguin Classics *Ibsen: Plays* (1965), together with *The League of Youth* and *The Lady from the Sea*; and the Oxford World's Classics *Henrik Ibsen: Four Major Plays* (1981) includes *A Doll's House*, together with *Ghosts*, *Hedda Gabler*, and *The Master Builder*, trs. by James McFarlane and Jens Arup (the *Doll's House* translation dates from 1961). Both read well, but the other plays in the Oxford World's Classics collection are better value than those in the Penguin collection. Ibsen is also included in the Methuen Drama series, well translated by Michael Meyer.

August Strindberg, 1849–1912

August Strindberg's father was a middle-class shipping controller who had married beneath him, and the boy had a cramped, emotionally-tangled upbringing in Stockholm, at several addresses as the family moved house. From the ages of seven to eleven he attended a strict and repressive day-school for young gentlemen; and then, after a year at a school for poorer boys, he spent the last six years of his schooldays at the excellent Stockholm Lyceum,

---

[6] Michael Meyer, *Ibsen*, Sphere 1992, p. 478. If you doubt this, try watching the fine BBC television production of 1992, with Juliet Stevenson as Nora.

where he got a good grounding in Latin and other academic subjects. In 1867 he moved on to the University of Uppsala, which he disliked but to which he remained attached as a mostly non-resident student until 1872, when he failed to graduate.

During this time Strindberg had flung himself into other activities, first with an attempt at acting, and then with writing plays. His first notable play was a historical prose drama, *Master Olof* (1872), which, although it was at first rejected in both its prose and later verse forms, was eventually staged in 1881 as it was originally written. From 1874 to 1882 he earned a pittance as a part-time Assistant Librarian at the Royal Library, and made what extra he could from teaching and from a considerable output of fiction, plays, translations, and polemical newspaper articles. It was never quite enough to meet his expenditure, the difference being met by loans and, in 1879, by declaring himself bankrupt.

In 1876 Strindberg married a well-born Finnish actress, Siri von Essen (she had been married before, but divorce was easier then in Scandinavia than in the rest of Europe), with whom he stayed for six years and had three children. A semi-autobiographical novel, *The Red Room*, appeared in 1879 (the year of *A Doll's House*); and in 1884 the Strindbergs went abroad for five years, staying mostly in France and Switzerland. Strindberg was never satisfied for long wherever he was: when abroad he wanted to be back in Sweden, when in Sweden he wanted to be abroad. And all the time they were plagued by money troubles, not so much because Strindberg did not make enough money as because he was extravagant and could not manage the money he did make. Towards the end of this first exile he wrote a trio of short anti-feminist plays that were among his greatest works, and on which his reputation still largely rests: *The Father* (1887), *Miss Julie*, and *Creditors* (both 1888; each of these plays being written in no more than two or three weeks. We shall be looking at *Miss Julie* in the next section.) It was difficult to find producers for them, and in 1889 Strindberg attempted to set up his own experimental theatre, but it foundered as a result of his incompetence.

Strindberg and Siri were finally divorced, with much acrimony on his part, in 1891; and in 1892 he wrote two more short plays of high quality, the black social comedies *Playing with Fire* and *The Bond*. In 1893 he married Frida Uhl, an Austrian journalist, but left her the following year to go and live in Paris; they were divorced in 1896. *Inferno*, a compelling account in purported diary form of his own hallucinations and near-madness in 1896, was published in 1897; and among the several plays he wrote in his final years was *To Damascus* (the fine Parts I and II in 1898, and the less successful Part III in 1901), which concerns a famous writer like himself, struggling against the misfortunes that fate brings him, but accepting in the end that his destiny is controlled by a higher power. In 1901 he was married for the third time, to a Norwegian actress twenty-nine years younger than himself called Harriet Bosse, but she left him within a year; they were reunited for a while, but were finally divorced in 1904. He spent the last three years of his life writing miscellaneous pamphlets, and died in Stockholm of stomach cancer in 1912, aged sixty-three.

Throughout his career Strindberg wrote fast, copiously, and without revision, an output that was grossly uneven in quality. In the first place he could never concentrate, as Ibsen could, on doing mainly what he did best – writing drama – but continually veered aside to write fiction and tendentious autobiography that was as bad in some parts as it was good in others; to turn out numerous didactic and polemical books and articles about politics, sociology, and science that were a waste of his great talent; to immerse himself in futile alchemical experiments and the occult; and to paint (quite successfully) in oils. But, besides this intellectual profligacy, there was a wild element in his writing as in his life, which expressed disturbances deep inside him.

Strindberg's mental health was generally precarious: alternately manic and depressed, he manifested schizophrenic and paranoid symptoms in his relations with other people,[7] and he loved and hated with irrational, monomaniac passions that came to include an ugly anti-Semitism, and a frenzied hatred of women – the Enemy, as he saw them. He could exercise great charm and project a charisma which was immediately attractive, but he could not sustain his three marriages, and he turned eventually against virtually all his relatives, friends and supporters, exhibiting violence and brutality towards them both on paper and in person. Politically he moved from socialism to nihilism, and thence to a denial of the basic human rights that were championed by Ibsen, whom he came to hate and despise. He recognised as kindred spirits Edgar Allan

---

[7] Whether Strindberg was actually a paranoid schizophrenic is doubtful; the symptoms, notably hallucinations, which were at their worst in the 1890s, could have been the result of drinking absinthe regularly for many years.

Poe (who had died in the year of his birth) and Nietzsche (with whom he had a brief but mutually appreciative correspondence in 1888).

All these contradictory characteristics were poured with an insane intensity into much of his fiction and polemical writings. With drama it was another matter: here he might still be driven by his passions, but the control required by the form itself denied access to most of the irrelevant and unpleasant rubbish that disfigured much of his other writing; and, although some of his plays were unbalanced and carelessly written, when at his best they were brilliant, original, and masterly in technique, taking drama on from realism to expressionism:[8] plays that (like his paintings) presented a world violently distorted by the intensity of his moods, ideas, and emotions, in which the characters are driven by their emotions to the edge of madness, in settings where reality merges into fantasy. He was hated by most of his Swedish contemporaries, but his admirers included (amongst our subjects) Chékhov, Górky, Mann, and Kafka.

Miss Julie, 1888

Miss Julie, the centrepiece of Strindberg's three anti-feminist dramas of 1887–8, is a short, intense, one-act play with only three characters (*The Father* had five – the same number as *A Doll's House* – and *Creditors* three), set ostensibly in real time in the kitchen of the Count's great house. Miss Julie, the daughter of the Count (who is temporarily away from home and who is never seen, but whose spirit broods aristocratically over the whole action), has recently broken off her engagement to a local official and, as the play begins, she is dancing off-stage with some of the servants. Two of the servants, Kristin the cook and Jean the footman[9] (who are engaged), are discussing her behaviour – she has been dancing unrestrainedly with Jean, amongst others – which they see as being inappropriate to her station. Miss Julie comes in and hauls Jean off for another dance. At the end of it he leaves her on the dance floor and returns to Kristin in the kitchen, but Miss Julie soon comes

---

[8] Expressionism is a style in which the artist seeks to express emotional experience rather than to describe the external world. Strindberg was acquainted with the great Norwegian expressionist painter Edvard Munch (1863–1944) and spent some time with him, in Berlin in 1892–3 and in Paris in 1896.

[9] The footman, who wants to better himself, has adopted the French name 'Jean' in place (presumably) of his native 'Johan'.

after him again, and engages him in flirtatious conversation; Kristin first falls asleep in a chair, and then goes off to bed, leaving Jean alone with Miss Julie. Their talk becomes more and more intimate and eventually, when they hear a group of villagers approaching, singing a bawdy song which Jean claims is about Miss Julie and himself, they take cover off-stage in Jean's bedroom, where it is understood that they have sex – Miss Julie's desire for 'rough trade' being at least as great as his less complicated desire to have her.

They reappear after the villagers have gone, Jean exultant, Miss Julie upset. She asks him to love her – he cannot, he is still, and will remain, a servant – and he suggests that they go away together to Switzerland and start a hotel. She disagrees; they quarrel; she agrees; they have no money; she will steal some from her father's bureau; she goes off to get it and to prepare for their journey. Kristin returns briefly; she is appalled when she realises what has happened but holds Jean to his promise to marry her, and leaves to dress for church. Miss Julie reappears in travelling clothes, carrying her pet greenfinch in a cage. Jean refuses to take the bird with them – kill it, then, she says – and he promptly chops off its head with a cleaver, demonstrating the superiority of his lower-class practicality to her aristocratic sentimentality. Kristin comes in on her way to church; they try to persuade her to leave with them and cook in their hotel, but knowing that it is not right, she refuses, and goes to church. All at once the Count is heard to return and ring for Jean, who is immediately the obsequious servant. Miss Julie has come to the end of her tether: she is debased, she cannot stay, she cannot leave, her father will find out about Jean and the stolen money. She is given a razor by Jean and goes off to cut her throat in the stables, while Jean answers the Count's summons.

This is an enthralling story which plays very well. In his attitudes to women and his exploration of the lower classes Strindberg differed markedly from Ibsen; but *Miss Julie* was not very different in its degree of realism, in its characterisation of personalities at war with themselves, and even in its melodrama, from several of Ibsen's plays of the same period (*Rosmersholm*, 1886, and *Hedda Gabler*, 1890, for instance). Where *Miss Julie* differed most from Ibsen's social dramas was, first, in its extreme dramatic concentration; it is half their length, yet it seems to pack just as much in, which increases the emotional intensity of the characters and their reactions. Secondly, the speeches in *Miss Julie* do not always follow a logical progression, but in moments of stress become disjointed and inconsequential just as dialogue often does in real life. Thirdly, Strindberg was prepared to deal more frankly with sex than was Ibsen; he makes it plain that Miss Julie was not seduced by Jean but wanted him to have sex with her, and to have it crudely ('my womb wanted your seed'); and he shows, here and elsewhere, how sexual desire can co-exist with dislike and even hatred of the sexual partner.

Miss Julie was published in Sweden in a slightly bowdlerised text in November 1888, receiving uniformly hostile reviews, and four months later received its first, private, performance in Copenhagen University's Student Union; but public performance was banned for the moment in Denmark, Sweden, and Germany, and its Swedish première did not take place until 1906.[10]

Translations

Peter Watts is again the translator of *Miss Julie* in Penguin Classics (Strindberg, *Three Plays*, 1958, including *The Father* and *Easter*); but a better choice is Michael Meyer's translation in *Strindberg: Plays I* (Methuen Drama 1964, revised 1976, including *The Father* and *The Ghost Sonata*) which is taken from an unexpurgated text and adds Strindberg's important Preface to *Miss Julie*. There are several other translations of *Miss Julie* in print, but none in Oxford World's Classics.

Knut Hamsun, 1859–1952

Knut Hamsun was born Knud Pedersen[11] to a peasant family in south-central Norway, which moved north of the arctic circle to the remote village of Hamerøy (on the coast opposite the Lofoten Islands just south of Narvik) while he was still an infant. Here the family had a farm called Hamsund; but when the boy was nine he was sent to live with a sadistic uncle who mistreated him, psychologically and physically – and gave him a lifelong hatred

---

[10] There were several fine stage productions and films of *Miss Julie* in the mid- to late twentieth century; and its continuing power was demonstrated in a notable television adaptation by Patrick Marber (*After Miss Julie*, BBC2 1995), which successfully transferred the action into the setting of an English country-house kitchen of 1945.

[11] Hamsun changed his name from the Danish-sounding Knud Pedersen to the more Norwegian Knut Pederson; then added Hamsund (Hamsund being the name of the family farm) to make Knut Pederson Hamsund; and finally decided, by 1884, to call himself Knut Hamsun.

of authority – until he was old enough at the age of fourteen to leave and, going south, to get a job near his birthplace as a shop assistant in his godfather's general store. Besides this he tried schoolteaching (his hated uncle had at least taught him something useful) and travelling as a pedlar; and he also tried writing stories, even having one published when he was nineteen.

Encouraged, but seeing that he needed to escape the limitations of his peasant background, Hamsun wrote a begging letter in 1879 to a self-made millionaire saying that he needed a loan with which to go and try his luck with publishers in Copenhagen. The millionaire was so impressed that he sent Hamsun the very large sum of 2,000 kroner in two instalments, as a gift. But it became clear in Copenhagen that Hamsun was not yet ready to become a professional writer, and he spent most of the next ten years doing a variety of jobs, with intervals of great poverty, while he matured. In Norway he first worked as a navvy, building roads; there were two visits to the United States (1882–4 and 1886–8) where he worked as a grocery clerk in Wisconsin, as secretary to a Unitarian minister in Minneapolis, as a farm labourer in several states, and as a tram-conductor in Chicago; and back in Norway he gave lectures on literature and picked up what he could from journalism. His first major literary breakthrough came with the anonymous publication of a part of what became his first great novel, *Hunger*, in a Danish periodical in 1888. This was followed by a pot-boiler on American culture, and then by *Hunger* itself (the subject of the next section) in 1890.

Hunger was followed in the 1890s by three more astonishing novels of psychological realism: the extraordinary *Mysteries* (1892), which brings the reader even closer than *Hunger* to the apprehension of another consciousness, and one that is equally disturbing; *Pan* (1894), a haunting love story; and *Victoria* (1898), a story of love going wrong. Hamsun was influenced in writing them by Nietzsche, by Strindberg, and – most of all – by Dostoévsky, but there was nothing second-hand about this remarkable quartet of novels. They ensured that he was recognised from now on as a novelist of great power and originality, in Germany as well as in Scandinavia; indeed he quickly became a cult figure in Norway, hero-worshipped by young intellectuals.

Having tried his hand at writing short stories and plays (notably the *Kareno* trilogy, 1895–8), Hamsun's next novel, *Swarming*, appeared in 1904, and it introduced a change of direction in his fiction that was to prove permanent. Technically it was a slight, conventional novel with a complicated plot, and a cheerful mood very different from the brooding works of the 1890s with their mysterious, wandering heroes. There were better novels to come, but Hamsun's earlier style was gone for good; and the last nine novels, from *The Children of the Age* (1913), were written with third-person narrators who tended to be garrulous. They earned him great popularity, nevertheless, especially in Scandinavia and Germany (he became a cultural icon in both countries); and his work as a whole had a vast influence on the development of twentieth-century literature in Europe and the United States, his admirers including Samuel Beckett, Bertolt Brecht, André Gide, Maxím Górky, Ernest Hemingway, Hermann Hesse, Franz Kafka, Thomas Mann, Henry Miller, Robert Musil, Borís Pasternák, Isaac Bashevis Singer, and H. G. Wells.[12]

Notable among the later works were *The Growth of the Soil*, Hamsun's Nobel Prize novel of 1917, an attempt to show Norwegian society as he would have liked it to be, strong and reliable, based on agriculture rather than industry; and *The Women at the Pump* (1920) a ribald comedy about pompous small-town worthies and the wily, amoral cripple who takes advantage of them. Hamsun's last novel, *The Ring is Closed* (1936), the story of a self-centred layabout, deliberately looked back to *Hunger*, and was a closing of the fictional circle.

Hamsun was a big man whose labourer's arms and fists were matched by a powerful personality: he was a lively companion, loyal and honourable in his dealings with other people, independent-minded, and a natural leader; but he was also arrogant, vain, bossy, and too sure of his own rightness; while underneath it all he was lonely and deeply insecure. He did not make an easy husband. His first marriage in 1898 to a wealthy divorcée began badly, and ended in divorce. His second one in 1909, to a much younger actress (he was fifty, she twenty-four), lasted his lifetime, but went through some very bad patches towards the end.

Politically, Hamsun was driven by an extreme and irrational hatred of England and the English, and by an equally passionate love of Germany and the Germans (who appreciated his work).[13] In the First World War he supported the Germans, and felt sure that,

[12] James Joyce also read Hamsun, having the *Kareno* trilogy of plays (1895–8) in Norwegian in his personal library at Trieste (Richard Ellmann, *The Consciousness of Joyce*, Faber 1977, p. 111).

[13] In a characteristic paradox, Hamsun learned to speak English but not German.

even if they were beaten then, that great people would eventually 'punish England to death'. He applauded Hitler and the Nazis in the 1930s for giving power and self-respect back to Germany; and during the Second World War he again supported the Germans even when they invaded and occupied his own country, believing it desirable and inevitable that the Germanic peoples should eventually triumph. (Yet when he had an audience with Hitler at the Berghof in 1943 he infuriated the great dictator by complaining about the conduct of his deputy in Norway, Reichskommissar Josef Terboven, and became heated himself when Hitler kept changing the subject; Hamsun and Hitler were indeed two of a kind in their resistance to contrary opinions.) But by that time Hamsun was in his eighties, deaf, and, although not senile, limited in his knowledge of what was really going on. After the war he was tried and convicted of treason, and heavily fined.[14] He died, aged ninety-two, in 1952, having written, amongst other things, twenty-two full-length novels, five stage plays, and a verse drama.

Hunger, 1890

Hunger is the first-person narrative of a few months in the life of a young man, poor and adrift in Christiania – then a small city in which everyone knew each other – as he tries unsuccessfully to keep body and soul together by writing ambitious stories and articles for the newspapers. This study of urban alienation is divided into four parts, the first two of which see the hero brought to the brink of starvation, and then temporarily rescued by the unexpected acquisition of a small sum of money. In Part III he has a relationship with a young woman, which only just avoids ending in rape; and in the fourth part, which finds him involved in the squalid life of a low boarding house, he finally signs on as deck–hand on a collier, and sails out of the story.[15] There is no real plot, just a series of episodes strung together which take their often tenuous connection with reality from Hamsun's recollections of his own periods of extreme poverty in Christiania in 1880–1 and 1886–7.

---

[14] The puppet leader Quisling was shot, and Hamsun's wife was sentenced to three years' hard labour for her active membership of Quisling's fascist party; but, in spite of Hamsun's treasonable war-time activities on behalf of Nazi propaganda, he was nearly ninety when he was tried and it would have been embarrassing to put him in prison.
[15] The Captain of his ship says surprisingly that they are sailing 'with ballast to Leeds [which had no ship canal], to take in coal for Cádiz'.

What is most remarkable about *Hunger* is how close the reader gets to the character and consciousness of the narrator, how one seems sometimes to enter his very mind. His absurd fantasies, his elation and depression, his illogical loves and hatreds, his horror at his situation and his paradoxical refusal to take steps to relieve it, all have an awful familiarity. We may never have been in precisely the narrator's position, but we feel that *this is how we are*.

Hamsun achieves this feat both by the accuracy of his psychological observation, and by a style of writing which (even in translation) slips and slides as if through the narrator's mental processes. There are mixtures of formal language and demotic vernacular; direct speech becoming reported speech as the narrator's viewpoint shifts; abrupt changes of tense as narration of the past blends into re-experience in the present; patches of interior monologue that ring in the memory; and all this in short simple sentences that ultimately derived, via the 'Norwegianisers' of the mid-nineteenth century such as Hamsun's hero Bjørnstjerne Bjørnson, from the Old Norse sagas.

Hunger was immediately acclaimed, not only for its technical brilliance, but for its originality. Here was a completely new and modern form of fiction – so modern in fact that (if the streets of the story were filled with cars rather than carriages) it could have been written yesterday; and we realise, with some alarm, that the narrator would recognise his *semblables*, his brothers, hunched in the doorways of any great modern city.

Translations

There have been only three translations of *Hunger* into English. The first, by Mary Dunne (*c.* 1920), was expurgated and has been long out of print. The second, by Robert Bly (1967), was published in paperback by Picador but is also now out of print. The third, Sverre Lyngstad's translation of 1996, currently a Rebel Classic, is much the most accurate of the three, as the translator takes care to point out in his Introduction and textual notes; fortunately it reads very well, and carefully follows the twists and turns of Hamsun's style.

Further reading

There is no convenient concise political or cultural history in English of nineteenth-century Scandinavia (as there is of France and Germany and Russia), but Michael Meyer's biographies of

Ibsen and Strindberg, and Robert Ferguson's biography of Hamsun, include a wealth of background material.

Michael Meyer's *Ibsen*, two vols, Rupert Hart-Davis 1967, 1971, and abridged by the author in one volume, Sphere 1992, is the essential introduction to Ibsen's life and works. Ibsen was presented – rather quirkily – to British readers by Bernard Shaw in *The Quintessence of Ibsenism*, 1891, revised edition 1913. James McFarlane's *Ibsen & Meaning*, Norvik 1989, contains a valuable collection of studies, essays and prefaces; and *Approaches to Teaching Ibsen's A Doll House*, ed. Yvonne Shafer, MLA 1985, includes stimulating material. See also *The Cambridge Companion to Ibsen*, Cambridge University Press 1994.

For Strindberg we are largely dependent on Michael Meyer's excellent *Strindberg: a Biography*, Secker and Warburg 1985. Nearly all the other secondary sources are in languages other than English, apart from the introductions to the several translations of a few of Strindberg's plays.

The only modern biography of Hamsun (in any language) is Robert Ferguson's *Enigma: the Life of Knut Hamsun*, Hutchinson 1987, which is full and very readable, and deals intelligently with Hamsun's fiction as well as his life and politics.

XI Chékhov and Górky

Russia at the end of the old régime

Tsardom and all the trappings of the Russian autocracy came to seem increasingly anachronistic as the nineteenth century wore on. There had been some ideological opposition to the régime even in the eighteenth century, and there was the abortive Decembrist rising of aristocratic officers against Nicholas I in 1826; but it was the mid-nineteenth century that saw the development of a more general opposition to the autocracy by educated Russians. The 'intelligentsia', as it came to be called – the educated, enlightened, 'progressive' elements in society – was in fact the only group willing to stand up to the régime; and it did so both by its political activities and through the medium of literature.

The intelligentsia, divided as we have seen into 'Westernists' and 'Slavophiles' (p. 122 above), had institutions for sharing ideas ready to hand in the salons, universities, study circles, periodicals, and local administrations that they frequented; and they were further divided into radicals – ranging from liberals to nihilists and terrorists – who wanted to reform the whole system, and conservatives who wanted to improve certain aspects of the state but who were opposed to fundamental reform. In the earlier part of the century, up to the accession of Alexander II in 1855, the reformers were chiefly concerned with finding out who they were and what they believed; while in the later part of the century their focus of interest changed to what was to be done.

The reformers wanted to see change in four main areas of Russian life. These were the rigidity of the autocracy itself; the inefficiency and corruption of the administration; the curbs on freedom (of the press, of expression, of travel, and so on); and the status and outlook of the peasants. It was plain that the Tsar, supported by the court, would refuse to delegate any real power from the throne unless he was forced to do so; and that the corruption of the administration (which involved favouritism and sinecures as well as bribery) was so deep-seated that nothing but wholesale, enforced reform could have much effect. Therefore those liberal reformers who rejected the use of force concentrated on the questions of individual freedom, and of the peasants.

In fact, as we have seen (p. 122) the censorship became notably less onerous during the reign of Alexander II. There was, moreover, little official objection to orderly liberal discussion groups, and it was not difficult for members of the intelligentsia to obtain passports for foreign travel; even known subversives – such as the socialist Alexánder Hérzen and the anarchist Mikháil Bakúnin – travelled abroad and set up their revolutionary headquarters in Western Europe. But everyone still needed passports, and censorship and the laws against dissent remained in force, and were even more strictly interpreted under Alexander III.

The great change in the status of the peasants came with the emancipation of the serfs in 1861, which had been helped along by liberal writers such as Turgénev. It was objected by some of the reformers, however, that in the event the peasants had been shabbily treated in the amounts of land that they were allotted, and in the rents that they were required to pay. For this reason the more extreme radicals proposed in the 1870s that the emancipated peasants were revolutionary material and needed only a push to set them going; and they encouraged young, educated Russians 'to go to the people', to live with the peasants and educate them in their revolutionary role. In fact the radicals who promoted this scheme had very little idea of what the peasants were actually like, and the movement was a fiasco. Large numbers of young liberals, especially university students, went to live in the village communes around 1874, where they were not welcome, and where they found that the peasants were interested in becoming capitalists, not communists.

Realising that the peaceful reform was getting nowhere, the most extreme radicals turned to a campaign of terror by assassination and bombing, and in 1878–81 small groups of extremists killed prominent supporters of the status quo, including the reform-minded Tsar Alexander II. This resulted in increased repression, at first by the government and then by the reactionary Tsar Alexander III. But although the terrorists were subdued for the moment, their campaign had hastened the destabilisation of the state; and it was only a matter of time before the cycle of revolutionary activity alternating with state repression built up to the point of open revolt, which duly came in 1905, the first stage on the road that was to lead to the final overthrow of tsardom in 1917.

Antón Pávlovich Chékhov, 1860–1904

The three great Russian novelists discussed in chapter IX all came from the Estate of the Gentry (and in Tolstóy's case from the aristocracy as well), but the two subjects of this chapter came from much lower levels of society. Chékhov's grandfather was born a serf, and his father was a shopkeeper, a humble 'town-dweller' of Taganróg on the Sea of Azov in southern Russia.

Antón, the third of the six Chékhov children, was born into a disordered family. The father, Pável, was a bully and an incompetent who went bankrupt and fled to Moscow in 1876, followed by his wife and five of the children, leaving the sixteen-year-old Antón to complete his schooling on his own at the grammar school in Taganróg. He was not an outstanding pupil, but he was sensible and hardworking, and when he took his final examinations in 1879 he was awarded a scholarship of twenty-five roubles a month to support him at Moscow University. There he was to read medicine until he qualified as a physician in 1884.

Antón duly went to Moscow, where the twenty-five roubles disappeared into the family's financial deficit; and soon after the beginning of his university course he began to bring in a little more money for the common pot by writing short stories and articles at a few kópecks a line for a St Petersburg comic weekly. He continued to write these pieces of light journalism by the dozen – he signed most of them 'Antósha Chekhónte' – for various Petersburg periodicals throughout his medical studies, and for some years afterwards. Some of them were rubbish, others very light-weight, but they did include some good jokes and worthwhile stories.[1]

In 1886 Chékhov received an encouraging letter about his work from the elderly novelist Dmítri Grigoróvich – the same Grigoróvich who had shared rooms with Dostoévsky in 1844 and helped to get *Poor Folk* noticed – and in 1888 he had a story ('The Steppe', one of his best) published for the first time in a 'thick' literary journal. Chékhov was now recognised as a short-story

---

[1] There is a good collection of Chékhov's *Early Stories* (1883–8), translated by Patrick Miles and Harvey Pitcher, in Oxford World's Classics (1994).

writer of the first rank, and the fifty-four tales he wrote from 1888 to 1904 – a period of some seventeen years – were nearly all of outstanding quality, showing great range, deep psychological perception, and masterly technique; they were variously funny and moving, morally ambiguous, and immensely readable. To mention a few of the finest of them, 'A Dreary Story' (1889), 'Ward Number Six' (1892), 'The Russian Master' (1894), 'Peasants' (1897), and 'Lady with a Dog' (1899) are among the best short stories ever written, and they are as fresh and challenging today as they were then.[2]

Chékhov's interest in the theatre was slower to mature. An early play, *Ivánov*, had a mixed reception in Moscow in 1887; and the next important one, *The Seagull*, did badly at its première in St Petersburg in 1896 (though it had a successful revival in Moscow two years later); and it was not until 1899, with the production of the wonderful *Uncle Vánia* in Moscow, that the full power of his genius as a playwright emerged and was recognised. This was followed by two more superb plays: *Three Sisters* in 1901, and his last work *The Cherry Orchard* (the subject of the next section) in 1903–4.

Chékhov always took his medical practice seriously, and believed that it both kept his feet firmly on the ground and provided him with essential material for his fiction and drama. As a medical scientist, too, he was pragmatic, and was determined to write truthfully in the sense of incorporating in what he wrote nothing but material that he considered to be a reflection of what he himself had observed. He had avoided radical politics as a student, and he still believed, as a doctor and a writer, in the vital importance of opposing the violence and lies of both right and left. As a doctor, however, he had one serious defect: he would not – perhaps he could not – diagnose in himself the tuberculosis that was to kill him, and that would have been apparent to any other experienced physician as early as 1885, when a cure might have been possible. He would not acknowledge his disease, indeed, until 1897, when other doctors obliged him to do so but when it was too late to hope for recovery, despite wintering at Yalta in the Crimea from 1898.

Apart from this, Chékhov was a sane, practical, and enterprising man. In 1890 he made the punishing overland journey through

---

[2] The fifty-four stories of 1888–1904, translated by Ronald Hingley, are collected in vols 4–9 (1965–80) of the Oxford *Chékhov*.

Siberia to the penal colony of Sakhalín – Russia's 'Devil's Island' – where he undertook a meticulous survey of the prisoners and their conditions which was of real scientific and sociological importance; and in 1891 he travelled for the first time to Western Europe. He was liked and respected for his charm and good nature; he could be sardonically waspish (like a Russian Jane Austen) but he was essentially a good man, gentle, kind, and charitable, without being sententious or priggish; at the same time guarding himself against close personal involvement with other people. He accepted his role as the main support of his feckless family as soon as he could afford it, and he had his parents and some of his siblings to live with him at the small estate of Mélikhovo, fifty miles south of Moscow, that he bought in 1892; but he remained aloof from their tantrums and squabbles. He was particularly close to his younger sister Mária, and looked with disfavour on anyone who wanted to marry her. At Mélikhovo he was an energetic and enlightened landowner, running his farm efficiently, and building a medical centre and three schools for the peasants.

Chékhov was also guarded in his love life. He liked women, and several of them adored him, but he shied away from emotional commitment, drawing back when his lovers became too serious. He met the actress Ólga Knípper in 1898, who became his mistress. They were married in 1901; and this was possible for him, perhaps, only because she was as determined to keep her emotional independence as he was to keep his, and carried on with her theatrical life largely as before.

Chékhov died of tuberculosis in Germany in 1904, aged forty-four, drinking a glass of champagne with his wife.

The Cherry Orchard, 1903–4

Chékhov's last major work is a play of great charm and subtlety. He called it a comedy, and indeed it is very funny in parts, but it is a comedy infused with sadness and nostalgia. The Gáiev estate is heavily mortgaged but there is no money to pay the interest, and the gentry family which owns it is incapable of coming to any decision, sensible or otherwise, that will enable them to keep it from being sold. Leoníd Gáiev is silly, selfish, and ineffective; while his self-centred sister Liúba Ranévskaia (a widow just returned from a prolonged stay with her lover in Paris) lives in a romantic dream of being a rich and generous landowner; yet for all their foolishness they are not unattractive. Squeamish about commerce, neither of them will contemplate the sensible suggestion made by Lopákhin, the son of one of their former serfs but now in business and a very rich man, that they should fell their beautiful and celebrated cherry orchard and lease the land out as building plots – the unprofitable cherry orchard which stands for the old way of life on the estate, and which, Lopákhin urges, should now go to make way for a new sort of 'summer countrymen', urban tenants of country cottages. Gáiev and Ranévskaia procrastinate until the estate is sold over their heads; and the purchaser turns out to be Lopákhin. Gáiev takes a modest job in a bank (a job that he seems unlikely to keep), and Ranévskaia returns to her lover in Paris, intending to live on 15,000 roubles that has been wheedled out of a rich aunt 'to save the estate'.[3]

Among the other characters are Ranévskaia's daughters Vária, a serious young woman who has done her best to manage the estate and who would like to marry Lopákhin but is disappointed, and the dreamy teenager Ánia who indulges in idealistic fantasies and admires the 'student' Trofímov. This radical twenty-seven-year-old, who has been expelled from two universities for his political views, is the only one who can see that the old-style landowners are parasites, 'living on credit, at the expense of others', and that 'to start living in the present we have to redeem our past' (as he says to Ánia, who hears but does not care to understand him).

Besides the major symbol of the cherry orchard itself, Chékhov introduces the sound of a winding cable snapping in a distant mine, symbolising the moment of parting between past and future. Also symbolic is the fate of the ancient servant, Firs, the ex-serf who is supposed to be delivered into the care of an old-people's home when the family finally leaves; in the event he is forgotten by everybody and is locked up in the empty house, which echoes, as the final curtain comes down, with the snapping of another distant cable and with the clunk of a felling axe in the orchard.

The Cherry Orchard is a beautiful but elusive play. When we consider Ibsen's *A Doll's House*, or Strindberg's *Miss Julie*, or Górky's *The Lower Depths* (to be discussed later in this chapter), their tendencies are on the whole clear. But in Chékhov the lights and shades of rights and wrongs subtly overlap. The Gáievs

---

[3] It is not made clear why Ranévskaia has to use the aunt's money in this way. Lopákhin has paid the interest on the mortgage plus 90,000 roubles for the estate, money which is presumably due to her and her brother (unless it is immediately swallowed up by debts to Lopákhin and others).

contribute very little to society, but they mean well and it is impossible not to sympathise with them as the old order changes and yields to the new; Lopákhin works hard and is clearly a decent man, but lacks the education and *savoir-vivre* to make best use of his decency; while it is apparent that Trofímov, the utopian 'perpetual student', will never put his great ideals into practice. And some of the play's melancholy may have its roots in the fact that Chékhov, knowing from his own experience at the age of sixteen what it was like to be evicted from the family home, wrote *The Cherry Orchard* as he was preparing – still a relatively young man – to leave home for the last time.

Translations

The Cherry Orchard has been translated into English many times. It is included in Chékhov's *Plays* in Penguin Classics, trs. by Elisaveta Fen (1959) (with *Three Sisters*, *Ivánov*, *Uncle Vánia*, and three one-act 'vaudevilles'); in Chékhov's *Five Plays* in Oxford World's Classics trs. by Ronald Hingley (1964) (with *Ivánov*, *The Seagull*, *Uncle Vánia*, and *Three Sisters*); and in Chékhov's *Plays* in Methuen Drama trs. by Michael Frayn (1978) (with *The Seagull*, *Uncle Vánia*, *Three Sisters*, and four one-act 'vaudevilles'). All three translations read well, Michael Frayn's for Methuen being perhaps the liveliest.

Maxím Górky, 1868–1936

Maxím Górky was born Alexéi Maxímovich Peshkóv in Nízhni Nóvgorod on the Volga,[4] the son of a carpenter working in a shipyard and of the daughter of a self-important 'town-dweller'. When Maxím Peshkóv died in 1872, Alexéi, aged four, was taken by his mother to live in her father's house. This grandfather was a brutal old man whose business was in decline, and whose increasingly harsh treatment of the child was only partly alleviated by the kindness of his grandmother; meanwhile his mother married an idle spendthrift. Not surprisingly Alexéi became delinquent, stealing lumber with his gang, and leaving school when he was ten. When his mother died the following year, Alexéi's grandfather refused to keep him at home any longer, and sent him out to earn his own living.

---

[4] From 1932 to 1991 Nízhni Nóvgorod was called Górky.

Thus Alexéi set out at the age of eleven on a wandering life that lasted from 1879 to 1892, going from one menial job to another, coming into contact with all sorts of people, and travelling all over Russia. He worked on river boats and building sites, in shops and small factories; he lived in dosshouses, and starved and froze with down-and-outs; he tramped the roads of southern Russia, from the Caucasus to the Ukraine; returning from time to time to his home city of Nízhni Nóvgorod.

At thirteen he became a voracious reader of literature, starting with Balzac (in translation) and going on during the next few years to Púshkin, Turgénev, Dostoévsky, Tolstóy, Scott, Dickens, Goncharóv, and Flaubert. At sixteen he tried to matriculate at Kazán University but was thwarted by his lack of general education. At nineteen his beloved grandmother died, and feeling hopeless and alone he attempted suicide but succeeded only in shooting himself through one of his lungs.

By this time – 1887 – Alexéi's political views were crystallising. He was coming to hate the gentry and the bourgeoisie as parasitical bloodsuckers, and to despise the intelligentsia for talking a lot but doing nothing; he had scarcely more respect for the peasants, whom he saw as unenlightened, superstitious, and reactionary; and he turned against religion. The future, he decided, belonged to the workers, the proletariat: they alone were capable of instituting reform, and he was attracted (by way of social-democracy) to Marxism. In discussing these matters with like-minded acquaintances he came to the attention of the police, and was several times arrested and briefly imprisoned; but each time he was released for lack of evidence or on account of his ill-health (his damaged lung had become tubercular).

By this time, too, he was writing stories and prose poems, and in 1892 one of his stories was admired and published. He decided to use a *nom de plume*, choosing Maxím (after his father) and Górky (meaning 'bitter' in Russian); by which name he was known for the rest of his life. Settling for a while in Nízhni Nóvgorod, Górky worked in a lawyer's office and published more stories. His writing was undisciplined – the words poured out, direct, guileless, passionate – with everything seen in black and white, tormentors and victims clearly defined; but the passion and the style were in tune with the times, and his work rapidly gained an audience. In 1895 he got a job as a newspaper columnist, and a better newspaper job the following year, both in Nízhni

Nóvgorod; he met an intelligent young woman called Elizavéta Vólzhina, whom he married in Samára in 1896; and his two volumes of *Sketches and Stories* were published to great acclaim in Moscow in 1898.

Górky, already something of a cult figure in Russia, now decided to become a professional writer. He wrote a polemical novel (*Fomá Gordéev*, 1899), another novel (*The Three of Them*, 1900), and his first play (*The Petty Bourgeois*, 1900), but none of them had the literary quality of the preceding stories. He made friendly contact with Chékhov (who gently chided him for his lack of restraint) and Tolstóy (who was attracted to him as 'a man of the people'). He became increasingly famous, and increasingly objectionable to the authorities, who now feared him; and it was now that he wrote his masterpiece, *The Lower Depths* (1902), which is discussed in the next section.

The rest of Górky's life may be described more briefly. Five more plays were staged in 1904–8. In 1905 he protested against 'Bloody Sunday' and was imprisoned in the Peter and Paul Fortress in St Petersburg, but was released almost immediately following an international outcry. In 1903 he had left his wife for the actress María Andréeva, also a Marxist, with whom he travelled to New York in 1906, hoping to raise funds for Lenin and the Bolsheviks; later they moved to Capri, where they settled for the next seven years. Górky set up a school for Russian revolutionaries on Capri in 1909; Lenin objected, but they were reconciled the following year, and Górky continued to give financial assistance to the Bolsheviks. He returned to Russia with María in 1913; opposed Russia's entry into the First World War; and after the February Revolution of 1917 opposed the plans for a Bolshevik coup. Although friends again with Lenin, Górky continued to criticise the Bolshevik régime, and he was encouraged to live abroad again from 1921. He visited Russia from 1928 (he was now reconciled with his wife, having broken up with María Andréeva in 1920, and had in addition a mistress-secretary called Móura Búdberg), and returned for good in 1932, in which year his home town was renamed after him. But although he actively supported the Soviet regime and was fêted as Russia's leading proletarian writer, he was never quite comfortable with Stalin. He died suddenly in 1936, and it has been suspected (but not proved) that he was murdered on Stalin's orders because it was feared that he might speak out against the show trials of the old Bolsheviks.

As we have seen, Górky continued to write drama and fiction throughout his life, but nothing to equal *The Lower Depths* in literary quality. His best work of the later period was in the three volumes of his autobiography: *My Childhood* (1913–14), *In the World* (also known as *My Apprenticeship*, 1915–16), and *My Universities* (1923), which described his life up to 1888.

The Lower Depths, 1902

When Górky read through his new play with the actors he told them that 'I'll be satisfied if you can shake the audience so much that they can't sit comfortably in their seats';[5] and, to improve their chances of doing so, the cast went out into Moscow's lower depths – to the dosshouses in the slums where the vagrants, whores, and drunken down-and-outs passed their miserable days – to see the reality for themselves. It was familiar enough to Górky, of course, for he had lived the life himself; and he was now determined to rub the noses of the bourgeoisie and the intelligentsia in the mess for which he held them partly responsible.

To present this turbulent life on the stage he brought together a large group of characters – the play has seventeen speaking parts – who represent various states of degradation in desperate interaction: the grasping landlord of the dosshouse, Kostilëv, his vicious wife Vassilíssa, Vassilíssa's downtrodden younger sister Natásha, and their uncle Abrám, a corrupt policeman; Kváshnia, a cheerful street-vendor; Váska Pépel, a professional thief; Aliócшka, a wild young cobbler; Nástia, a romantic whore; Keshch, an unemployed locksmith, and his dying wife Ánna; two street-porters, the Tartar and Zob; and four unemployed and unemployable drunks: Búbnov, a homespun philosopher; the Actor, far gone in alcoholism; the Baron, formerly a gentleman; and Sátin, an intellectual.

The mechanism of the play turns on an affair that Váska the thief has been having with Vassilíssa, the landlord's wife. Vassilíssa asks him to kill her husband, but he suspects that she not only wants her husband dead but also wants him out of the way in prison because she suspects, rightly, that he is about to transfer his affections to her younger sister Natásha. Into this situation wanders Luká, an old travelling pilgrim, who overhears Vassilíssa's plotting, and advises Váska to run away with Natásha. But before Váska can do so Natásha is assaulted by Vassilíssa, and in the subsequent brawl

5 Henri Troyat, *Gorky*, W. H. Allen, London 1989, p. 85.

Váska kills Kostilëv. As a result, Váska is arrested but escapes from custody, Natásha also disappears, Vassilíssa is imprisoned, and Luká wanders off again on his travels.

In the context of the play as a whole, the plot is not much more than a device which allows Górky to develop his main themes: the near-hopeless position of the down-and-out community; the personal responsibility, or lack of it, of its individuals; and the competing claims of truth and compassion in dealing with them. The character around whom these themes revolve is the old pilgrim, Luká, one of the 'holy fools' who tramped round Russia, wandering from shrine to shrine. He stops in the dosshouse for a short while, kindly, tolerant, unshockable, always seeing hope in the most hopeless cases. He is ever ready with a wise saying or the solace of religion; he comforts Ánna as she dies with tales of heaven; he tells the alcoholic Actor that there is a fine treatment centre for him if he really wants to be cured of his addiction; and he implicitly defends such 'lying' when he says – concerning the romantic fantasies of Nástya the prostitute – ''Tisn't the word that matters. But why has the word been spoken, that's what matters.' For him, compassion comes before truth; and this is recognised, even by the intellectual Sátin, as justifiable lying. But, as Sátin says later on, 'there's another lie. [...] it blames the man who's dying of hunger! [...] Whoever's weak in the soul, and lives off the sap of others, he needs that lie. [...] Lies – they're the religion of slaves and bosses.' But Luká too has his weakness, for when a situation arises which cannot be seen off with a cheerful word – the brawl at the end of Act III in which Kostilëv is killed – he quietly disappears, wandering off to investigate a new religion in the Ukraine that he has heard about.

In fact the brawl at the end of Act III results in the departure from the play of five interesting characters – Kostilëv, Vissilíssa, Natásha, Váska, and Luká – which weakens the final Act, as Chékhov was quick to point out. But it may be that this slow winding down to the final shock (when the Actor, shattered at being refused a place in the Tartar's prayers, hangs himself) is what Górky wanted: to give an account of the life of the dosshouse as a process without beginning or end, a process so evil and corrupt that some way would have to be found to replace it with something better.

There was a good chance that the censor would ban *The Lower Depths* altogether in 1902 but – probably because it was thought that the play would flop – it was allowed to be performed. To the dismay of the authorities, it was an enormous success, a bemused Górky taking fifteen curtain calls on the first night. It was promptly banned in ordinary theatres but it remained in the repertoire of the Moscow Arts Theatre; and 75,000 copies of the printed text were put on sale in the first year alone.

Although most of Górky's plays were politically slanted with stereotypically 'good' (worker) and 'bad' (drone) characters, *The Lower Depths* was the great exception, a compelling work of art that was more dramatically effective and less obviously polemical. It was also new and influential in showing the underclass from the bottom up as seen by one who had been a member of it, rather than from the top down by a middle-class intellectual.

Translations

The only translation of *The Lower Depths* currently available is included in Methuen Drama's *Gorky: Five Plays*, translated (1973) by Kitty Hunter-Blair and Jeremy Brooks, which deals satisfactorily with the difficult problem of putting the speeches of Górky's down-and-outs into credible demotic English. The other plays in this collection are *Summerfolk* (1904), *Children of the Sun* (1905), *Barbarians* (1906), and *Enemies* (written 1907 but not performed until 1935). *The Lower Depths* was also included in *The Storm and Other Russian Plays*, well translated by David Magarshak, Mac-Gibbon and Kee 1960, but now out of print.

Further reading

As was suggested in chapter VI, for the general background see Richard Pipes's *Russia under the Old Régime*, Weidenfeld and Nicolson 1974 (now in Penguin Books). For the literary background, Ronald Hingley's *Russian Writers and Society in the Nineteenth Century*, 2nd rev. edn, Weidenfeld and Nicolson, London 1977, is an excellent guide. *The Cambridge History of Russian Literature*, ed. Charles A. Moser, rev. edn Cambridge University Press 1992, has useful sections on the authors and plays discussed here.

We are fortunate in having two first-rate biographies of Chékhov: *A New Life of Chékhov*, Oxford University Press 1976, by Ronald Hingley, a translator of all of Chékhov's plays and all of his stories from 1888; and Donald Rayfield's rich and crowded *Antón Chékhov: a Life*, HarperCollins, London 1997.

The best approach to Górky's life up to 1888 (well before he wrote *The Lower Depths*) is to be found in his three volumes of autobiography: *My Childhood* (1913–4), *In the World* (also known as *My Apprenticeship*, 1915–16), and *My Universities* (1923), which are all available as Penguin Modern Classics. A good general biography is Henri Troyat's *Górky*, trs. by Lowell Bair, W. H. Allen, London 1991.

France and Germany at the end of the nineteenth century

The defining event for France and Germany in the later nineteenth century was the Franco-Prussian War of 1870–1. Deliberately provoked by the Prussians, France foolishly embarked on a war in which she was decisively beaten. As a result France was not only humiliated but also lost the eastern provinces of Alsace and Lorraine; while Bismarck was able to improve on the earlier Prussian successes in the wars of 1864 against Denmark and of 1866 against Austria by extending the North German Confederation southwards to create a new German Empire. As the Second French Empire fell, so the Second German Reich arose.

The Second Empire was followed by the Third French Republic, and – very briefly – by the Paris Commune and the horrors of its suppression by government forces. The Monarchists missed their chance of a restoration, but remained dominant in the 1870s; and they were followed in government by conservative republicans for the rest of the century, who held the balance between the extreme politics of right and left, with the aid of a state education system that was no longer dominated by the Church. There was a rightist revival in the 1890s, in which anti-German chauvinists, the military, and the Church combined to combat the socialists and other liberal republicans. The conflict was epitomised by the Dreyfus Affair, which revealed the deep enmity that existed between right- and left-inclined Frenchmen: a Jewish army officer was falsely accused of espionage, convicted as the result of the fabrication of evidence by the authorities in 1893–4, sent to Devil's Island, and not fully rehabilitated until 1906. When the Affair, and its detestable anti-Semitism, had subsided, the French turned to preparing themselves for the war against Germany that they could see was coming; and when war did break out in 1914 the mood in France was not so much of chauvinistic euphoria as of resignation and of resolution to see it through, to pay the Germans back and to recapture Alsace-Lorraine.

Following social unrest in the 1840s, there was an unsuccessful attempt at the unification of Germany but, despite its failure, some constitutional reform was achieved, and rapid industrialisation followed, in which Britain, hitherto the industrial leader, was overtaken by the North German Confederation in the 1860s. In the new German Empire of the 1870s – the result more of the Prussian desire to expand than of pan-German nationalism – the unusual Prussian combination of political reaction and progressive economic policies continued to bring wealth and power to the whole country. Industrialisation went from strength to strength – the rate of German economic growth was double that of Britain – along with tariff-protected agriculture. The German population exploded, from forty-one million in 1871 to sixty-eight million in 1914 (the population of France grew from thirty-six million to only forty million in the same period). It was a federal empire, with the real power in the hands of the *Bundesrat* or Federal Council working in harness with the Emperor and his Chancellor, the army being more or less independent of the government.[1] The old landowning (*Junker*) class continued to dominate German politics and the army, even though their economic power was relatively less than it had been; and there was no serious left-wing opposition. This worked well enough under Kaiser Wilhelm I, but the grandson who succeeded him as Wilhelm II in 1888[2] – he was also a grandson of Queen Victoria – was an arrogant, intemperate, and unstable man who dismissed Bismarck and took his over-confident country down the path of imperialist aggression that led to the débâcle of 1914–18.

The late-nineteenth and early-twentieth century was a period of great cultural change in the West: in science (atomic physics, relativity, quantum theory), technology (especially in transport, communications, and weapons of war), sociology (family planning, Freudian psychology), and the arts. In painting there were the Post-Impressionists and Dada; in music and dance there were Debussy, Stravinsky, the Ballet Russe, and jazz; and in literature the beginnings of Modernism in fiction, poetry, and drama, including the

[1] There was also a democratically-elected *Reichstag*, but it did not have the power to initiate or veto legislation.

[2] Wilhelm I's son reigned for three months as Frederick III, but he was dying of cancer, so Wilhelm II did in effect succeed his grandfather.

work of several of the authors discussed in chapters X to XIV of this book, together with such writers in English as Conrad, Joyce, Pound, T. S. Eliot, and Wyndham Lewis. It will be seen in this chapter, too, that Zola, Fontane, and Proust, who were writing in the late-nineteenth and early-twentieth century, were affected in different ways by this cultural upheaval.

Modernist developments in the arts were concentrated in the capital cities of the West, and especially in Paris, where many of the most original painters, musicians, and writers either lived or stayed for lengthy visits. This meant that the French language and French culture had a disproportionately large influence on the development of Modernist art, even though many of its greatest practitioners were not of French origin; and that Frenchmen continued to believe in the innate superiority of their civilisation. London was next after Paris in importance in the arts; while a number of Scandinavian and Eastern European painters and writers congregated with their German colleagues in Berlin in the 1890s before moving on to Paris.

Émile Zola, 1840–1902

Émile Zola, an only child, was born in Paris, but was brought up in the southern town of Aix-en-Provence, where his father – a distinguished Italian civil engineer – worked to divert water into the drought-stricken region. François Zola died just before the child's seventh birthday, leaving his wife and son to increasing poverty. The boy attended the Collège Bourbon in Aix, where he made some close and lasting friends including the painter Paul Cézanne, but he did not shine academically. Mother and son migrated to Paris in 1857–8, where Zola entered the Lycée Saint-Louis on a scholarship, and failed at the age of nineteen in two attempts to gain his *baccalauréat*. In 1862 he became a naturalised French citizen. Over the seven years after leaving school he worked as a clerk in the Customs service, and then, after a spell of unemployment, as director of publicity for the bookseller Hachette. He also began to write, *Les Contes à Ninon* appearing in 1864.

In 1866 Zola decided to turn to writing full-time. He left Hachette to become a freelance journalist; and in the following year his first major novel, a lurid tale of love, sex, and murder called *Thérèse Raquin*, was published; he was now twenty-seven, and for the rest of his life he was to combine the life of a prolific novelist with occasional journalism. Three years later Zola worked out a plan for a series of ten – later expanded to twenty – 'naturalistic' novels based on the evolution of an extended family, the Rougons and the Macquarts, which was grudgingly accepted by his unimaginative publisher Albert Lacroix. (In 1872 Zola was able to transfer his work to a more genial and sympathetic publisher, Georges Charpentier, who looked after him for the rest of his life.) The first Rougon–Macquart novel, *La Fortune des Rougon* came out in 1870 (not a good year for launching Zola's series), and the twentieth and last, *Le Docteur Pascal* in 1893.

'Naturalism', of which Zola was the chief practitioner, used the descriptive realism that had been developed by Balzac and others earlier in the century to expound a 'deterministic positivism', or 'scientific' point of view. ('Determinism' is the doctrine that all actions are determined by causes external to the will; while 'positivism' – deriving from Auguste Comte's recognition of observable phenomena only, and consequent rejection of metaphysics and belief in God – recognises heredity, environment, and the historical moment as the three principal determinants.) The general theme that emerged in Zola's novels, therefore, is that men and women are dependent on their inherited physical natures in the context of where and when they were brought up; which they may express in ruthless ambition, artistic genius, sexual and other passions, alcoholism, and so on.

Although gratefully acknowledging the formal influence of *La Comédie humaine*, Balzac's great series of novels with reappearing characters (pp. 93, 96 above), Zola said that, with Rougon–Macquart, he was attempting something different. Where Balzac intended to hold up a mirror to contemporary society, Zola's intention was to be more scientific than social in his approach, to anatomise and dramatise the interplay of race and milieu in representatives of the different branches of a single family.

The two main branches of this family derived from a single ancestor, Adelaïde Fouque (Tante Dide, born 1768) who had a son, Pierre, from her marriage to Rougon, a wily peasant from Plassans (Aix), and two illegitimate children, Antoine and Ursule, by Macquart, a violent alcoholic smuggler.[3] The Rougons turned out to be clever, ambitious, unscrupulous people who rose through

---

[3] Zola constructed an elaborate genealogical tree for the members of the Rougon–Macquart family, specifying the characteristics of each one. He amended it as the novels progressed, and finalised it in 1893. The resulting series of trees is reproduced in the Gallimard edition of Zola.

the ranks of society, while the Macquarts were more unstable, alcoholic, and violent, and included losers, criminals, and geniuses.

It is the children and grandchildren of Antoine Macquart (born 1789) who are the chief characters in the finest of the novels of the series, ostensibly set in the time of the Second Empire (1852–70). Antoine's son Jean Macquart is a leading character in *La Terre* (1887, a bleak account of peasant life), and his daughter Gervaise slides inexorably downhill in *L'Assommoir* (1877, about alcoholism and urban slum-dwellers). Four more of the best of the series are dominated by Gervaise's children: Claude Lantier the frustrated artist in *L'Oeuvre* (1886); Jacques Lantier the psychopathic engine-driver in *La Bête humaine* (1890); the proletarian Étienne Lantier – the least deviant of the four – in *Germinal* (1885, to be discussed in the next section); and their half-sister Anna Coupeau, the prostitute and courtesan in *Nana* (1880). Two other outstanding Parisian novels in the series concern Octave Mouret, a young southerner on the make who is decended from both the Rougon and the Macquart sides of the family: *Pot-bouille* (1882, about bourgeois hypocrisy) and *Au Bonheur des dames* (1883, the anatomy of a great department store).[4] But as with Balzac's *La Comédie humaine*, each individual novel stands up on its own, and does not have to be read as part of the series.

Zola never lost his journalistic flair for attracting attention to his work and stimulating controversy by surprising and shocking his readers. Virtually all his novels abound with forceful accounts of brutality, squalor, crime, and sexual licence that would not be sniffed at by a tabloid editor today, but which had not hitherto been attempted in serious literature. But he was also both a deeply committed artist, and a dedicated, hardworking craftsman who planned his novels in great detail and carried out exhaustive research on their many different settings. No other novelist of any period, perhaps, could have planned in advance, and then actually written according to plan, twenty novels on the heroic scale of the Rougon–Macquart series.

[4] The titles of some of these novels are difficult to translate. Zola uses *La Terre* to mean both 'The Earth' which is cultivated and 'The Land' which is owned; *L'Oeuvre* is a little more than 'The Work' but less than 'The Masterpiece'; while *une bête*, in *La Bête humaine*, is primarily 'an animal', a distinctly weaker word than what is usually meant in English by 'a beast'. *Pot-bouille* means something like 'Ordinary Fare' (not 'Restless House' as in its only English translation), while *Au Bonheur des dames* (based on the *Bon Marché* department store) has been felicitously translated as 'The Ladies' Paradise'. (*L'Assommoir, Germinal*, and *Nana* are proper names.) See also the note on translating the title *À la recherche du temps perdu*, p. 185 n. 10 below.

Although enormously successful, Zola never lost a feeling of insecurity and inferiority resulting from the poverty of his provincial background and his lack of formal education. He was sociable, interested in everything and everybody, and not averse to displaying his wealth. In 1865 he set up house with Alexandrine Meley – they were married in 1870 – and she was a good and faithful wife to him. Unhappily the marriage was childless, and in 1888, when he was approaching fifty, Zola fell in love with one of their maids, an intelligent and sensible girl called Jeanne Rozerot, who was twenty-one to Alexandrine's forty-nine. He set the girl up in a flat as his mistress, where she bore him two children. Inevitably Alexandrine found out about the liaison, and the rest of their married life was blighted by her jealousy and his feelings of guilt. But they stayed together, while Zola continued to see and support his mistress and his children.

When Captain Alfred Dreyfus was first wrongfully accused and convicted of espionage in 1894, Zola paid little attention to the matter; but when, three years later, he became aware of the monstrous way in which evidence in Dreyfus's favour had been suppressed and evidence against him had been fabricated with the active connivance of army generals and defence ministers, he was outraged beyond bearing. Determined to speak out for truth and honesty, he audaciously published in a newspaper a polemic against these guilty men, despite the support they were getting from the many Frenchmen who believed passionately that the 'honour' of France and her army should be preserved at whatever cost to a mere individual, and a Jew at that. This was the famous *J'Accuse ... ! Lettre au Président de la République par Émile Zola*, which appeared on the front page of the new daily paper *L'Aurore* for 13 January 1898, and presented the whole sorry story in detail. The sensation this caused was enormous and, as he had foreseen, Zola was prosecuted for slander, and was convicted on the showing of more falsified evidence. Following the advice of his own supporters he spent a year in hiding in England – unwisely, perhaps, for he might have promoted Dreyfus's cause more effectively from jail. When he returned to France in 1899 the climate had changed;[5] the case against him was dropped and the good eventually prevailed

---

[5] It appears that Zola's intervention came too late to be a major factor in Dreyfus's release; but it did give Dreyfus's supporters considerable extra publicity at home and abroad.

over the bad, though Zola did not live to see Dreyfus fully rehabilitated. He died in his bedroom in 1902, aged sixty-one, from carbon-monoxide poisoning; and it is possible that he was murdered by supporters of Dreyfus's conviction.

Germinal, 1885

Germinal – the seventh month of the French Revolutionary Calendar,[6] equivalent to 21 March to 20 April – seems at first an odd title for a novel about a late-nineteenth-century industrial dispute in the coalfields of northern France, but it is explained in the last two sentences of the book (in Leonard Tancock's translation): 'Men were springing up, a black avenging host was slowly germinating in the furrows, thrusting upwards for the harvests of future ages. And very soon their germination would crack the earth asunder.' For this novel is about the practical politics of revolution. Its original French readers, moreover, would have known that 12 Germinal Year III (1 April 1795) saw the beginning of severe rioting for bread by the starving poor of Paris.

To write the novel Zola began with several months of concentrated research: he read numerous technical and sociological works on the coal industry, and talked to as many experts as he could find. Most importantly he toured the mining district himself (called *le pays noir*, 'the black country', in France just as in England), went down a coal mine, talked to the miners and their families, saw for himself the conditions in which they lived and worked, and discussed the politics of wages and strikes with their leaders. He saw how the miners' standard of living depended not only on their skill and sobriety – for they were piece-workers – but also on how many in their families were old or fit enough to work down the mine and contribute to the cost of food and clothing; how injury, disease, drunkenness, or the departure of a working child to get married could wreck a family's economy; and how few were the rewards for the back-breaking labour which led to lung disease and premature death: bread but very little meat; an occasional beer; and the cheapest pleasure of all, sex. As he saw it, promiscuous sex pervaded the

---

[6] The names of the months of the Revolutionary calendar – which began on 1 Vendémiaire Year I (22 September 1792) – are irresistably evocative: *vendémiaire* (≃ October), *brumaire* (≃ November), *frimaire* (≃ December), *nivôse* (≃ January), *pluviôse* (≃ February), *ventôse* (≃ March), *germinal* (≃ April), *floréal* (≃ May), *prairial* (≃ June), *messidor* (≃ July), *thermidor* (≃ August), and *fructidor* (≃ September).

whole community: haulage girls had frequent sex, willingly or not, down the mine, boys and girls did it out of doors, husbands and wives (not always their own) did it indoors: for sex was the means whereby the workers reproduced and got by, their recompense, the universal symbol of their potency and ultimate survival.

The plan of the book is a simple one. Its first third is taken up with setting the scene at a coal-mining complex in the neighbourhood of Lille-Douai-Valenciennes, where the miners, who already live from hand to mouth in appalling working conditions, are threatened by their employers with a cut in wages – forced on the owners by a recession which has hit all the industries in the area. The rest of the book describes the resulting strike and its outcome: the walk-out of the miners, starvation increasing, resistance by the owners and managers, despair and political agitation among the people leading to mob attacks on the mines and bourgeois property, troops brought in, and the strike finally broken after more than two months as the fabric of the mine is sabotaged and wrecked. Nobody wins, and nothing is solved.

The third-person narrator tells how Étienne Lantier, an unemployed engineer, comes to the mine looking for work, and is taken on by Maheu, a skilled miner leading a small co-operative which cuts coal by hand at the face, runs it back in tubs for collection, and fits pitprops to keep the roof from caving in. He is attracted to Catherine, Maheu's pre-nubile daughter, but she is raped and captured by the villain of the team, Chaval. When the wage-cut is announced Étienne takes a political stand on the miners' behalf, egged on by his desire to shine in rivalry with an older agitator, and by the arguments of an exiled Russian nihilist, Souvarine. He leads the strike, but loses control when the mob's attacks on people and property get out of hand, and when the miners, rejecting his leadership, are eventually forced back to work by hunger. The owners and managers are half ruined; and a shareholder in the mine, whose family has lived comfortably on the labour of the miners for more than a century without doing anything at all, is punished by the murder of his effete daughter by a retired miner who has lost his reason. In the end Étienne, Catherine, and Chaval are trapped down the mine as a result of Souvarine's sabotage, and Étienne – having killed Chaval in a fight and possessed the dying Catherine – is the only one to be rescued.

Germinal is an intensely exciting book, fascinating as industrial and social history, and skilfully presented with characters that are sufficiently well realised. It was deservedly successful – though not in Britain, where Zola's publisher Henry Vizetelly was first fined and then imprisoned in the late 1880s for publishing translations of obscene books such as *L'Assomoir* and *Nana* – and it was chosen by André Gide as one of the ten best novels in French.

Translations

Peter Collier's Oxford World's Classics version (1993) is very well done; it also has a valuable Introduction and other apparatus, including a map of the mining area descibed in the book. The Penguin Classics version by Leonard Tancock (1954) lacks the apparatus but also reads well.

Theodor Fontane, 1819–98

On 30 December 1819 Henri Théodore Fontane was born, as his baptismal names suggest, to parents of French origin. The Fontanes had been part of the wave of Huguenot emigration to Prussia following the revocation of the Edict of Nantes in 1685; but their Frenchness when Fontane was born was largely imaginary, for his ancestors on both sides had lived in Prussia for over a century, and the family was thoroughly Prussian in all but name.

Born near Berlin, Fontane went to a vocational school in the capital to study pharmacology when he was thirteen, and three years later he followed his father by setting out to become first an apprentice and then a journeyman pharmacist. His interest in literature grew at the same time; he had a novella published in a Berlin literary journal when he was only nineteen, and over the next few years he joined various literary societies. He did a year of military service in 1844 (when he was twenty-four); made his first visit to England; and finally qualified as a hospital pharmacologist in 1847.

Fontane was active in support of the attempted revolution of 1848 in Berlin, though exactly what he did is unclear, since he played it down in later life. In 1849 he took the major step of giving up his hospital job to become a freelance writer (he published a volume of poems in 1851) and journalist for the Prussian government press office and the official government newspaper. He was sent to England in 1853, and again from 1855 to 1859, as the official Prussian correspondent and press attaché, where he became an enthusiastic Anglophile, well acquainted with English ways; and on returning to Germany he wrote notable travel books, first about England and Scotland, and then about his own home province of Brandenburg. He did three stints as a war correspondent with the Prussian armies, in the wars against Denmark in 1864, Austria in 1866, and France in 1870–1. In the Franco-Prussian War he was captured by the French and held as a prisoner of war for three months, narrowly escaping from being shot as a spy, and being released through the direct intervention of Bismarck.

It was not until 1878, when he was already fifty-eight, that Fontane's first mature novel was published. It was the historical *Vor dem Sturm* ('Before the Storm'), about Prussia's involvement in the Napoleonic Wars; but it was followed in the last two decades of his life with fifteen more novels and collections of stories, nearly all concerning contemporary Prussian society, together with several volumes of poems and memoirs. Outstanding among the novels were *L'Adulterá* ('The Woman Taken in Adultery', 1882); *Schach von Wuthenow* (1883, 'a man of honour' at the beginning of the nineteenth century); *Irrungen, Wirrungen* ('Delusions, Confusions', 1888, about sexual liaisons across class boundaries); *Unwiederbringlich* ('Beyond Recall', 1892, a novel of marriage and middle age); *Frau Jenny Treibel* (1893); *Die Poggenpuhls* and *Effi Briest* (1895); and *Der Stechlin* (1897, an atmospheric novel of old age). Considering their consistently high quality, this was an extraordinary achievement by a 'new' novelist writing in his sixties and seventies.

As a man Fontane worked hard and honourably; he had many friends and few enemies; he was not quarrelsome or contentious; he was a good husband and father; and he loved his country with all its faults. But not all of his country loved him. Although Fontane the novelist was admired by the younger German critics, and although he himself had an amused fondness for the fossilised Prussian aristocracy, his work was not appreciated by the Prussian upper classes that he portrayed with such a keen and unsentimental eye in his novels. He rather touchingly hoped that the aristocracy would understand that his ironical criticism of its anachronistic ways came from affection, not dislike, but of course it did not. It was the new bourgeoisie, which he tended to disdain, that most appreciated Fontane's novels; for the middle classes could see in them, even if he did not care to, that it was they who would ultimately come out on top.

Fontane died, an Honorary Doctor of the University of Berlin, in 1898, aged seventy-eight.

Effi Briest, 1895

Effi Briest is the third of the great nineteenth-century European novels of adultery to be discussed here, the other two being *Madame Bovary* (1856–7, p. 103) and *Ánna Karénina* (1874, p. 130).[7] It is the story of an innocent, inexperienced upper-class girl of seventeen who is pushed by her family into marriage with a man twice her age: Geert von Instetten, an aristocrat whose breeding and prospects satisfy her parents' ambitions, and who was formerly the suitor of her own mother. He takes her off to the little seaside town of Kessin (based on Swinemünde in western Pomerania[8]) where he is a senior civil servant, and where, despite his reasonable and proper behaviour, she becomes bored, alienated, and rebellious, especially during his absences on official business. When he is away she allows herself to be seduced by the wiles of a married womaniser, Major von Crampas, an affair that is in the event short and unsatisfying.[9] Some six years later, when the Instettens have a young daughter, Effi's husband accidentally finds some letters written to her by von Crampas at the time of their affair which she has foolishly kept, and he realises that she has been unfaithful to him. Instetten immediately calls out von Crampas and kills him in a duel, knowing that his quixotic act will ruin Effi and their family; but as 'a man of honour' he believes that he has no choice. The result is disaster for Effi: divorced, ostracised from society, unloved by her daughter, and rejected by her own parents, she is broken in health and spirit. Eventually her parents relent and let her return home, but it is too late and she dies.

This uncomplicated story has an elegant symmetry, beginning and ending at Effi's home, with two central sections at the seaside town (the seduction) and the Prussian capital (the discovery of the letters and the divorce); and it is told by a third-person narrator in a quiet, compassionate style, rich in symbolic and metaphorical

---

[7] See 'Women and adultery in the nineteenth century', pp. 98–103 above. Although Fontane's novel was the last of the three to be published by more than twenty years, he was two years older than Flaubert and nine years older than Tolstóy.

[8] Fontane knew Swinemünde well, having spent part of his childhood there; it is now Swinoujscie, just over the border in Poland.

[9] It is not made clear whether Effi becomes von Crampas's mistress in the technical sense, though the presumption must be that she does.

suggestion, very different from the heavy, determined naturalism of some of Fontane's contemporaries. Effi is introduced as scarcely more than a child, young for her years, emotional and impressionable, and unprepared for the sacrifice that will be required of her as a Prussian wife and mother; and it is as a victim that she is duly sacrificed to the unforgiving morality of the Prussian aristocracy when she lets herself give way to her own weakness and desire. Instetten, for his part, is the incarnation of that morality: correct, objective, efficient – and emotionally repressed. He is locked into the social code; and when he finds the incriminating letters and has to decide what to do, the demands of the rigid social code are unhesitatingly preferred to the love and compassion that he should have been able to find in himself – and this in connection with an offence that occurred more than six years before. What is perhaps even more shocking is the reaction of Effi's father and mother, who are plainly decent people at heart: for even they feel obliged at first by the laws of their society to tell Effi that they cannot receive her as a disgraced wife in what had once been her own home.

It is a sad, haunting tale, and was always unlikely to please the Prussian aristocracy; but *Effi Briest* – arguably Fontane's masterpiece – achieved the best sales of all his novels, going into three printings in the first year of publication.

Translations

The standard translation of *Effi Briest* is the one by Douglas Parmée (1967) in Penguin Classics, and is the only one currently available; it reads well, and has a good Introduction but no notes or other apparatus.

Marcel Proust, 1871–1922

Seen from outside, the relatively short life of Marcel Proust was not an exciting or even an interesting one. The elder of the two sons of the distinguished medical specialist Doctor Adrien Proust and his Jewish wife, Marcel was a sickly child who was obsessively devoted to his mother, and who remained a hypochondriac all his life, never worked for his living, preferred homosexual and aristocratic society so far as he cared for society at all, dabbled (as it seemed) in literature, and chose to spend much of the later part of his life in bed. But of course it was his inner life that was interesting: his perspicacity, his fascination with human nature (especially his own), and his ability to penetrate into the inner workings of social beings in his huge and unprecedented semi-autobiographical novel *À la recherche du temps perdu*, 'In Search of Lost time'.[10]

Memories of Marcel Proust's childhood form the background to *Swann's Way*, the first part of *In Search of Lost Time*. He was born two months after the fall of the Paris Commune at the house of his mother's uncle in Auteuil, on the edge of Paris, and grew up in the family home in the city itself. His brother Robert was born eighteen months after Marcel; his arrival was inevitably the cause of some fraternal jealousy, though Marcel managed to retain the first place in his mother's heart, and the brothers got on reasonably well with each other. (Robert grew up to resemble their kind and sensible father, and became a distinguished physician himself.)

Marcel resembled his sensitive, doting mother, and their relationship was exceptionally close. He sought repeated proofs of her love for him, placing special importance on her good night kiss, and feeling betrayed and resentful when she was prevented (for instance, by the presence of dinner guests or by Dr Proust's ridicule) from giving it to him. He discovered early on that she seemed to love him most when he was hurt or ill; and so he contrived to be ill as often as possible. His hypochondria seemed to be justified and was entrenched when, at the age of nine, he suffered his first violent, life-threatening attack of asthma – in his case an extreme form of hay fever which, while it was not self-induced, probably did have a psychosomatic element. (It may be that later on his asthma served a purpose similar to Flaubert's and Dostoévsky's epilepsy in opening his mind for his writing.)

The key memories of Marcel's childhood derived from family holidays at the small town of Illiers south-west of Chartres (called 'Combray' in the novel), the birthplace of Dr Proust. Here the family stayed for Easter from 1878 with a Proust aunt, and Marcel revelled in the magic that children find in special places – his bed, the lavatory, gardens, hedges, footpaths, secret dens – and in family walks. From Illiers they would normally walk either to the village of

---

[10] *À la recherche du temps perdu* was eccentrically rendered by Proust's first English translator C. K. Scott Moncrieff as *Remembrance of Things Past*. The French title translates literally as 'In Search of Lost Time', implying a search for aspects of the narrator's past that are missing from his memory, but which he hopes to find; and the final section of the book is called *Le Temps retrouvé*, 'Time Found Again' (Scott Moncrieff's 'Time Regained'). But note that *Perdre son temps* also means 'to waste one's time', so that there is the parallel suggestion of 'In Search of Wasted Time'.

Méréglise, a couple of miles west of the town ('the Méréglise way', which was to become 'Swann's way'), or to the church of Saint-Éman, a mile-and-a-half to the north ('the Saint-Éman way', later 'the Guermantes way'). These magical places and walks came to represent a paradise that was lost when the climate and pollen of Illiers were judged to be bad for Marcel's asthma, and later family holidays were taken at various seaside resorts on the Normandy coast (combined in the novel as 'Balbec'). They had a symbolic value for him which was connected with later people, places, and events in his life, and which were all woven back together in his book.

The rest of Proust's life must be described more briefly. He was educated at the Lycée Condorcet in Paris and, after a year of voluntary army service (1889–90), as a law student, graduating in law in 1893 and in philosophy in 1895. This period saw the beginning of the Dreyfus Affair, in which he and the rest of the Proust family were *Dreyfusards* from the start, and which temporarily alienated him from his fashionable acquaintances who tended to believe that Dreyfus was guilty. His emotional life, being homosexually oriented, was necessarily secret and sometimes sordid; and his literary efforts were sporadic, his first major publications being translations of Ruskin's *Bible of Amiens* (1904) and *Sesame and Lilies* (1906). When Dr Proust died in 1903 he had no reason to suppose that his elder son would ever be anything more than an intelligent and charming imaginary invalid who was a literary dilettante; and although Marcel's mother believed in his exceptional gifts, there was again little evidence for her belief when she died, having never recovered from the loss of her husband, in 1905. Predictably, Marcel took his mother's death very hard; he had an emotional collapse lasting several months – he was now in his mid-thirties – and mourned her for the rest of his life.

From 1906, when he moved into a flat in the Boulevard Haussmann,[11] until his death in 1922 from pneumonia at the age of fifty-one, Proust lived as a recluse, staying for the most part in bed in a cork-lined room, with summer holidays by the sea, untroubled by the need either to earn his living or to overcome his hypochondria. By 1910 he had started work on what was to become *À la recherche du temps perdu*, the first part of which, *Swann's Way*, was published at his own expense in 1913. He was found unfit for the army

[11] He stayed in this rather noisy flat until 1919, when he was obliged to move house twice, finally settling in the rue Hamelin.

in 1914, and during the war he simply got on with his novel, compulsively rewriting and adding to the parts that had been 'completed'. He was awarded the Prix Goncourt for *À l'ombre des jeunes filles en fleurs* (Scott Moncrieff's 'Within a Budding Grove') which was published commercially in 1919; and further parts of the book were published in 1920, 1921, and 1922. Proust went on writing and revising until the very last moment, and the final parts were brought out, as far they could be put together from the confusion of his papers, in 1923, 1925, and 1927. There were subsequent recensions of the whole enormous work – it runs to about 1,240,000 words, the length of four or five substantial nineteenth-century novels – the most recent one appearing in 1987–8.

Swann's Way, 1913

Both *Germinal* and *Effi Briest* were, in their different ways, conventional third-person novels narrated chronologically, but *À la recherche du temps perdu* is startling in its much greater difference and originality. It does contain third-person sections (there is one in *Swann's Way*), but much of the work is occupied by a first-person narrator who finds himself sometimes meditating in the present, sometimes remembering the past with more or less immediacy and numerous chronological dislocations, and whose experiences can match Proust's (the narrator's name turns out to be 'Marcel') but can also be fictional. The style is unhurried and discursive, drawing the reader into close intimacy with the narrator.

Du côté de chez Swann, or 'Swann's Way', the first part of *À la recherche du temps perdu*, is itself divided into four sections which are known as 'Overture'; 'Combray'; 'Swann in Love' (*Un amour de Swann*); and 'Place-names, the Name' (*Noms de pays, le nom*). In the 'Overture' the narrator reaches back during sleepless nights in the present to what he can ordinarily remember of his childhood in Combray, such as his agonies over bedtime and his mother's missing kiss; but he then has a transcendental experience in which, as a result of tasting a particular sort of cake (a *petite madeleine*) soaked in tea, he gains almost total recall of what was magical in that period of his childhood. These extraordinarily vivid memories are explored, interpreted, and meditated upon in the second section of *Swann's Way*, 'Combray': the wonder of the child 'Marcel's' sensitive insight into the world he finds about him, and the family's activities and its acquaintance with Swann, the Guermantes, and others; and they end with the light of dawn beginning to show above the curtains of the narrator's bedroom window. The third section, 'Swann in Love', has a third-person narrator who manages the transition from the first person by addressing the reader in an almost metafictional way,[12] but then unobtrusively occupies Swann's point of view to tell the story – which belongs to a period before 'Marcel's' birth in the social setting of the Paris salon of Madame Verdurin – of his love for Odette de Crécy. The final section, 'Place-names: the Name', which reverts to first-person narration, begins with a short discussion of place names and an evocation of a seaside holiday at Balbec, but is mostly taken up with memories of the adolescent 'Marcel's' acquaintance in Paris with Swann's daughter Gilberte, whom he used to meet in the Bois de Boulogne; and it ends with a sudden jump forward to a meditation on the state of the Bois de Boulogne at the time of writing.

Here is a paragraph from 'Place-names: the Name', describing the young Marcel's developing relationship with Gilberte in the Bois de Boulogne:

> And there was another day when she said to me: 'You know, you may call me "Gilberte". In any case, I'm going to call you by your first name. It's too silly not to.' Yet she continued for a while to address me by the more formal '*vous*,' and when I drew her attention to this, she smiled and, composing, constructing a phrase like those that are put into the grammar-books of foreign languages with no other object than to teach us to make use of a new word, ended it with my Christian name. Recalling, some time later, what I had felt at the time, I distinguished the impression of having been held for a moment in her mouth, myself, naked, without any of the social attributes which belonged equally to her other playmates and, when she used my surname, to my parents, accessories of which her lips – by the effort she made, a little after her father's manner, to articulate the words to which she wished to give a special emphasis – had the air of stripping, of divesting me, like the skin from a fruit of which one can swallow only the pulp, while her glance, adapting itself to the same new degree of intimacy as her speech, fell on me also more directly and testified to the consciousness, the pleasure, even the gratitude that is felt by accompanying itself with a smile.[13]

The first part of this paragraph, down to 'ended it with my Christian name', is simple first-person narration, strengthened by

---

[12] On 'metafiction' see p. 85 n. 7 above.

[13] *Remembrance of Things Past*, trs. by C. K. Scott Moncrieff and Terence Kilmartin, vol. 1, Chatto and Windus, London 1981, pp. 437–8. The French text of this passage (p. 237 below) gives a good idea both of the precision of Proust's prose despite its convolutions, and of the fidelity of the Moncrieff–Kilmartin translation.

the simile of the grammar-book sentence which refers light-heartedly to 'the name'. The second part, however, is one long meditative sentence, beginning with the key phrase 'Recalling, some time later, what I had felt at the time'. It is typically Proustian, not only on account of its length but also in way the narrator's experience is followed, clause by clause, along the complicated path that takes the reader through exactly what 'Marcel' felt as Gilberte spoke his name, and what her smile told of her feelings as she did so.

This brief introduction to *Swann's Way* is intended to show the way into a novel of great power and beauty which is too long to be treated here in full, but which the reader is urged to explore at length once an understanding of this first part has been gained. As with Joyce's *Ulysses*, all seven parts of *À la recherche du temps perdu* are threaded with a web of cross-references which are mutually supporting in their treatment of characters and events, and in the end the novel turns out to be a coherent whole which should be read as a whole like any other novel. It contains some justly celebrated characters – Swann himself, Odette, tante Léonie, Albertine, M. de Charlus, the Duchesse de Guermantes, Robert de Saint-Loup – but of course it is 'Marcel' who dominates the book, and who is investigated in greater psychological detail and with more revealing intimacy than any other character in fiction.

The remaining six parts of the novel, with their usual English titles and with indications of who and what appear in them, are as follows:

> *À l'ombre des jeunes filles en fleurs* ('Within a Budding Grove'): Madame Swann at home; the Marquis de Norpois; place names; first stay at Balbec; introduction of M. de Charlus, Robert de Saint-Loup, and Albertine.
>
> *Du côté de Guermantes* ('The Guermantes Way'): Names of people; the Duchesse de Guermantes; illness and death of my grandmother; Albertine; M. de Charlus.
>
> *Sodome et Gomorrhe* ('Cities of the Plain'): Men who are also women; M. de Charlus; Swann and the Prince de Guermantes; final visit to Balbec; Albertine, her jealousy and mysteries; M. de Charlus's 'duel'.
>
> *La Prisonnière* ('The Captive'): Life with Albertine; the Verdurins quarrel with M. de Charlus; Vinteuil's concert; the disappearance of Albertine.
>
> *Albertine disparue* ('The Fugitive'): Grief and forgetting; Mlle de Forcheville; Gilberte; Venice; a new aspect of Saint-Loup.
>
> *Le Temps retrouvé* ('Time Regained'): Tansonville and the German occupation; M. de Charlus during the War; the sanatorium; fighting

round Combray; air raids; Saint-Loup killed; reception at the Princesse de Guermantes'; 'Marcel's' notion of Time.

Translations

C. K. Scott Moncrieff's twelve-volume translation of À *la recherche du temps perdu* (1922–31) was a notable landmark, but it was in some respects quirky and in need of general revision, not least because of advances in the recovery of the text made since it was published. This was very adequately done in what was partly a new translation, based on the recension of 1954, by Terence Kilmartin: Marcel Proust, *Remembrance of Things Past*, three vols, Chatto and Windus, London 1981 (since reprinted in paperback). Terence Kilmartin also compiled *A Guide to Proust*, Chatto and Windus, London 1983, which consists of useful indexes to characters, persons, places, and themes in the three volumes of his translation.

Further reading

For the general background of France and Germany in this period, see Roger Price, *A Concise History of France*, Cambridge University Press 1993; and Mary Fulbrook, *A Concise History of Germany*, Cambridge University Press, rev. edn 1992.

For Zola, Frederick Brown's recent biography, *Zola: a Life*, Macmillan, London 1996, is a first-rate study: thorough, intelligent, and well written; it supersedes all its predecessors, though Joanna Richardson's *Zola*, Weidenfeld and Nicolson 1978, is a notable critical biography. It is always worth reading novelists on their fellow-novelists, and Angus Wilson's *Émile Zola: an Introductory Study of his Novels,* Secker and Warburg, London 1952, remains a valuable critical essay. (Wilson also wrote good introductions to the translations of Zola's novels that were published in the 1950s but are now out of print.) Naturalism in fiction is discussed in Roger Pearson's fine Introduction to his translation of one of Zola's most 'naturalistic' novels, *La Bête humaine*, Oxford World's Classics 1996.

William L. Zweibel's Theodor *Fontane*, Twayne, New York 1992, is a satisfying critical biography; Professor Zweibel is also the translator (into American English) of Fontane's superb *Irrungen, Wirrungen*, or 'Confusions, Delusions' (with *Die Poggenpuhls*), Continuum, New York 1989. Stanley Radcliffe's monograph,

Fontane: Effi Briest, Grant and Cutler, London 1986, is excellent but does not supply English translations of the numerous quotations in German – unlike Alan Bance's *Theodor Fontane: the Major Novels*, Cambridge University Press 1982, which is a good general survey.

In the vast literature concerning Proust, George D. Painter's *Marcel Proust: a Biography*, two vols, Chatto and Windus, London 1959, 1965, stands out; it is one of the great twentieth-century biographies, and a revised edition is now available in a single paperback volume, Pimlico, London 1996. Sheila Stern's *Proust: Swann's Way*, Cambridge University Press 1989, is a valuable introductory monograph. *The World of Marcel Proust* by André Maurois, Angus and Robertson, London 1974, is short on text but is full of marvellous photographs and other illustrations of Proust and his milieu. There is also Alain de Botton's *How Proust Can Change Your Life*, Picador, London 1997, an affectionately amused commentary on aspects of *À la recherche du temps perdu* which, like Julian Barnes's *Flaubert's Parrot* of 1984, includes entertaining critical insights.

XIII   Mann and Kafka

The central powers before 1914

As we have seen (p. 174), the German Empire from 1871 to 1914 was not a unitary state, but a federation dominated by Prussia, some of its constituent states being kingdoms, grand duchies, free cities, and so on. The non-Prussian states had a good deal of domestic autonomy, but their foreign and defence departments were ultimately controlled from Berlin. Thomas Mann was born in the free city of Lübeck, adjacent to the Grand Duchy of Mecklenburg-Schwerin; then, after his father's death, the family moved from the north to the south of the Empire, to Munich in the Kingdom of Bavaria.

The Austro-Hungarian Empire, even larger than the German one, was a ramshackle assemblage of ethnically distinct provinces, economically backward and bureaucratically inefficient. It included all of present-day Austria, Hungary, the Czech Republic, Slovakia, Slovenia, Croatia, and Bosnia; together with parts of southern Poland, western Ukraine, north-western Romania, the western rim of Serbia, and north-eastern Italy. Within its borders were the cities of Vienna, Prague, Budapest, Cracow, Lemberg (Lvov), Brassó (Brasov), Sarajevo, Zagreb, Trieste, and Trento. Although the Emperor ruled, after a fashion, from Vienna with German as the language of official business and with a bureaucracy dominated by Austrians, the Empire's German-speakers were in a minority; and the central government was opposed by numerous nationalist movements in the non-German-speaking provinces, most formidably in what is now the Czech Republic. Franz Kafka, a German-speaking Jew, was born and lived his whole life in Prague, the capital of the Czech-speaking 'kingdom' of Bohemia.

Modernist fiction

'Modernism' is a term applied retrospectively to early-twentieth-century developments that affected all the arts, and especially literature. It was coeval with a time of great cultural change, not only in the arts, but in Western society generally. By the early 1900s, nineteenth-century optimism, and its moral certainties – for some certainties did survive Darwinism and the retreat of the sea of faith – were threatened by new political and sociological ideas, as well as by the rapid advance of science and technology; and they were finally seen off by the First World War and its gross demonstration of the inability of 'civilisation' to control men's darker and more primitive sides when armed with weapons of mass destruction: barbed wire and machine guns, artillery barrages, poison-gas, and submarine torpedoes.

Modernism in fiction was diverse in its manifestations, which included the manipulation of form; the influence on the presentation of narrative and the analysis of character of classical and later mythology, Freudian psychology, and the anthropology of Frazer's *The Golden Bough*; the use of interior monologue; and the introduction, to a much greater extent than in nineteenth-century fiction, of symbolic themes and leitmotifs.[1] Philosophically it was strongly influenced by Nietzsche (1844–1900), who had himself been influenced by Schopenhauer (1788–1850), and who, having abolished God, believed in a quasi-religious human 'life-force' which parallelled the 'reason' of the eighteenth-century *philosophes* and the 'nature' of Goethe. Many Modernist features and trends in literature, which were cosmopolitan both in their origin and in their practice, had been foreshadowed in the nineteenth century, for instance by the later Dostoévsky, the French Symbolist poets, Strindberg, and Hamsun's novels of the 1890s. Some early-twentieth-century writers, on the other hand, such as Kipling and E. M. Forster, did not altogether reject nineteenth-century literary forms and conventions (of realism, for instance) and remained relatively unaffected by Modernism; even Proust, though his treatment of chronology and narrative point of view presented aspects of Modernism, still wrote in an essentially pre-Modernist style. The Modernists who wrote fiction in English included the later Henry James, Conrad, Joyce, Virginia Woolf, Ford Madox Ford, and Faulkner.

---

[1] A 'leitmotif' in a novel is a repeated phrase, image, or event, which emphasises a theme, partly by giving the reader a sense of *déjà vu*.

Thomas Mann, 1875–1955

Thomas Mann's father was a north-German bourgeois, a prosperous merchant in the old Hanseatic free port of Lübeck on the Baltic, while his mother was of more exotic stock, a latin beauty whose own mother was a Portuguese creole whom her father – another Lübecker – had married in Brazil. He was educated at a secondary school in Lübeck which he did not care for; but, his father having died in 1891, his mother removed the family to Munich in 1894 – a move from the stern grey north to the sunnier, more artistic south, which remained his base for the next four decades. After a brief spell of office work, he began to write fiction, following his elder brother Heinrich who was already a writer.[2] The brothers were very different from each other – Heinrich liberal and expansive where Thomas was conservative and uptight – and they were at odds, and in competition, with each other for much of their lives.

Thomas Mann's first notable work of fiction was a short story, 'Little Herr Friedemann', which was published in 1897. This was soon followed by an extraordinarily accomplished first novel, *The Buddenbrooks*,[3] a long and ironical saga of the decline of a family which was based on the history of the Manns of Lübeck. Completed in 1900 when Thomas was staying with Heinrich in Italy, it was published in 1901. German readers recognised it as an intriguing mirror of their society, and it was an immediate success, selling thousands of copies, turning the 25-year-old Thomas into a celebrity, and incidentally putting him well ahead of his brother Heinrich, a pre-eminence that he would retain for the rest of their lives.

Among the short stories that followed *The Buddenbrooks* were the wonderfully accomplished 'Tristan' (1902) and 'Tonio Kröger' (1903), which, along with 'Little Herr Friedemann' we shall be looking at briefly in the next section. In 1905 Mann married the daughter of a prominent Jewish family, Katia Pringsheim, eight years younger than himself, a satisfactory and successful union that produced six children[4] and lasted the rest of his life. His next major

---

[2] Heinrich Mann (1871–1950) is best remembered for his novels *The Land of Cockaigne* (1901) and *Professor Unrat* (1904). He lived in Italy for much of his life; then in France from 1933 to 1940; and finally in the United States.

[3] *Buddenbrooks* – a family name – is its German title but, as David Luke points out, an English novel (unlike a German one) about the Smith family would be called *The Smiths*, not *Smiths*.

[4] One of them (Erika, b. 1905) married W. H. Auden in 1935 in order to obtain a British passport.

work, *Death in Venice*, appeared in 1913, and he was just starting on another novel when the First World War intervened. Although Mann had volunteered for his army service on completing the manuscript of *The Buddenbrooks* in 1900, he was quickly discharged on medical grounds; and now in 1914, although his sentiments were strongly patriotic, he chose not to join the forces, arranging to be declared unfit for the rest of the war. It was of course a distressing time for him, but the family continued to live fairly comfortably. His support for the war and the monarchy, and Heinrich's objections to both, led to an open breach between the brothers that was not healed for many years.

Having lived through the revolution and the short-lived Bavarian soviet republic of 1919, Mann went back to the novel that he had abandoned in 1914, which was completed and published in 1924 as *The Magic Mountain*. This second substantial novel was set in a clinic in Switzerland (where Katia Mann had been briefly resident before the war with suspected tuberculosis), in which a patient, Hans Castorp, experiences the moral and intellectual disintegration of the sanatorium, parallelling the disintegration of pre-war European civilisation. It is a long and serious book, heavy going in places, and lacking the incisive clarity of the short story 'Tristan', which had had a similar setting. At the same time Mann was a prolific critic and essayist; and in 1929 he was awarded the Nobel Prize for Literature (for *The Buddenbrooks*, he noted with displeasure, rather than for *The Magic Mountain*).

The Mann family passed the 1920s prosperously at their town house in Munich, at their country house in Bad Tölz south of the city, and on holidays abroad, but by the early 1930s night and fog were gathering in Germany. At first the Nazis, of whom he strongly disapproved, did not seem much of a threat, but Hitler's seizure of power in the 'constitutional' *coup d'état* of 1933 could not be ignored. Mann earned his living from German publishers, but the Nazi regime was intolerable – and, besides, his wife was Jewish – so in 1933 the Manns moved to Switzerland. However, the Nazi government was not yet in the mood to strip this German Nobel Prizewinner of his citizenship, even though he was now an émigré known to be opposed to the Third Reich.

The situation was obviously unstable, and in 1938 the Manns emigrated again, this time to the United States, where they were to remain. After a brief period of Czech citizenship, Thomas and Katia had applied for US citizenship in 1937, and were granted it in 1944. Settled in Los Angeles, Mann produced his last major novel, *Dr Faustus*, in 1947, a retelling of the sixteenth-century legend of a bargain with the Devil[5] in a story of the life and tragic end of a composer, Adrian Leverkühn, in which art and politics are brought together in a treatment of German disintegration in the two world wars. Like *The Magic Mountain*, it is written with a high seriousness that deprives it of the vitality of *The Buddenbrooks* and the lean precision of the early short stories.

The two strains in Mann's family – from his bourgeois north-German father and his beautiful latin mother – seemed to be opposed in him: the bourgeois versus the artist, the demands of each preventing the fulfilment of the other. There was another contradiction in him too, a current of homosexuality that ran alongside his successful marriage and six children, which was probably never acted out physically but which continued to trouble and excite him into his fifties; this found its most notable expression in *Death in Venice*, to be discussed in the next section. These conflicts meant that he always had the sense of being an outsider, someone who did not quite belong: a bourgeois who was tainted by being an artist and vice versa, a husband and father who was erotically excited by male beauty. Not surprisingly there was a stiffness about him, and a keen sense of self-protection that found expression in egotism and mild vanity, and in a selfish care for his own comfort; while in politics he was at first anti-democratic, and always something of an authoritarian. He was yet another example of a type that we have kept coming across: an imperfect human being who was nevertheless a great artist.

Mann was taken ill with arteriosclerosis while on holiday in The Netherlands in the summer of 1955, and died in August, with Katia by his side, in hospital in Zurich at the age of eighty.

Death in Venice, 1912

Mann is the only author to be represented here by a short story (or *Novelle*[6]). This is because, magisterial as his full-length novels

---

[5] See p. 63 above.

[6] The term *Novelle* is used in German for a story (of whatever length) that concentrates on a single event or situation, usually with a surprising conclusion; whereas the English term 'novella' is used for a story of any sort intermediate in length and complexity between a short story and a novel. *Death in Venice* is a 'Novelle' but not quite a 'novella'; it runs to about 25,000 words in English translation, somewhere between the average short story (10,000–20,000 words) and the average novella (30,000 to 50,000 words).

were, he was even more impressive as a master of the short story in the great age of that form which lasted roughly from 1885 to 1915; an age which included the short stories (and novellas) of, amongst others, Chékhov, Kipling, Conrad, and Joyce. Short stories, moreover, were Mann's favourite form as a writer of fiction; and, as was also the case with Conrad, his long novels were projected, and usually begun, as short stories and were extended later.

'Little Herr Friedemann', written when Mann was no more than twenty-one and published in 1897, was his first great achievement: the story of a cripple – an outsider by definition – who determines to contract out of life by foregoing love, but who is betrayed and overcome by an overwhelming sexual passion for a married woman, whose rejection of him causes him to drown himself. This sharply told, gripping tale with an only slightly ironical third-person narrator is more 'naturalist' (or determinist) than Mann's later stories, but he is already tackling the plight of the outsider.

In 'Tristan' (1902), written after the successful publication of the great saga of *The Buddenbrooks*, the narrator is even further removed from the author, an ironical figure standing between Mann and his characters who is well suited to the story's comic elements. Here the mission of the writer-protagonist, Spinell (representing, Mann said, an undesirable element in himself), is to uncover the uncomfortable truth that beauty in art (created in this case at the piano by the consumptive young married woman, Gabriele) is more important than the survival of the artist; while Spinell himself remains a sterile seducer who shortens the young woman's life by encouraging her to live in the music of Wagner.

In both these stories, an autobiographical element is evident; and 'Tonio Kröger' (1903) is even more strongly autobiographical in following Mann's actual experiences: discussions with the painter Lisavéta Ivánovna in Munich about the difficulties of being an artist with bourgeois leanings (the conflict between the exotic 'Tonio' and the north-German 'Kröger' in him); his journey of self-discovery to his old home in Lübeck; and from there on to Denmark where he finds himself reliving his early and contradictory passions for two young people: his schoolfriend Hans Hansen and the beautiful blonde Ingeborg. The tone of the story has something in common with Joyce's *A Portrait of the Artist as a Young Man*, especially with *A Portrait* in its original form as *Stephen Hero* (1902–4).

There followed eight years in which Mann wrote no further major work, though he continued to busy himself with criticism and reviews; but then, during a visit to Venice in 1911 with Katia and his brother Heinrich, a series of experiences came together ready to be transmuted into the miraculous *Death in Venice* (1913). In this most finely-wrought of all his books, Mann tells the story of how Gustav von Aschenbach, a writer and aesthetic moralist, becomes increasingly obsessed by the classical beauty of Tadzio, an aristocratic Polish adolescent, until he finds himself compulsively following the boy about the canals and crooked alleys of Venice. Aschenbach first falls erotically in love with Tadzio, against all his training and beliefs, and then 'falls' morally by failing to warn his Polish family that they are in danger from a cholera epidemic, for fear of scaring them and Tadzio away from Venice. But he contracts the disease himself, and quickly dies, in sight of a god-like Tadzio who seems to be beckoning him out to sea.

Death in Venice is to some extent a reworking of Mann's own experience, for there was an actual Polish boy in Venice who strongly attracted him (although not to the point of active pursuit), though he was ten-and-a-half to Mann's thirty-six, where Tadzio is made to be fourteen to Aschenbach's fifty-three. It is also a classical tragedy in which the hubristic Aschenbach is destroyed for presuming to challenge the love-god rather than following his duty as an artist. This is a brilliantly-told story, richly satisfying even though the opposites in Aschenbach – and of course in Mann himself – remain in the end unresolved.

Translations

Much of Mann's fiction is available in English only in the unreliable translations of Helen Lowe-Porter, who for many years had a monopoly as Mann's translator.[7] Recently *Death in Venice* and the best of the early short stories have been excellently retranslated by David Luke (who has already appeared here as the translator of Goethe's *Faust*): Thomas Mann, *Death in Venice and Other Stories*, 1990 (now a Minerva paperback, London 1996); this collection (which includes 'Little Herr Friedemann', 'Tristan', and 'Tonio Kröger') has a particularly valuable Introduction. (*Buddenbrooks* has also been admirably retranslated by John E. Woods, 1993, and is available in Everyman Classics.)

---

[7] See p. 221 n. 2 below.

Franz Kafka, 1883–1924

The German-speaking Jews of Prague in Austro-Hungarian Bohemia were doubly outsiders in the late nineteenth and early
twentieth century, accepted neither by the native Czech majority
nor by the gentile German-speakers whose loyalty was to Austria
and the greater Germany. It was not a small or a poor community – there were many more German Jews in Prague than there
were German gentiles, and they included a flourishing middle
class – but they were denied employment in the civil service, and
they were persecuted by both the other groups in anti-Semitic
riots and pogroms. They also included a high proportion of
writers, artists, and other intellectuals, most of whom either
emigrated to Palestine after the foundation of Czechoslovakia
in 1918, or were murdered by the Nazis during the Second World
War.

Franz Kafka's father Hermann came to Prague, where he
founded a fancy-goods store, from a Czech village in which
his father had worked as a kosher butcher; and Franz's self-
effacing mother Julie was the daughter of a prosperous brewer,
with an exotic ancestry of Talmudic scholars. Although she had
six children – Franz, two more boys who died young, and
finally three girls – Julie considered that her first duty was to
act as carer and partner to her demanding, valetudinarian
husband, leaving the children to be looked after by the servants;
and Franz felt 'betrayed' by what he saw as her preference for
his domineering father (a classic Oedipal triangle), so that he
saw himself as an outsider even in a family and community of
outsiders.

Suffering throughout his life from abysmally low self-esteem
and difficulty with authority-figures (especially his father), Kafka
was a clever boy whose regular successes at his high school (he
called it 'a conspiracy of the grown-ups'), at which most of the
pupils were German-speaking Jews, were interpreted by himself
as 'not being found out'. Besides his native German, he was
fluent in Czech, and also knew some French and English, together
with the Latin that was uninspiringly taught at school. By the age
of fifteen he was already anti-nationalist and pro-underdog –
though he never became a radical activist – and was beginning to
make like-minded, intellectual friends. His closest friend of all
may have been his youngest and most rebellious sister Ottla, with

whom he formed an alliance against their family that lasted all his life.[8]

Kafka graduated moderately well from high school in 1901, and moved on to Prague's German university. After unsuccessful attempts at philosophy and chemistry, he settled down without enthusiasm to study law, one of the few subjects that could lead to a career for a Jew in the Austro-Hungarian Empire. Most of the ethnic-German students were right-wing reactionaries, showing off their uniforms and duelling scars, but Kafka consorted with more compatible companions: first Hugo Bergmann, and later Max Brod, Felix Weltsch, and the blind Oskar Baum. These talented men were all writers from the German-Jewish community with whom he enjoyed conversation, café society, and expeditions into the countryside, to the detriment of his law studies. From now on writing was a compulsion for Kafka, though he kept it secret for years even from these close friends; part of him was always alone in a crowd, kept apart from society by his need for personal privacy and by the clarity of his perception. But the law bored him, he had no intention of becoming a lawyer, and he only scraped through his finals and the orals for his doctorate in law in 1906.

What was he going to do with his life now, his father wanted to know? In 1906 he started work with a clerkship in the court system, and followed that in 1907 with employment in a go-getting insurance company, neither of which suited him. But in 1908 he found his niche in the Workingmen's Accident Insurance Institute for Bohemia, a semi-government organisation which, as a Jew, he was allowed to join only as a special case. Although he let it be known to his friends that he considered the job to be a *pis aller*, he was very good at it, being given responsible work, gaining promotion, and earning an adequate salary; best of all the hours were 8am to 2pm, leaving the rest of the day and night free for writing. He was employed by the Institute until he died, being withheld from military service during the First World War because of his 'indispensability'; after the War he was kept on and even promoted when the Institute was taken over by the Czechs in 1918 and most of the

---

[8] Ottla (short for Ottilie) married a gentile and, when the Czechoslovakian Jews were being rounded up by the Germans in 1941, she felt that her exemption as the wife of an 'Aryan' contradicted everything that she believed in. She divorced her husband (who, with her two children, survived the War), was deported as a Jew to Terezin in 1942, and murdered in Auschwitz in 1943. Kafka would have understood why she did it.

German employees were sacked; and he was still retained when he was so ill that he had to take long paid leaves.

Although he wrote compulsively, Kafka did not publish a great deal in his lifetime, rarely being satisfied with what he had achieved. A collection of short pieces, *Meditations*, appeared in 1912, and was favourably noticed but sold few copies; two other modest collections followed (*A Country Doctor*, 1919, and *A Hunger-artist*, 1922), and some individual stories, the best-known of which was 'The Metamorphosis' (1915); but much of Kafka's finest and eventually most influential work – especially *The Trial*, the greater part of *America*, and *The Castle* – remained unfinished and un-published at the time of his death. What is more, Kafka left a note for Max Brod with his papers saying that all his unpublished writings should be burned, unread. In the event Brod did not do what his friend asked but edited and published Kafka's manuscripts within a few years of his death, arguing that, when Kafka had asked him previously to destroy them when he died, Brod had replied that he could not in conscience do so, and that Kafka had accepted his refusal and yet had not destroyed the papers himself. Whether or not we feel that Brod acted properly, there is surely no doubt that, from our point of view, the outcome was a fortunate one.

Tall, gangling, and thin, seeming with his dark-eyed good looks always younger than his age, Kafka was attractive to both men and women, and his intelligence, good nature, and honesty were appre-ciated by everyone, Czechs and Germans alike. On the other hand he was deeply reserved and frightened of exposing himself in any way. Although he earned a good salary and could easily have afforded his own flat, he chose to live at home for most of his life, cramped and inconvenient as it was with a family he found difficult to tolerate. He had several attachments to women, but was unable to support a lasting relationship. The most enduring of these was with a German-Jewish professional woman from Berlin, Felice Bauer. In an absurd on-off courtship, mostly by correspondence, Felice was twice engaged to Kafka over a period of five years from 1912 to 1917 and twice broke it off; whenever she pressed him to name the day, he immediately retreated, claiming that he was ill, impotent, and as a committed writer impossible to live with. He even complicated things further by having some sort of affair with Grete Bloch, the confidante whom Felice sent to negotiate with him. He fell more deeply in love in 1920 with Milena Jesenská, a married woman who would not leave her husband; and he lived for a short while just before his death with a nineteen-year-old Jewish girl in Berlin, Dora Diamant.

Kafka's health was never robust. He suffered from agonising tension headaches and other psychosomatic pains; and then in 1917 he was diagnosed as suffering from tuberculosis. Paradoxically this pleased him, because it proved that he really was unfitted for marriage, and besides the disease was not yet life-threatening. His headaches disappeared and he seemed to be recovering when, in 1918, he was struck by Spanish flu followed by double pneumonia; the tuberculosis broke out again in a more virulent form, and eventually killed him in 1924. He was forty-one.

The Trial, written 1914, published 1925

Joseph K., a junior bank official, is lying in bed on the morning before his thirtieth birthday, waiting for his breakfast to be brought up, when he discovers that his rooms have been entered without permission by two warders and an inspector, who inform him that his 'case' is being investigated, and that he is under arrest. This is shocking news for K., who is not aware of any such case or that he has done anything wrong; but he takes the accusation seriously, for it has been made by 'the authorities'. However, it appears that being 'under arrest' does not involve physical restraint, and that he may go to work provided that he makes himself available for interrogation. There then follows a series of loosely linked episodes in which the increasingly fearful and anxious K. visits the examining magistrate's court and the court offices; is the unwilling witness of the corporal punishment of the two warders who came to his rooms; seeks help for his 'case' from an advocate, a commercial traveller, and a painter; and is preached at by a priest in the cathedral. During some of these episodes K. has encounters with women which are titillating but inconsequential. There seems at this point no reason why K.'s pursuit of his 'case' should not go on and on from one unsuccessful attempt at clarification to another; but it is brought abruptly to an end when he is physically arrested on the eve of his thirty-first birthday by a pair of executioners, frogmarched out of the house, and stabbed in the heart on some waste ground. Despite his anxiety and feelings of guilt, which steadily increase as he blunders on, K. never does discover what wrong he is supposed to have done; neither does he ever doubt that his 'case' and its outcome represent justifiable behaviour on the part of the authorities.

Such is the strange plot of *The Trial*. Its 'meaning' has been variously explained: Brod was inclined to see it as a parable of 'justice'; others have seen it as Kafka's reaction to paternal authority; or as a parody of a 'trial' to which he was actually subjected in 1913 by Felice Bauer and Grete Bloch when they jointly (and not unreasonably) accused him of infidelity and deception; or even as a clairvoyant vision of the fate of the innocent victims of the police states of the twentieth century. Some of these things could have influenced Kafka while he was writing the novel; but there may be no need to search for 'meaning' beyond the text itself, which takes the form of a waking dream.

Quite early in the story places and events begin to take on an unreal and dreamlike character. The examining magistrate's court turns out to be inappropriately housed on the upper floor of a slum tenement, and the court offices to be ranged above it along the cramped and dirty corridor of a crazy attic; the interrogation takes unexpected and illogical turns; a sadistic whipping of the two warders occurs in an ordinary lumber room at the Bank where K. works; K. is fondled by the advocate's cook in the shadows outside his bedroom door; he is jeered at in the painter's studio (which turns out to be adjacent to more court offices) by three malicious adolescent girls; the ambitious Deputy Manager of the Bank steals K.'s files from his desk and intrigues for his position; as the priest begins to speak the cathedral becomes menacingly dark at midday; and so on. Throughout the narrative time is variously stretched out and compressed, day mysteriously turns into night, sexual opportunities are offered and missed; K.'s vision is impaired, he can barely move his limbs, he is too tired to work; and scenes follow each other without much logical connection between them but the increasing pain and anxiety that K. experiences.[9]

All this is the familiar stuff of anxiety dreams – familiar to me, at any rate.[10] What is so original and compelling about *The Trial* is that it transfers the dream material in a convincing way into the waking world which we usually inhabit and, by putting it in the

---

[9] It is not even certain that the chapters of *The Trial*, as Brod arranged them for publication, are in the order that Kafka would have chosen if he had revised the book himself; but in the event this scarcely matters.

[10] I wonder if the reader, too, dreams of being found out in his or her neglect of responsibilities and duties; of pointless journeys that are interrupted by mechanical breakdowns, lost tickets and passports, missed connections; of shifting locations, inexplicable darkness, blindness, inability to move, unfulfilled sexual encounters, and so on – in other words, the sort of thing that goes on in *The Trial?*

place of everyday reality, makes us newly aware of the anxieties and fears that lie just below the surface of our daily lives and influence so much of what we say and do. It may be that Kafka himself actually lived in just such a waking dream; more probably he was vividly aware of what the states of mind described in his book – which is fiction, after all, not a textbook of psychoanalysis – can tell us about a vital part of our inner selves.

The Trial is narrated in the third person, in German of unusual clarity and simplicity; but it could just as well be in the first person, for nothing is said or done that is not directly experienced by K. In fact when Kafka began to write *The Castle* (which follows 'Joseph K.' into another dream world), he started in the first person and then, changing his mind, simply went back and changed the 'I's in the manuscript to 'K's. This very plain, direct narration is appropriate to the nature of the story, telling it in the way dreams might be recalled in all their strange inconsequentiality to a disinterested listener.[11]

Translations

The standard English translation of *The Trial* is by Willa and Edwin Muir (1935), available as a Penguin Modern Classic. The Muirs also translated the Penguin Modern Classics *The Castle* (1930) and *Metamorphosis and Other Stories* (1933, including 'The Penal Settlement').

Further reading

There are a great many good histories of the early twentieth century, the First World War, and the rise of the dictatorships for the reader to choose from. For Modernism in literature, see the collection of writings in *The Modern Tradition: Backgrounds of Modern Literature*, ed. Richard Ellmann, Oxford University Press 1965; and *Modernism 1890–1930*, eds Malcolm Bradbury and J. McFarlane, Penguin 1976.

Donald Prater, *Thomas Mann: a Life*, Oxford University Press 1995, is a first-rate modern biography. See also the excellent

---

[11] The narrative method of *The Trial* may be compared with that of the 'Circe' episode in James Joyce's *Ulysses* (1922), which sets out a series of dreamlike hallucinations in the form of dramatic dialogue with stage directions and speech headings – an entirely different technique but one which can have a similar effect on the reader.

Introduction by David Luke to Thomas Mann, *Death in Venice and Other Stories*, Minerva, London 1990, 1996.

The Nightmare of Reason: a Life of Franz Kafka by Ernst Pawel, Collins Harvill, London 1984, 1988, is a compelling and sympathetic biography that is particularly strong on Kafka's Jewish background. Ronald Gray's *Franz Kafka*, Cambridge University Press 1973, is a stimulating critical approach to Kafka's writings.

XIV   Pirandello and Brecht

The years of *l'entre deux guerres*[1]

The 1920s and 1930s – two decades still within living memory –
were dominated by the effects of the First World War and expectations of the Second. In fact, the twenty-one years from 1918 to
1939 were barely long enough for any of the participants in the first
of these appalling conflicts to recover from it: from the collapse of
confidence in the sufficiency and virtue of Western civilisation;
from the huge losses of young men in battle and of the even greater
number of people of all ages who died in the flu pandemic of 1918;
and from the cost of the vast and profligate dispersal of European
economic strength on armaments.

The greatest political change took place in Russia, where a
Bolshevik dictatorship was set up following the revolutions of
1917, resulting in a police state that was far more repressive than
Tsardom had ever been, but which was seen by starry-eyed Western
left-wingers as the socialist utopia in the making. A Communist
revolution was unsuccessfully attempted in Germany, and the
defeated country spent much of the 1920s struggling with repara-
tions, inflation, and inter-party squabbling under the unpopular
Weimar government; while in Britain, France, and Italy communist
and socialist parties expanded and entered constitutional politics,
opposed by fascist parties which sought to establish right-wing
dictatorships. The Fascists were successful in Italy, where Mussolini
became *Duce* in 1925–6; and the German Nazi party, increasing in
strength from the late 1920s, took power following the coup of
1933 when Hitler became *Führer*. The rest of the 1930s were
characterised by the general rearmament of Europe, with Germany

---

[1] 'Twenty years largely wasted, the years of *l'entre deux guerres* –' (T. S. Eliot,
East Coker 1940, l. 173).

eager to get her own back for the humiliation of 1918, while France and Britain – their economies weak and their empires faltering – were becoming resigned to the probability of another conflict but putting off the evil day for as long as possible.

The arts – and especially literature – in this anxious and unsettled period were strongly affected by these political developments. Writers throughout Europe took up political positions – the younger ones overwhelmingly on behalf of the left – and frequently used their work to promote political causes, such as support for the Soviet Union, for unemployed workers during the Great Depression (1929–34), and for the Republican side in the Spanish Civil War (1936–9). Fascism – represented for left-wing writers by the dictatorships in Italy and Germany and by the Spanish insurgents, but not by 'the dictatorship of the proletariat' in Russia – was perceived to be the enemy; and 'fascist' was also used as a term of abuse for the relatively innocent centre and centre-right parties of the democracies. Left-wing intellectuals in Britain and France generally managed to overlook the Stalinist terror of the late 1930s (afterwards they pretended, unconvincingly, to have been unaware of it at the time), but even they – apart from the most deeply committed Communists, for whom Stalin was God in his Soviet heaven – were disturbed by the Nazi-Soviet pact of 1939; and hardly any of them declined to take some part in the war which soon followed.

Modernist literary techniques were quite widely employed in the 1920s and 1930s, especially in poetry, but there were also many competent novelists who continued to use forms of fiction that were not essentially different from those of the later nineteenth century. The greatest change took place in the theatre, where the realist drama that had been pioneered by Ibsen and Strindberg was taken into new territory.

New forms of drama were assisted in the early years of the century by new styles of acting. The Russian director[2] Konstantín Stanislávsky (the stage name of K. S. Alexéev), although he had

---

[2] The 'Director' of a play, like the director of a film, is the person who puts it through rehearsals and tells the actors what to do. Formerly this functionary was known in the theatre as the 'Producer', which can be confusing since the producer is now the person who – again like the producer of a film – organises the mounting and financing of a play. In John Linstrum's translation of Pirandello's *Six Characters in Search of an Author* the 'Director' ('*il Capocomico*') is called the 'Producer' for the sake of period authenticity.

irritated Chékhov with the flamboyant and sentimentalised style of his acting and directing in the early days of the Moscow Arts Theatre, developed a 'system' shortly before the First World War which encouraged actors not to approach dramatic parts from the outside but to immerse themselves so completely in their roles – off-stage, if possible, as well as on – as to 'become' the characters they were playing.[3] This increased the degree of realism in acting, and encouraged playwrights, directors, and actors to reconsider the fundamentals of dramatic characterisation and presentation.

Luigi Pirandello, 1867–1936

The most original and influential playwright to experiment with new dramatic forms was Luigi Pirandello, who was an academic and an established writer of fiction before he took to writing plays. The eldest child of a prosperous family of mine owners, Pirandello was born near Girgenti (now Agrigento[4]) in southern Sicily, in a land of natural beauty and material poverty, into an anachronistic, near-feudal society in which social behaviour was strictly prescribed and the Mafia imposed obedience and silence. His parents, who had both been followers of Garibaldi in the unification of Italy, encouraged the boy's education at the classical Lyceum and then the university in Palermo, and later at the universities of Rome and Bonn, at the last of which he earned a doctorate with a dissertation on the dialect of his native region in 1891.

Although offered a lectureship at Bonn, he returned to settle in Rome, living chiefly on an allowance from his father, and beginning to write. In 1894 he unwisely agreed to an arranged marriage with Antonietta Portulano, a pretty but intellectually limited Sicilian girl, which brought them three children but which was, in the long run, a disaster. Antonietta resented the time he spent writing and never bothered to read his books,[5] and as time went on she

---

[3] Stanislávsky's 'system', with some alterations, was to become the 'method' acting of the 1950s.

[4] Agrigento had a distinguished history as the early Greek colony of Acragas, founded *c.* 580 BC.

[5] Some writers' spouses, such as Antonietta Pirandello and Nora Joyce, took little interest in their partners' work and did not read their books; while others such as Countess Tolstóya, Emma Hardy, and Leonard Woolf took the greatest interest, and helped their spouses with criticism, copying, and protection from interruption. Each method had its advantages and disadvantages.

developed paranoid suspicions of his behaviour, accusing him of betrayals, infidelities, and even incest; she had repeated mental breakdowns, and in 1919 was committed to a mental institution where she survived for forty years more. The difficulty of communication between human beings became a central idea in Pirandello's work.

Meanwhile, Pirandello took a job in 1897 as a lecturer at a women's teacher training college in Rome, which was just as well because the Pirandello-Portulano mining company went bankrupt in 1903, whereby he lost his private income and his wife's dowry. From then on he was the sole support of his wife and family, remaining at the training college (where he became a professor in 1908) until his success as a writer enabled him to resign in 1922.

In the early years he also had to work as a tutor and journalist, and to write, in order to survive. His output was enormous, eventually including (besides essays, reviews, and academic works) several books of verse, hundreds of short stories, seven novels, and over forty plays. His most distinguished early work was the novel *The Late Mattia Pascal* (1904, a tale of social exclusion), and his mature work for the theatre began with two one-act plays in 1910. His greatest and most original work, the unprecedented Modernist play *Six Characters in Search of an Author*, which will be discussed in the next section, was first produced in 1921; other dramas of this period included *So It is (If you Think So)* (1917, truth is what you think it is), *The Rules of the Game* (1919, the limits of social norms), and *Henry IV* (1922, role-playing at the edge of madness).

Pirandello was now living for, and largely in, the theatre, travelling around the world on his own to attend productions of his plays, and sometimes directing them himself. He upset his liberal friends and colleagues by becoming an enthusiastic adherent of Fascism in 1924, which helped him to enter the Italian cultural establishment despite the hostility of critics such as Benedetto Croce. In fact he had always been a semi-establishment figure: however singular and passionate his intellect, he was at the same time bourgeois, well-mannered, and dapper in his dress (though when he was alone he would act out his characters in a thoroughly uninhibited way). He directed the Rome Arts Theatre from 1925 to 1928; was nominated for the Italian Academy by Mussolini in 1929; and was awarded the Nobel Prize for Literature in 1934. He died, aged sixty-nine, in 1936.

Six Characters in Search of an Author, 1921

A Director is unenthusiastically rehearsing a group of Actors in a play – it happens to be Pirandello's *The Rules of the Game*,[6] which he does not admire – when six Characters (a Father, a Mother, and four children) are brought through the auditorium by the Door-keeper, demanding a hearing. Who are they? What do they want? And what are they doing coming down through an audience which finds itself watching a rehearsal which should not have an audience in the first place? The opening of Pirandello's extraordinary play is an open assault on the conventions of the theatre of his time, blurring the distinction between the auditorium and the stage, and drawing the audience into the theatrical illusion to investigate the relationship between life and art.

It appears that the Characters have come into existence in the creative imagination of an absent and anonymous author, who has failed to realise them in a work of art; and that they are now adrift, hoping to be able to realise themselves in this theatre by acting out their stories so that the Director and Actors can make a play from them. The idea that Pirandello is developing here, which he had been thinking about for more than a decade, is that when an author's characters are created in his mind they demand to be realised in the immutable form of art; and he was himself 'a man haunted by his own creations', which obsessed him until he had put them down in writing.[7] Towards the end of the play the Character of the Father explains:

> When the characters are really alive and standing in front of their author, he has only to follow their words, the actions that they suggest to him: and he must want them to be what they want to be: and it's his bad luck if he doesn't do what they want! When a character is born he immediately assumes such an independence even of his own author that everyone can imagine him in scores of situations that his author hadn't even thought of putting him in, and he sometimes acquires a meaning that his author never dreamed of giving him. (*Six Characters*, Act III, translated by John Linstrum.)

However, if the characters were to take human form in an effort at self-realisation – as they do in this play – they would become subject to change. Thus they are both imaginary Characters with limited, unchangeable histories and activities – immutable repre-

---

[6] Or, in another version of the text, Pirandello's *The Play of Parts* (1913).
[7] Alfred Mortier, quoted in F. A. Bassanese's *Understanding Pirandello*, University of South Carolina Press 1997, p. 97.

sentatives of art – and living people who suffer from the neglect of the artist who created them and, by engaging in the living world, are necessarily changed by life – as of course are the Director, the Actors, and the audience.

At first the Director tells the Characters to go away and let him get on with his rehearsal, but then, as they begin to explain themselves, he becomes interested and allows them to tell their story; and a wild, melodramatic story it turns out to be. Many years ago the Father and the Mother had a Son, now aged twenty-two; but then the Mother fell in love with the Father's male secretary, and the Father sent the two of them off to live together somewhere nearby. The Mother and the secretary had three illegitimate children – the Stepdaughter, now eighteen, the Young Brother, fourteen, and the Little Sister, four – and the Father, something of a voyeur, liked to watch them grow up – especially the eldest of the three, the Stepdaughter, by whom he was attracted – attracted (the Stepdaughter now says) as an incestuous paedophile. The Mother then moved some distance away with her new family, and has only recently returned following the death of her lover. She gets a job with a dressmaker, Madame Pace ('peace'), not realising that the dressmaking business is a front for a brothel, and that, in employing the Mother, Madame Pace is chiefly interested in getting the Stepdaughter to work for her as a prostitute. The Father, an old customer of the brothel, only realises at the last moment that the girl he is about to have is the Stepdaughter; the Mother feels deeply guilty on account both of her earlier abandonment of the Son and of the Stepdaughter's prostitution; the Son refuses to recognise his Mother and his bastard half-siblings; the Little Girl is drowned in a fountain; and the Young Brother shoots himself.

The missing author's exciting plot, with its passions and betrayals, is more attractive to the Director than Pirandello's obscure Modernist plays – which, he says, are written 'on purpose so that nobody enjoys them, neither actors nor critics nor audience' – and he takes a break to work out the story for the theatre, during which the stage is empty and the audience has twenty minutes in which to stretch its legs. The Father and the Stepdaughter then act their crucial meeting in the brothel for the benefit of the Actors (for it is the Actors, not the Characters, who will have to perform it on stage); but it is plainly incomplete without the brothel-keeper, and the Father invokes sympathetic magic, using the Actors' coats and hats, to bring Madam Pace into existence on the stage, terrifying the

Director and the Actors. But when the live Actors attempt to play the same scene they inevitably change it, to the dismay of the Characters for whom it has a fixed form; and in the muddle the curtain is let down by accident, giving the audience another break. In the third Act the rest of the Characters' ineluctable tragedy is acted out, culminating in the drowning of the Little Sister and the suicide of the Young Brother (both having been mutes throughout the play), the Actors finding themselves unable to decide whether his death is real or make-believe. In this way Pirandello's Modernist play not only encapsulates a tale of traditional melodrama in an unprecedented, strikingly original frame, but it also strictly observes the classical unities of action, time, and place.

Pirandello considerably revised *Six Characters* following a famous Paris production by Georges Pitoëff (an acquaintance of Stanislávsky's) in 1924, and added an explanatory Preface; it is the revised version that is available to us today. He wrote two further 'theatre plays': *Each in His Own Way* (1924) and *Tonight We Improvise* (1929–30), which continued his investigation of the relationship between art and life. However, it was the astonishing novelty of *Six Characters* – which can still seem almost as startling today as it did to the outraged audience at its première in Rome in 1921 – that made the break in theatrical form which decisively affected the direction taken later by such mid-twentieth-century playwrights as Brecht, Ionesco, Beckett, Pinter, and Stoppard.

Translations

John Linstrum's translation of *Six Characters* (1979) in Methuen World Classics, together with *The Rules of the Game* and *Henry IV* (both by other translators), is admirable; but the translation by Mark Musa (1995), together with *Henry IV* and *So It Is (If You Think So)* in Penguin Twentieth-century Classics also reads very well. Both versions have good introductions, but neither, unfortunately, includes Pirandello's important Preface to *Six Characters* of 1924–5.

Bertolt Brecht, 1898–1956

Berthold Brecht, notwithstanding his later attempts to present a proletarian appearance and his preference for being called 'Bertolt' or 'Bert', came from a prosperous bourgeois family – his father was the manager of a paper mill – of Augsburg in Bavaria.

At the grammar school in Augsburg he was a moderately success-ful and moderately rebellious pupil, moving on in 1917 to become a medical student in Munich; he did not pursue his medical studies, however, and his registration at the university was finally cancelled in 1921. Although he was already eighteen in 1916, he was able as a medical student to avoid military service for another two years, when he was called up in the autumn of 1918 to serve for a few months as a medical orderly in the army while still living at home.

By this time Brecht was immersed in the theatre, writing his first experimental play, *Baal*, in 1918 and doing theatre reviews for the local newspaper. Further cynical, anarchic plays followed – *In the Jungle of Cities* (1923), *Man Is Man* (1926) – and then his first great success, *The Threepenny Opera* (1928, to be discussed in the next section). He visited Berlin in 1920–1, settling there in 1924, and in 1922 he was married to Marianne Zoff, one of a number of Brecht's relationships with women as lover and husband in which his partners came off badly. Brecht and Marianne were divorced in 1927; he married the actress Helene Weigel who had borne him a son five years before, in 1928, and they had a daughter in 1930; and he was also closely involved with his secretary Elisabeth Hauptmann (the translator of *The Beggar's Opera*) and with Ruth Berlau and Margarete Steffin, some of them simultaneously.

Clever, ambitious, and self-confident, Brecht was an elusive and ambiguous figure, attractive when it suited him, using and dom-inating people yet commanding their loyalty. In the theatre he failed to recognise the weaknesses and needs of others, but he still had his way and always got himself to the centre of things. In politics he moved in the late 1920s from youthful anarchic cynicism to Com-munism, but he avoided the final commitment, not criticising the Soviet Union but not joining the Party either; and he spent most of the War years in California rather than in Europe. After the War he had a theatre in East Berlin, but his roots remained fixed in the West.

From 1926 Brecht was reading Marx and moving to the left, though it was not until after *The Threepenny Opera* that his writing shifted decisively to encompass specifically Communist themes. He soon became unpopular with the Nazis and other nationalists, and in 1933 left Germany with his family for a wandering life of exile in Europe and the United States that was to last until 1948. During this period he cocked a snook at Hitler with the caustic satire of

Fear and Misery of the Third Reich (1938); and he wrote the first versions of his best-known, 'epic' plays: *Life of Galileo* (1938, concerning the ethics of science); *Mother Courage and Her Children* (1939, a warning to those who profit from wars that you need a long spoon to sup with the devil), *The Good Person of Szechwan* (1941, the relationship between money and goodness), and *The Caucasian Chalk Circle* (1944, the relationship between the peasant commune and the state). The period ended in Hollywood with a narrow escape from the anathema of the House Committee on Unamerican Activities. He was always a successful evader.

The short remainder of Brecht's life – he died of a heart attack in 1956 at the age of fifty-eight – was spent in close connection with, and some of the time actually in, the DDR (East Germany), mostly in Berlin. The epic plays were revived, in Western as well as in Eastern Europe, and Brecht was recognised as the leading 'socially-aware' dramatist of the age, as well one of formidable power and originality. He was awarded the Stalin Peace Prize in 1954.

The Threepenny Opera, 1928

The idea of adapting John Gay's *The Beggar's Opera* (1727) came up as a quick way of meeting the need to find a new play to open a theatre that was being funded by Ernst-Josef Aufricht, an actor who had come into money. Brecht had been collaborating for the past year with the composer Kurt Weill, and the two of them agreed in April 1928 to write new sets of words and music for the play, which was to open on 31 August.

The Beggar's Opera had been one of the great theatrical successes of the eighteenth-century. Gay had had the original notion of writing a musical about London criminals – a class scarcely touched on in the theatre since Jacobean times – which would satirise both the Italian opera of the period and its political corruption. Funny and hard-hitting, it had a singable score by Christoph Pepusch based on the popular tunes and ballads of the day and has often been successfully revived. Brecht's friend Elisabeth Hauptmann had been translating it into German, and now Brecht and Weill (aged thirty and twenty-eight respectively) believed that they could create a new musical on the same theme in the four months available to them.

They only just made it, the last of the words and the best of the songs being added while rehearsals were already in progress; but perhaps the speed with which they had to work contributed to the freshness and verve of the result. For *The Threepenny Opera* turned out to be not only their collaborative masterpiece, but also an essentially new work, something more than a mere reworking of *The Beggar's Opera*.

Peachum, the master of a beggar's co-operative in a vaguely late-Victorian London, is disgusted to learn that his daughter Polly has married the notorious robber Macheath – disgusted not because he disapproves of robbery but because he could have made something out of his daughter's virginity if she had hung on to it. However, Macheath, who is already involved with Jenny Diver, cannot keep away from the ladies, and Peachum – the name means 'informer' – has little difficulty in arranging with Macheath's whores to have him arrested and condemned to death. Polly and Jenny do their best to cut each other out and to comfort Macheath, but there is no hope for him until a happy ending is contrived by means of an absurd last-minute reprieve.

The basic plot of this simple tale does not stray very far from that of *The Beggar's Opera*; and Brecht's and Weill's intention was to satirise the corrupt society and vacuous opera of the time, just as Gay's had been. What was fresh and exciting about *The Three-penny Opera* was the authentic life of the 1920s that Brecht breathed into the characters; his mordant dialogue and mocking song texts (including a version of Villon's *Ballade des pendus*[8]); Weill's original, jazz-influenced score, which for the first time dispensed with Pepusch's tunes altogether, and included 'Mac the Knife', one of the great popular songs of the century; the play's attack on respectable society that was mirrored by its greedy villains and corrupt policemen; its debunking of contemporary conservative opera, which Brecht and Weill called 'culinary opera', a mere confection of song, music, and spectacle, without critical interest or artistic value; and various Modernist techniques of production, such as exaggerated make-up, unrealistic sets, special lighting, and explanatory signs for the songs.

The Threepenny Opera was a huge success in Germany, though not for very long, for the Nazis banned it as soon as they could. Since the Second World War it has continued to be performed there, and in many other countries in translation: it was the greatest musical of the years of *l'entre deux guerres*; and it lives on as our final landmark.

[8] See pp. 25 and 237.

Translations

The Methuen Collected Plays of Bertolt Brecht includes *The Three-penny Opera* (1979) as Part 2 of Volume 2, trs. by John Willett and Ralph Manheim. This splendid version includes an Introduction, and variants and notes by Brecht and Weill. Brecht's notes, which date from 1931, were affected by the Communist party line, but the text of the play was fortunately not altered to accord with them. (The 'epic' plays are included in this Methuen series.) A recording of the songs made by the original cast and orchestra in 1930 is available on the Pearl label as a two-CD set, and Pabst's film of 1931 is occasionally revived.

Further reading

Many writers of the 'wasted' years of *l'entre deux guerres* have touched on their political development in the 1920s and 1930s. The best collection is *The God that Failed*, Hamish Hamilton, London 1950, essays by six left-wing writers about how and why they became first enchanted and later disenchanted with Communism and the Soviet Union: the novelists Arthur Koestler, Ignazio Silone, Richard Wright, and André Gide, the journalist Louis Fischer, and the poet Stephen Spender. It gives an illuminating commentary on the whole period.

Fiora A. Bassanese's *Understanding Luigi Pirandello*, University of South Carolina Press 1997, is an excellent introduction to the playwright and his work, including chapters on Pirandello's life and on *Six Characters* and the other theatre plays. There are also four interesting articles on *Six Characters* in *A Companion to Pirandello Studies*, ed. J. L. Digaetani, Greenwood Press, Westport CT 1991. See also the Introductions to the two translations of *Six Characters* mentioned above.

There are recent biographies of Brecht by Ronald Speirs, *Bertolt Brecht*, Macmillan Modern Dramatists, Basingstoke 1987; and John Fuegi, *The Life and Lies of Bertolt Brecht*, HarperCollins, London 1994, which argues that substantial parts of some of Brecht's plays were drafted by Elisabeth Hauptmann and others. *The Cambridge Companion to Brecht*, eds Peter Thomson and Glendyr Sacks, Cambridge University Press 1994, has valuable chapters on Brecht's Germany, his life, and *The Threepenny Opera*.

Appendix A

Translating Flaubert

The following paragraph is taken from the original French text of *Madame Bovary*. Describing Emma's awed reactions to the evening party at the château of the Marquis d'Andervilliers, it is written with scrupulous attention to the choice of words, and to the style and balance of the sentences and of the paragraph as a whole.

Emma se sentit, en entrant, enveloppée par un air chaud, mélange du parfum des fleurs et du beau linge, du fumet des viandes et de l'odeur des truffes. Les bougies des candélabres allongeaient des flammes sur les cloches d'argent; les cristaux à facettes, couverts d'une buée mate, se renvoyaient des rayons pâles, des bouquets étaient en ligne sur toute la longueur de la table, et, dans les assiettes à large bordure, les serviettes, arrangées en manière de bonnet d'évêque, tenaient entre le bâillement de leurs deux plis chacune un petit pain de forme ovale. Les pattes rouges des homards dépassaient les plats; de gros fruits dans des corbeilles à jour s'étageaient sur la mousse; les cailles avaient leurs plumes, des fumées montaient; et, en bas de soie, en culotte courte, en cravate blanche, en jabot, grave comme un juge, le maître d'hôtel, passant entre les épaules des convives les plats tout découpés, faisait d'un coup de sa cuiller sauter pour vous le morceau qu'on choisissait. Sur le grand poêle de porcelaine à baguette de cuivre, une statue de femme drapée jusqu'au menton regardait immobile la salle pleine de monde. (Madame Bovary, Pt I, ch. 8; 189 words)

Next come one nineteenth-century and four twentieth-century translations of the same paragraph into English, all but the first of which are still in print:

1. Emma, on entering, felt herself wrapped round by the warm air, a blending of the perfume of flowers and of the fine linen, of the fumes of the viands, and the odour of the truffles. The silver dish-covers reflected the lighted wax candles in the candelabra, the cut crystal covered with light steam reflected from one to the other pale rays; bouquets were placed in a row the whole length of the table; and in the

217

wide-bordered plates each napkin, arranged after the fashion of a bishop's mitre, held between its two gaping folds a small oval-shaped roll. The red claws of lobsters hung over the dishes; rich fruit in open baskets was piled up on moss; there were quails in their plumage; smoke was rising; and in silk stockings, knee-breeches, white cravat, and frilled shirt, the steward, grave as a judge, offering ready-carved dishes between the shoulders of the guests, with a touch of the spoon gave you the piece chosen. On the large stove of porcelain inlaid with copper baguettes the statue of a woman, draped to the chin, gazed motionless on the room full of life. (Trs. by Eleanor Marx-Aveling, 1886, the first translation into English; reprinted Everyman 1928; 189 words)

2. As soon as Emma entered the room, she felt herself enveloped in a gust of warm air which smelled of flowers, fine linen, roast meat and truffles. The flames of the candles in the sconces rose long and straight above bell-shaped casings of silver. The cut-crystal lustres, misted over with a dull sheen of moisture, gave back a dull glow. There were bunches of flowers all down the long table, and, on the wide-bordered plates, the napkins, in the form of bishops' mitres, held small oval rolls in the yawning gap between their folds. The red claws of lobsters hung over the china rims of dishes. Luscious fruit, set in open baskets, stood piled on beds of moss. The quails were served with all their plumage. A cloud of steam rose to the ceiling. The butler, in silk stockings, knee-breeches, a white cravat and a lace frill, looking as solemn as a judge, handed the courses, ready carved, between the shoulders of the guests, and, with a deft movement of his spoon, picked out for each the portion she had indicated as her choice. From the great porcelain brass-fitted stove, the stature of a woman, draped to the chin, gazed at the crowded room in frozen immobility. (Oxford World's Classics translation by Gerard Hopkins, 1949, revised 1981; 208 words)

3. As she went in, Emma felt herself plunged into a warm atmosphere compounded of the scent of flowers and of fine linen, of the savour of meat and the smell of truffles. The candles in the chandeliers glowed on the silver dish-covers with elongated flames. The pieces of cut glass had steamed over, and reflected a dull glimmer from one to the other. Bunches of flowers were set in a row down the whole length of the table, and on the wide-rimmed plates stood serviettes folded in the form of a bishop's mitre, each with an oval-shaped roll inside the fold. The red claws of the lobsters lay over the edge of the dishes. Luscious fruits were piled on moss in open baskets. The quails still had their feathers on them. The fumes rose. Solemn as a judge in his silk stockings and knee-breeches, his white cravat and frilled shirt, the major-domo handed the dishes, ready carved, between the guests' shoulders, and flicked the piece you chose onto your plate with his spoon. On the big porcelain stove with its copper rod, the statue of a woman draped to the chin stared fixedly at the roomful of people. (Penguin translation by Alan Russell, 1950; now a Penguin Popular Classic; 197 words)

4. Emma, as she entered the room, felt herself immersed in warmth, a mixture of the scent of flowers and fine linen, the smell of roast meat and the odour of truffles. The candle-flames were mirrored from the curves of silver dishes; the cut glass, blurred under a dull film of moisture, glistened faintly; there were posies in a line along the table; and, on the large-bordered plates, the serviettes, made into the shape of a bishop's mitre, each held a little oval loaf down between their folds. Purple-red lobster claws straddled the plates; fresh fruit was piled in shallow baskets lined with moss; the quails were unplucked, the steam was rising; and, in silk stockings, knee-breeches, white cravat and frilled shirt, solemn as a judge, the butler, handing the dishes, each already carved, between the shoulders of the guests, would drop onto your plate with a sweep of his spoon the very morsel of your choice. On the great copper-railed porcelain stove, the statue of a woman, swathed up to her chin, gazed steadily down upon the crowded room. (Penguin Classics translation by Geoffrey Wall, 1992; 180 words)

5. Here the air was warm and fragrant; the scent of flowers and fine linen mingled with the odor of cooked meats and truffles. Candle-flames cast long gleams on rounded silver dish-covers; the clouded facets of the cut glass shone palely; there was a row of bouquets all down the table; and on the wide-bordered plates the napkins stood like bishops' mitres, each with an oval-shaped roll between its folds. Red lobster claws protruded from platters; oversized fruit was piled up on moss in openwork baskets; quail were served in their plumage; steam rose from open dishes; and the platters of carved meat were brought round by the maître d'hotel himself, grave as a judge in silk stockings, knee breeches, white neckcloth and jabot. He reached them down between the guests, and with a flick of his spoon transferred to each plate the piece desired. Atop the high copper-banded porcelain stove the statue of a woman swathed to the chin in drapery stared down motionless at the company. (Everyman Classics translation by Francis Steegmuller, 1993 [deriving from his translation of 1957]; 168 words)

Four short passages, with their five translations, are now extracted for detailed comment on how the translators have expressed – or in most cases have failed to express – Flaubert's precise meaning:

i. *Les bougies des candélabres allongeaient des flammes sur les cloches d'argent;* (Flaubert)

The silver dish-covers reflected the lighted wax candles in the candelabra, (Marx-Aveling; misses the sense of the 'elongated', 'stretched out' reflections of the candle-flames on the curved dish-covers indicated by *allongeaient*; and *bougies* are simply 'candles', not specifically 'wax candles')

The flames of the candles in the sconces rose long and straight above bell-shaped casings of silver. (Hopkins; *candélabres* are 'candelabra', branched candlesticks, not sconces on the walls; *allongeaient* refers to the reflections of the candle-flames, not to the flames themselves; and *cloches* ['bells'] means 'dish-covers' here)

The candles in the chandeliers glowed on the silver dish-covers with elongated flames. (Russell; gives the sense of *allongeaient* correctly; but *candélabres* are not 'chandeliers'; 'glowed' is not in the original)

The candle-flames were mirrored from the curves of silver dishes; (Wall; *candélabres* is omitted altogether; *allongeaient* is suggested by 'curves', but *cloches* is wrongly translated as 'dishes')

Candle-flames cast long gleams on rounded silver dish-covers; (Steegmuller; *allongeaient* and *cloches* are correctly translated; but *candélabres* is again omitted; and 'gleams' is not in the original)

ii. *tenaient entre le bâillement de leurs deux plis chacune un petit pain de forme ovale.* (Flaubert)

held between its two gaping folds a small oval-shaped roll. (Marx-Aveling; *bâillement* is more than a 'gap' [for which the French word *ouverture* might be used here], it is a 'yawn'; but 'gaping folds' does well enough)

held small oval rolls in the yawning gap between their folds. (Hopkins; this gets the sense perfectly)

each with an oval-shaped roll inside the fold. (Russell; misses the sense of 'yawning gap')

each held a little oval loaf down between their folds. (Wall; misses the sense of 'yawning gap'; and *petit pain* is a 'roll', not a 'little loaf')

each with an oval-shaped roll between its folds. (Steegmuller; misses the sense of 'yawning gap')

iii. *faisait d'un coup de sa cuiller sauter pour vous le morceau qu'on choisissait.* (Flaubert)

with a touch of the spoon gave you the piece chosen. (Marx-Aveling; the point here is that *faisait [...] sauter* the piece of meat with a *coup* of the butler's spoon means 'to make [it] jump' with a 'blow', 'hit' or 'knock' of the spoon; this translation lacks the sense of sharp movement)

with a deft movement of his spoon, picked out for each the portion she had indicated as her choice. (Hopkins; 'deft' is wrong, as is 'picked out'; and *on* should not be translated as 'she' when both men and women were being served)

flicked the piece you chose onto your plate with his spoon. (Russell; 'flicked' gets the sense of the original neatly and concisely)

would drop onto your plate with a sweep of his spoon the very morsel of your choice. (Wall; apart from 'drop onto', this is more or less correct, but lacks the precision of Russell's rendering)

and with a flick of his spoon transferred to each plate the piece desired. (Steegmuller; fairly accurate, but 'transferred' is clumsy)

iv. *le grand poêle de porcelaine à baguette de cuivre,* (Flaubert)

the large stove of porcelain inlaid with copper baguettes (Marx-Aveling; in this extract the main problem is the precise meaning of *à baguette*, which is avoided here simply by repeating the word. The first meaning of *baguette* is 'rod', but long rectangular *baguettes* (like the stones of 'baguette' finger-rings) could be 'inlaid' as decoration in cabinet-making and in some architectural contexts; and this is probably what is meant here.[1] *Cuivre* by itself can mean copper or brass [to be precise you have to say *cuivre-rouge* or *cuivre-jaune*], but brass is a more likely material than copper for use on stoves)

the great porcelain brass-fitted stove, (Hopkins; another solution that avoids the problem, though it is accurate as far as it goes; also the only one to translate *cuivre* as 'brass' rather than 'copper')

the big porcelain stove with its copper rod, (Russell; this can only confuse the reader)

the great copper-railed porcelain stove, (Wall; a brave try, but wrong)

the high copper-banded porcelain stove (Steegmuller; see footnote 1; but brass is the more likely material.)

The result of this survey of the verbal accuracy of the current English translations of *Madame Bovary* comes as something of a shock. The paragraph taken as an example was chosen virtually at random from the French text before I compared it closely with any of the English translations; and, of the twenty renderings of the four sample passages extracted from this paragraph, only three reach a reasonably high standard of accuracy (Marx-Aveling's and Hopkins's translations of the second passage, and Russell's of the third); three are fairly accurate (Wall's and Steegmuller's translations of the third passage, and Hopkins's of the fourth); and the other 14 (70 per cent) all contain serious verbal errors or omissions.[2]

As well as the question of the verbal accuracy of these five translations, we must also ask if they adequately represent the style and balance of Flaubert's prose. Here the answer is not quite so discouraging. Flaubert's sentences tend to be long and mellifluous, and to contain numerous subordinate clauses. In this paragraph, for instance, the sentence describing the appearance and actions of the *maître d'hotel* from *en bas de soie [...]* to *[...] qu'on choisissait* has

---

[1] Nineteenth-century porcelain stoves might also have brass rings round them; and little insulated metal rods that projected for operating the damper and removing tiles for putting in fuel.

[2] Another hair-raising example of mistranslation occurs in Helen Lowe-Porter's versions of Thomas Mann's novels and short stories. Mrs Lowe-Porter, who had a monopoly on translating Mann into English before copyright expired, not only made numerous verbal errors but also omitted whole sentences by mistake, some of them very important ones. See David Luke's Introduction to his translations of Mann's *Death in Venice and Other Stories*, Minerva, London 1996, pp. xlvii–li, which gives chapter and verse.

five short relative clauses before we get to its subject; and the subject is then followed by a long adverbial clause (from *passant* [...] to [...] *découpés*), which leads into an equally long predicate (from *faisait* [...] to [...] *choisissait*). Russell's and Wall's translations follow the pattern of this sentence fairly closely; Marx-Aveling's and Hopkins's versions shift the position of its subject; while Steegmuller radically rearranges its elements and splits it into two. My own feeling is that Geoffrey Wall (number four) makes the best job of the five in giving us the rhythm and flavour of Flaubert's prose; and he does not obscure the movement from Emma's subjective fascination with the scene to the narrator's objective description (which is like the 'steady gaze' of the statue). On the other hand, in three of the four extracts he makes serious verbal errors, and gets only a 'fair' for the fourth.

I find this analysis disturbing. If Flaubert's clear, precise French can be so misrepresented in these recent, standard English translations, how can we feel confident of the verbal accuracy of translations from languages such as Russian with which few readers can claim any acquaintance? There is no comforting answer; and, as I suggested in the Introduction, we can do little more than be aware of what may be happening, and make such allowances for it as we can.

Appendix B

Quotations from original texts
and selected translations

Dante (see pp. 11 and 13 above)

Inferno I

*Nel mezzo del cammin di nostra vita
mi ritrovai per una selva oscura
che la diritta via era smarrita.
Ah quanto a dir qual era è cosa dura
esta selva selvaggia e aspra e forte
che nel pensier rinova la paura!
Tant' è amara che poco è piu morte;
ma per trattar del ben ch'hio vi trovai,
dirò dell'altre cose ch'i' v'ho scorte.*
           (*Inferno* I, 1–9)

In the midway of this our mortal life,
I found me in a gloomy wood, astray
Gone from the path direct: and e'en to tell,
It were no easy task, how savage wild
That forest, how robust and rough its growth,
Which to remember only, my dismay
Renews, in bitterness not far from death.
Yet, to discourse of what there good befel,
All else will I relate discover'd there.
           (Hell I, 1–9, trs. by H. F. Carey, 1814)

Midway this way of life we're bound upon,
   I woke to find myself in a dark wood,
   Where the right road was wholly lost and gone.

Ay me! how hard to speak of it – that rude
   And rough and stubborn forest! the mere breath
   Of memory stirs the old fear in the blood;

223

It is so bitter, it goes nigh to death;
   Yet there I gained such good, that, to convey
   The tale, I'll write what else I found therewith.
     (Hell I, 1–9, trs. by Dorothy L. Sayers 1949,
     Penguin Classics)

Midway along the journey of our life
   I woke to find myself in a dark wood,
   for I had wandered off from the straight path.

How hard it is to tell what it was like,
   this wood of wilderness, savage and stubborn
   (the thought of it brings back all my old fears),

a bitter place! Death could scarce be bitterer.
   But if I would show the good that came of it
   I must talk about things other than the good.
     (Inferno I, 1–9, trs. by Mark Musa 1971,
     Penguin Classics)

Half way along the road we have to go,
I found myself obscured in a great forest,
Bewildered, and I knew I had lost the way.

It is hard to say just what the forest was like,
How wild and rough it was, how overpowering;
Even to remember it makes me afraid.

So bitter is it, death itself is hardly more so;
Yet there was good there, and to make it clear
I will speak of other things that I perceived.
     (Inferno I, 1–9, trs. by C. J. Sisson 1980,
     Oxford World's Classics)

Just halfway through this journey of our life
I reawoke to find myself inside
a dark wood, way off course, the right road lost.
How difficult a task it is to tell
what this wild, harsh, forbidding wood was like
the merest thought of which brings back my fear;
for only death exceeds its bitterness.
But I found goodness there; I'll deal with that
as I describe the various things I saw.
     (Inferno I, 1–9, trs. by Tom Phillips 1990, Thames and Hudson)

(The prose translation of this passage by John D. Sinclair, 1939, is quoted on p. 11 above.)

Inferno V

Noi leggiavamo un giorno per diletto
  di Lancialotto come amor lo strinse:
  soli eravamo e sanza alcun sospetto.
Per piu fïate li occhi ci sospinse
  quella lettura, e scolorocci il viso;
  ma solo un punto fu quel che ci vinse.
Quando leggemmo il disïato riso
  esser baciato da cotanto amante,
  questi, che mai da me non fia diviso,
la bocca mi baciò tutto tremante.
  Galeotto fu il libro e chi lo scrisse:
  quel giorno più non vi leggemmo avante.
(*Inferno* V, 127–38)

Petrarch (see p. 17 above)

Rime sparse

Benedetto sia 'l giorno e 'l mese et l'anno
e la stagione e 'l tempo et l'ora e 'l punto
e 'l bel paese e 'l loco ov' io fui giunto
da' duo begli occhi che legato m'ànno;

et benedetto il primo dolce affanno
ch' i' ebbi ad esser con Amor congiunto,
et l'arco e le saette ond' i' fui punto,
et la piaghe che 'nfin al cor mi vanno.

Benedette le voci tante ch' io
chiamando il nome de mia donna ò sparte,
e i sospiri et la lagrime e 'l desio;

et benedette sian tutte le carte
ov' io fama l'acquisto, e 'l pensier mio,
ch' è sol di lei si ch' altra non v'à parte.
(*Rime sparse*, 61)

Oh blessèd be the day, the month, the year,
the season and the time, the hour, the instant,
the gracious countryside, the place where I
was struck by those two lovely eyes that bound me;

and blessèd be the first sweet agony
I felt when I found myself bound to Love,
the bow and all the arrows that have pierced me,
the wounds that reach the bottom of my heart.

And blessèd be all of the poetry
I scattered, calling out my lady's name,
and all the sighs, and tears, and the desire;

blessèd be all the paper upon which
I earn her fame, and every thought of mine,
only of her, and shared with no one else.

(*Canzoni*, 61, trs. by Mark Musa 1985, Oxford World's
Classics)

Villon (see pp. 23–4, 25 above)

'Ballade des dames du temps jadis'

> *Dictes moy où, n'en quel pays,*
> *Est Flora, la belle Romaine,*
> *Archipiadès ne Thaÿs,*
> *Qui fut sa cousine germaine,*
> *Echo parlant quant bruyt on maine*
> *Dessus riviere ou sur estan,*
> *Qui beaulté ot trop plus qu'umaine.*
> *Mais où sont les neiges d'anten?*

> *Où est la tressaige Esloÿs,*
> *Pour qui chastré [fut] et puis moyne*
> *Piere Esbaillart à Saint Denys?*
> *Pour son amour eust ceste essoyne!*
> *Semblablement, où est la royne*
> *Qui commanda que Buriden*
> *Fut gecté en ung sac en Saine?*
> *Mais où sont les neiges d'anten?*

> *La Royne blanche comme liz,*
> *Qui chantoit à voix de seraine,*
> *Berte au plat pié, Bietrix, Aliz,*
> *Haranburgis qui tint le Maine,*
> *Et Jehanne, la bonne Lorraine,*
> *Qu'Engloys brulerent à Rouen,*
> *Où sont ilz, où, Vierge souveraine?*
> *Mais où sont les neiges d'anten?*

> *Prince, n'enquerrez de sepmaine*
> *Où elles sont, ne de cest an,*
> *Qu'à ce reffraing ne vous remaine:*
> *Mais où sont les neiges d'anten?*

'Ballad of the Dead Ladies'
Tell me now in what hidden way is
    Lady Flora, the lovely Roman?
Where's Hipparchia, and where is Thaïs,
    Neither of them the fairer woman?
Where is Echo, beheld of no man,
Only heard on river or mere,
    She whose beauty was more than human? ...
But where are the snows of yester-year?

Where's Héloïse, the learned nun,
    For whose sake Abeillard, I ween,
Lost manhood and put priesthood on?
    (From love he won such dule and teen!)
    And where, I pray you, is the Queen
Who willed that Buridan should steer
    Sewed in a sack's mouth down the Seine? ...
But where are the snows of yester-year?

White Queen Blanche, like a queen of lilies,
    With a voice like any mermaiden,
Bertha Broadfoot, Beatrice, Alice,
    And Ermengarde the lady of Maine,
    And that good Joan whom Englishmen
At Rouen doomed and burned her there,
    Mother of God, where are they then? ...
But where are the snows of yester-year?

Nay, never ask this week, fair lord,
    Where they are gone, nor yet this year,
Save with thus much for an overword,
    But where are the snows of yester-year?
      (trs. by Dante Gabriel Rosetti)

'Ballade des pendus'

Freres humains, qui après nous vivez,
N'ayez les cueurs contre nous endurcis,
Car, se pitié de nous povres avez,
Dieu en aura plus tost de vous mercis.
Vous nous voiez cy atachez, cinq, six:
Quant de la chair, que trop avons nourrie,
El est pieçà devorée et pourrie,
Et nous, les os, devenons cendre et pouldre.
De nostre mal personne ne se rie,
Mais priez Dieu que tous nous vueille absouldre.
('Ballade des pendus', first stanza)

Ronsard (see pp. 26–8 above)

'Sonnets for Helen'

You will become old. You will learn to knit
And read by candlelight when you are sleepless
The poems here, that made you marvelous.
You were beautiful.
                                    Already drowsy with firelight
And the tedious march of words, you catch
And start. The book makes blessings on you.
It is my name – Ronsard – against your fingers;
A name you have heard spoken with real sound.

I will be tangled in the roots of myrtle,
A boneless ghost, a shadow hovering
Below the skin of earth. You, crippled

With age, will find bare
Memory in your arms – my love, your proud refusal,
And the stripped stem from which the rose has fallen,
And its leaves; unless you take me, living, now.

('Sonnets for Helen' 5, trs. by Nicholas Kilmer
1979, University of California Press)

Cervantes (see pp. 39–40 above)

Don Quixote

At that moment they caught sight of some thirty or forty windmills, which stand on that plain, and as soon as Don Quixote saw them he said to his squire: 'Fortune is guiding our affairs better than we could have wished. Look over there, friend Sancho Panza, where more than thirty monstrous giants appear. I intend to do battle with them and take all their lives. With their spoils we will begin to get rich, for this is a fair war, and it is a great service to God to wipe such a wicked brood from the face of the earth.'

'What giants?' asked Sancho Panza.

'Those you see there,' replied his master, 'with their long arms. Some giants have them about six miles long.'

'Take care, your worship,' said Sancho; 'those things over there are not giants but windmills, and what seem to be their arms are the sails, which are whirled round in the wind and make the millstone turn.'

'It is quite clear,' replied Don Quixote, 'that you are not experienced in this matter of adventures. They are giants, and if you are afraid, go away and say your prayers, while I advance and engage them in fierce and unequal battle.'

As he spoke, he dug his spurs into his steed Rocinante, paying no attention to his squire's shouted warning that beyond all doubt they were windmills and no giants he was advancing to attack. But he went on, so positive that they were giants that he neither listened to Sancho's cries nor noticed what they were, even when he got near them. Instead he went on shouting in a loud voice: 'Do not fly, cowards, vile creatures, for it is one knight alone who assails you.'

At that moment a slight wind arose, and the great sails began to move. At the sight of which Don Quixote shouted: 'Though you wield more arms than the giant Briareus, you shall pay for it!' Saying this, he commended himself with all his soul to his lady Dulcinea, beseeching her aid in his great peril. Then, covering himself with his shield and putting his lance in the rest, he urged Rocinante forward at a full gallop and attacked the nearest windmill, thrusting his lance into the sail. But the wind turned it with such violence that it shivered his weapon in pieces, dragging the horse and his rider with it, and sent the knight rolling badly injured across the plain. Sancho Panza rushed to his assistance as fast as his ass could trot, but when he came up he found that the knight could not stir. Such a shock had Rocinante given him in their fall.

'O my goodness!' cried Sancho. 'Didn't I tell your worship to look what you were doing, for they were only windmills? Nobody could mistake them, unless he had windmills on the brain.'

'Silence, friend Sancho, replied Don Quixote. 'Matters of war are more subject than most to continual change. What is more, I think – and that is the truth – that the same sage Friston who robbed me of my room and my books has turned those giants into windmills, to cheat me of the glory of conquering them. Such is the enmity he bears me; but in the very end his black arts shall avail him little against the goodness of my sword.'

'God send it as He will,' replied Sancho Panza, helping the knight to get up and remount Rocinante, whose shoulders were half dislocated.

(*Don Quixote*, pt I, ch. 8, trs. by J. M. Cohen 1950, Penguin Classics)

Molière (see pp. 43–4 above)

Tartuffe

(1) TARTUFFE   (apercevant Dorine)
Laurent, serrez ma haire avec ma discipline,
Et priez que toujours le Ciel vous illumine.
Si l'on vient pour me voir, je vais aux prisonniers
Des aumônes que j'ai partager les deniers.

DORINE   *Que d'affectation et de forfanterie!*

TARTUFFE   *Que voulez-vous?*

DORINE   *Vous dire ...*

TARTUFFE   (il tire un mouchoir de sa poche)
                               Ah! mon Dieu, je vous prie,

Avant que de parler prenez-moi ce mouchoir.

DORINE *Comment?*

TARTUFFE   *Couvrez ce sein que je ne saurois voir:*
Par de pareils objets les âmes sont blessées,
Et cela fait venir de coupables pensées.

(2) TARTUFFE   *Laissez-moi vite, en m'éloignant d'ici,*
Leur ôter tout sujet de m'attaquer ainsi.

ORGON *Non, vous demeurerez: il y va de ma vie.*

TARTUFFE *Hé bien! il faudra donc que je me mortifie.*
Pourtant, si vous vouliez ...

ORGON   *Ah!*

TARTUFFE   *Soit: n'en parlons plus.*
Mais je sais comme il faut en user là-dessus.
L'honneur est délicat, et l'amitié m'engage
À prévenir les bruits et les sujets d'ombrage.
Je fuirai votre épouse, et vous ne me verrez ...

ORGON *Non, en dépit de tous, vous la fréquenterez.*
Faire enrager le monde est ma plus grande joie,
Et je veux qu'à toute heure avec elle on vous voie.
Ce n'est pas tout encore: pour les mieux braver tous,
Je ne veux point avoir d'autre héritier que vous,
Et je vais de ce pas, en fort bonne manière,
Vous faire de mon bien donation entière.
Un bon et franc ami, que pour gendre je prends,
M'est bien plus cher que fils, que femme, et que parents.
N'accepterez-vous pas ce que je vous propose?

TARTUFFE *La volonté du Ciel soit faite en toute chose.*

ORGON *Le pauvre homme! Allons vite en dresser un écrit,*
Et que puisse l'envie en crever de dépit!
        (*Tartuffe*, lines 853–62, 1163–84)

Goethe (see pp. 65–6 above)

Faust

MEPHISTOPHELES (tritt, indem der Nebel fällt, gekleidet wie ein fahrender
Scholastikus, hinter dem Ofen hervor)
Wozu der Lärm? was steht dem Herrn zu Diensten?

FAUST *Das also war des Pudels Kern!*
Ein fahrender Scholast? Der Casus macht mich lachen.

MEPH. *Ich salutiere den gelehrten Herrn!*
Ihr habt mich weidlich schwitzen machen.

FAUST *Wie nennst du dich?*

MEPH.   *Die Frage scheint mir klein*
Für einen, der das Wort so sehr verachtet,
Der, weit entfernt von allem Schein,
Nur in der Wesen Tiefe trachtet.

FAUST *Bei euch, ihr Herrn, kann man das Wesen*
Gewöhnlich aus dem Namen lesen,
Wo es sich allzudeutlich weist,
Wenn man euch Fliegengott, Verderber, Lügner heisst.
Nun gut, wer bist du denn?

MEPH.   *Ein Teil von jener Kraft,*
Die stets das Böse will und stets das Gute schafft.

FAUST *Was ist mit diesem Rätselwort gemeint?*

MEPH. *Ich bin der Geist, der stets verneint!*
Und das mit Recht; denn alles, was entsteht,
Ist wert, dass es zugrunde geht;
Drum besser wär's, dass nichts entstünde.
So ist denn alles, was ihr Sünde,
Zerstörung, kurz das Böse nennt,
Mein eigentliches Element.
   (*Faust*, Part I, lines 1322–44)

Schiller (see pp. 72–3 above)

Die Piccólomini

Mein bester Sohn! Es ist nicht immer möglich,
Im Leben sich so kinderrein zu halten,
Wie's uns die Stimme lehrt im Innersten.
In steter Notwehr gegen arge List
Bleibt auch das redliche Gemüt nicht wahr.
Das eben ist der Fluch der bösen Tat,
Dass sie, fortzeugend, immer Böses muss gebären.
Ich klügle nicht, ich tue meine Pflicht,
Der Kaiser schreibt mir mein Betragen vor.
Wohl wär' es besser, überall dem Herzen
Zu folgen, doch darüber würde man
Sich manchen guten Zweck versagen müssen.
Hier gilt's, mein Sohn, dem Kaiser wohl zu dienen,
Das Herz mag dazu sprechen, was es will.
   (*Die Piccolómini*, V, 1.3554–67)

Dear son, it is not always possible
Still to preserve that infant purity
Which the voice teaches in our inmost heart.
Still in alarm, for ever on the watch
Against the wiles of wicked men, e'en Virtue
Will sometimes bear away her outward robes
Soiled in the wrestle with Iniquity.
This is the curse of every evil deed,
That, propagating still, it brings forth evil.
I do not cheat my better soul with sophisms:
I but perform my orders; the Emperor
Prescribes my conduct to me. Dearest boy,
Far better were it, doubtless, if we all
Obeyed the heart at all times; but so doing,
In this our present sojourn with bad men,
We must abandon many an honest object.
'Tis now our call to serve the Emperor,
By what means he can best be served – the heart
May whisper what it will – this is our call!
  (*The Piccolómini*, III, 1, 206–24, trs. by
  S. T. Coleridge 1800)

Wallenteins Tod

Wär's möglich? Könnt' ich nicht mehr, wie ich wollte?
Nicht mehr zurück, wie mir's beliebt? Ich müsste
Die Tat vollbringen, weil ich sie gedacht [...]

Bahnlos liegt's hinter mir, und einer Mauer
Aus meinen eignen Werken baut sich auf,
Die mir die Umkehr türmend hemmt!
  (*Wallenteins Tod*, I, 4, 3897–9, 3914–6)

              Is it possible?
Is't so? I can no longer what I would?
No longer draw back at my liking? I
Must do the deed because I thought of it [...]

No road, no track behind me, but a wall,
Impenetrable, insurmountable,
Rises obedient to the spells I muttered
And meant not – my own doings tower behind me.
  (trs. by S. T. Coleridge, 1800[1]

What? I, no longer act as I might choose?
No longer turn back if I wanted? Must
The deed be *done* because I *thought* of it? [...]

---

[1] Coleridge's Act IV scene 4.

All paths cut off behind me, and a wall
Arises, piled on high, of my own building,
A barrier to all return!
    (trs. by F. J. Lamport 1979, Penguin Classics)

Can it be true? Are all my options closed?
Retreat impossible if I should choose?
Must I *perform* the thing I merely *thought*? [...]

Trackless terrain behind me, and a wall
Built of my own actions towering up
To block retreat.
    (trs. by T. J. Reed 1991, Oxford University Press)

Púshkin (see pp. 82–3 above)

Eugene Onégin

'My uncle, man of firm convictions ...
By falling gravely ill, he's won
A due respect for his afflictions –
The only clever thing he's done.
May his example profit others;
But God, what deadly boredom, brothers,
To tend a sick man night and day,
Not daring once to steal away!
And, oh, how base to pamper grossly
And entertain the nearly dead
To fluff the pillows for his head,
And pass him medicines morosely –
While thinking under every sigh:
The devil take you, Uncle. Die!'

*   *   *

He lay quite still and past all feeling;
His languid brow looked strange at rest.
The steaming blood poured forth, revealing
The gaping wound beneath his breast.
One moment back – a breath's duration –
This heart still throbbed with inspiration;
Its hatreds, hopes, and loves still beat,
Its blood ran hot with life's own heat.
But now, as in a house deserted,
Inside it – all is hushed and stark,
Gone silent and forever dark.
The window boards have been inserted,
The panes chalked white. The owner's fled;

But where, God knows. All trace is dead.
(*Eugene Onégin*, 1, 1, 6.32, trs. by James E. Falen
1990, Oxford World's Classics)

Baudelaire (see pp. 113–14 above)

Un Voyage à Cythére

*Mon coeur, comme un oiseau, voltigeait tout joyeux
Et planait librement à l'entour des cordages;
Le navire roulait sous un ciel sans nuages,
Comme un ange enivré d'un soleil radieux.*

*Quelle est cette île triste et noire? – C'est Cythère,
Nous dit-on, un pays fameux dans les chansons,
Eldorado banal de tous les vieux garçons.
Regardez, après tout, c'est une pauvre terre. [...]*

*– Cythère n'était plus qu'un terrain des plus maigres,
Un désert rocailleux troublé par des cris aigres.
J'entrevoyais pourtant un object singulier!*

*Ce n'était pas un temple aux ombres bocagères,
Où la jeune prêtresse, amoureuse des fleurs,
Allait, le corps brûlé de secrètes chaleurs,
Entre-bâillant sa robe aux brises passagères;*

*Mais voilà qu'en rasant la côte d'assez près
Pour troubler les oiseux avec nos voiles blanches,
Nous vîmes que c'était un gibet à trois branches,
Du ciel se détachant en noir, comme un cyprès.*

*De féroces oiseaux perchés sur leur pâture
Détruisaient avec rage un pendu déjà mûr,
Chacun plantant, comme un outil, son bec impur
Dans tous les coins saignants de cette pourriture;*

*Les yeux étaient deux trous, et du ventre effondré
Les intestins pesants lui coulaient sur les cuisses,
Et ses bourreaux, gorgés de hideuses délices,
L'avaient à coups de bec absolument châtré. [...]*

Ridicule pendu, tes douleurs sont les miennes! [...]

*– Le ciel était charmant, la mer était unie;
Pour moi tout était noir et sanglant désormais,
Hélas! et j'avais, comme en un suaire épais,
Le coeur enseveli dans cette allégorie.*

Dans ton île, ô Vénus! je n'ai trouvé debout
Qu'un gibet symbolique où pendait mon image.
– Ah! Seigneur! donnez-moi la force et le courage
De contempler mon coeur et mon corps sans dégoût!

Rimbaud (see pp. 118–19 above)

Ma Bohème (Fantaisie)

Je m'en allais, les poings dans mes poches crevées;
Mon paletot aussi devenait idéal;
J'allais sous le ciel, Muse! et j'étais ton féal;
Oh! là là! que d'amours splendides j'ai rêvées!

Mon unique culotte avait un large trou.
– Petit Poucet rêveur, j'égrenais dans ma course
Des rimes. Mon auberge était à la Grande-Ourse.
– Mes étoiles au ciel avaient un doux frou-frou.

Et je les écoutais, assis au bord des routes,
Ces bons soirs de septembre où je sentais des gouttes
De rosée à mon front, comme un vin de vigueur;

Où, rimant au milieu des ombres fantastiques,
Comme des lyres, je tirais les élastiques
De mes souliers blessés, un pied près de mon coeur!

My Gipsy Days

Off I would go, with fists into torn pockets pressed.
My overcoat became a wrap of mystery.
Under the great sky, Muse, I was your devotee.
Eh, what fine dreams I had, each one an amorous gest!

My only trousers gaped behind; and thus I went
Tom Thumb the dreamer, husking out some lyric line.
My nightly inn had always the Great Bear for sign.
My stars moved with a silken rustle of content.

And often, sitting by the roadside, I would listen,
On calm September evenings, with fine dew a-glisten
Upon my brow, like drops of cordial, sweet yet tart;

Where, rhyming in these shadowy, fantastic places,
As if I played a lyre, I'd gently pluck the laces
Of my burst boots, one foot hugged tight against my heart!
(trs. by Norman Cameron 1942, Anvil Press Poetry)

Les Chercheuses de poux

Quand le front de l'enfant, plein de rouges tourmentes,
Implore l'essaim blanc des rêves indistincts,
Il vient près de son lit deux grandes soeurs charmantes
Avec de frêles doigts aux ongles argentins.

Elles assoient l'enfant devant une croisée
Grande ouverte où l'air bleu baigne un fouillis de fleurs,
Et dans ses lourds cheveux où tombe la rosée
Promènent leurs doigts fins, terribles et charmeurs.

Il écoute chanter leurs haleines craintives
Qui fleurent de longs miels végétaux et rosés,
Et qu'interrompt parfois un sifflement, salives
Reprises sur la lèvre ou désirs de baisers.

Il entend leurs cils noirs battant sous les silences
Parfumés; et leurs doigts électriques et doux
Font crépiter parmi ses grises indolences
Sous leurs ongles royaux la mort des petits poux.

Voilà que monte en lui le vin de la Paresse,
Soupir d'harmonica qui pourrait délirer;
L'enfant se sent, selon la lenteur des caresses,
Sourdre et mourir sans cesse un désir de pleurer.

The Seekers of Lice

When the child's head, full of red torments, implores the white swarm of indistinct dreams, there come near his bed two charming grownup sisters with slim fingers and silvery nails.

They sit the child down in front of a casement, wide open to where the blue air bathes a tangle of flowers, and in his heavy hair on which the dew falls, their fine, fearful, magical fingers go moving.

He listens to the sigh of their apprehensive breath which smells of long roseate honeys of plants, and is interrupted now and then by a hiss: spittle caught on the lip or wishes for kisses.

He hears their dark eyelashes beating in the odorous silence; and their fingers, electrical, sweet, among his grey indolences make the deaths of the little lice crackle under their sovereign nails.

It is then that there rises in him the wine of Sloth; a sigh [like the resonance of a (glass)] harmonica, which could induce delirium; the child feels, according to the slowness of their caresses, surging and dying away continually a desire to cry.

(trs. by Oliver Bernard 1962, Penguin Classics)

Proust (see p. 188 above)

À la recherche du temps perdu

Et il y eut un jour aussi où elle me dit: 'Vous savez, vous pouvez m'appeler Gilberte, en tout cas moi, je vous appellerai par votre nom de baptême. C'est trop gênant.' Pourtant elle continua encore un moment à se contenter de me dire 'vous', et comme je lui faisais remarquer, elle sourit, et composant, construisant une phrase comme celles qui dans les grammaires étrangères n'ont d'autre but que de nous faire employer un mot nouveau, elle la termina par mon petit nom. Et me souvenant plus tard de ce que j'avais senti alors, j'y ai démêlé l'impression d'avoir été tenu un instant dans sa bouche, moi-même, nu, sans plus aucune des modalités sociales qui appartenaient aussi, soit à ses autres camarades, soit, quand elle disait mon nom de famille, à mes parents, et dont ses lèvres – en l'effort qu'elle faisait, un peu comme son père, pour articuler les mots qu'elle voulait mettre en valeur – eurent l'air de me dépouiller, de me dévêtir, comme de sa peau un fruit dont on ne peut avaler que la pulpe, tandis que son regard, se mettant au même degré nouveau d'intimité que prenait sa parole, m'atteignait aussi plus directement, non sans témoigner la conscience, le plaisir et jusque la gratitude qu'il en avait, en se faisant accompagner d'un sourire.

(*À la recherche du temps perdu*, II, Gallimard, pp. 249–50)

Brecht (see pp. 25, 215 and 227 above)

The Threepenny Opera

You fellow men who live on after us
Pray do not think you have to judge us harshly
And when you see us hoisted up and trussed
Don't laugh like fools behind your big moustaches
Or curse at us. It's true that we came crashing
But do not judge our downfall like the courts.
Not all of us can discipline our thoughts –
Dear fellows, your extravagance needs slashing.
Dear fellows, we've shown how a crash begins.
Pray then to God that He forgive my sins.

('Macheath Begs for Forgiveness', stanza 1, *The Threepenny Opera*, trs. by Ralph Manheim and John Willett 1979, Methuen)

Appendix C

The form and pronunciation of Russian names[1]

Form

Russian personal names take the form: Christian name + patronymic + surname; and women's names carry feminine suffixes: thus we have Vladímir Ilých Uliánov (Lenin) and Mária Ilínichna Uliánova (Lenin's sister). The normal, non-intimate, form of address is Christian name + patronymic, and this is used (within limits) both ways between superiors and inferiors as well as between equals. In conversation and correspondence the second-person pronoun (you) takes the singular (*ty*) or plural (*vy*) according to the degree of intimacy, superiority, or inferiority that is involved, as in French (*tu, vous*) and German (*du, Sie*); but this can rarely be indicated in English translations which are limited to 'you'.

Pronunciation

Like English, Russian is a stressed language, but the stressing of Russian names follows no obvious rules. For instance, the personal surnames 'Petróv' and 'Oblónsky' are stressed on the second syllable, but 'Flérov'[2] and 'Kérensky' are stressed on the first; again, 'Turgénev' is stressed on the second syllable (with the unstressed 'e' pronounced 'ye'), but 'Gorbachëv' is stressed on the third (with 'ë', which is always stressed, pronounced 'yó'). There are similar inconsistencies in place names: for example, there is 'Khárkov' but 'Tambóv'.

Since there is no way of telling for certain how an unfamiliar

---

[1] I am most grateful to Mrs Kitty Stidworthy for her help with this appendix and with the transliteration and stressing of the Russian names in the text.

[2] Though occasionally 'Fleróv'; similarly 'Maria' is sometimes pronounced 'Mária', sometimes 'María'.

Russian name is pronounced, we have to rely on the minority of those lexicographers, translators, historians, and critics who supply stress marks (as I have done here) when they transcribe Russian names. Contance Garnett's translations of Turgénev, Dostoévsky, and Tolstóy, and the Maude translations of Tolstóy, are particularly helpful in including lists of the characters' names with the stresses marked; and Richard Pipes's histories of twentieth-century Russia have stresses marked on the principal names in the indexes.

Transliteration

I have used the Library of Congress system for transliterating the Russian alphabet, but (1) retaining the final '-y' for '-i' and '-sky' for '-skii' in names that have become well-established (for instance 'Tolstóy' rather than 'Tolstói', 'Vrónsky' rather than 'Vrónskii'); and (2) omitting the apostrophe for the 'soft sign'.

Note that, in pronouncing transliterated Russian names,

    a = a in 'father'
    e = ê in 'fête'
    ë (always stressed) = yo in 'yonder'
    i = ee in 'meet' (but pronounced after a, e, o like
       'say', 'eye', 'boy')
    o = o in 'loch' (longer than in 'hot')
    u = oo in 'hoot'
    y = i in 'hit'

Appendix D

The value of money in the mid- to late-nineteenth century

It is notoriously difficult to translate the value of the money of other times and other places into today's currency, both because the relative value of commodities differs so widely between then and now, and because some of the things we buy now were not available in the past. For instance, the proportion of the average lower-middle-class income that would pay the wages of an indoor servant in the nineteenth-century was far less – by a factor of about ten – than the proportion that would be required for an indoor servant now; while a hundred years ago such things as simple domestic central-heating systems, microwave ovens, and washing machines (which take the place of indoor servants) could not be bought at all.

Nevertheless a rough idea of the value of the pound sterling of the mid- to late nineteenth century in today's currency may be had by multiplying it by fifty. This means that a meal in a modest restaurant, say, costing 2s (10p) then would now cost £5; and that the fourteen roubles (see below) Lévin paid for his share of a meal at an expensive Moscow restaurant would now be just under £50. A skilled tradesman earning £250 a year (more or less tax free) would now have £12,500 (£240 a week) after tax. An inheritance of £20,000 would now equal something like a million pounds (with no inheritance tax); and, in *The Importance of Being Earnest* (1895), Cecily Cardew's £130,000 'in the Funds' would now be worth a serious £6,500,000 – hence Lady Bracknell's interest.

Foreign currencies are even more difficult to translate, because their purchasing power did not always agree with the exchange rate, which itself fluctuated against the pound. However we can say that, in the mid- to late nineteenth century, the French franc was worth roughly 9½d (4p), the Russian rouble about 1s 5d (7p), and the German mark about 1s (5p). Multiplying these figures by fifty, we get one nineteenth-century French franc to about £2 in today's money, one Russian rouble to about £3.50, and one German mark to about £2.50. The value of the Norwegian and Swedish krone was roughly the same as that of the German mark.

The table of the value of nineteenth-century currencies below gives the approximate values in today's pounds sterling of 1/10 to 10,000 nineteenth-century pounds, francs, roubles, marks, and kroner.

Units	Pounds	Francs[1]	Roubles	Marks/Kroner
1/10	£ 5	£ 0.20	£ 0.35	£ 0.25
½	£ 25	£ 1.00	£ 1.75	£ 1.25
1	£ 50	£ 2.00	£ 3.50	£ 2.50
5	£ 250	£ 10.00	£ 17.50	£ 12.50
10	£ 500	£ 20.00	£ 35.00	£ 25.00
50	£ 2,500	£ 100.00	£ 175.00	£ 125.00
100	£ 5,000	£ 200.00	£ 350.00	£ 250.00
500	£ 25,000	£ 1,000	£ 1,750	£ 1,250
1000	£ 50,000	£ 2,000	£ 3,500	£ 2,500
10000	£500,000	£20,000	£35,000	£25,000

[1] In nineteenth-century French novels fractions of a franc were sometimes reckoned in 'sous', the sou being a pre-Revolutionary unit of currency. The convention was that one sou = five centimes, so that twenty sous = one franc, or about £2 today. The 20-franc gold piece (worth about 16s, or four-fifths of a British sovereign) was sometimes called a *louis*.

Copyright Acknowledgements

For permission to reprint copyright material, the publishers would like to thank: Harvard University Press for *Petrarch's Lyric Poems* by Robert M. Durling © 1976 by Robert M. Durling, reprinted by permission of Harvard University Press; Thames & Hudson for Dante *Inferno* V. 127–38 by Tom Phillips © 1989, Tom Phillips, reprinted by permission of Thames & Hudson; Grant & Cutler for Villon, *Poems*, translated by John Fox © 1984, John Fox, reprinted by permission of Grant & Cutler; A. P. Watt Ltd on behalf of Michael B. Yeats for 'When You Are Old' in *The Rose* by W. B. Yeats © 1950, A. P. Watt Ltd, reprinted by permission of A. P. Watt Ltd; Oxford University Press for Goethe's *Faust* Part I translated by David Luke © 1987, David Luke, reprinted by permission of Oxford University Press; Anvil Press Poetry for 'The Lice Pickers' taken from *Rimbaud: A Season in Hell & Other Poems* translated by Norman Cameron, published by Anvil Press Poetry in 1994; Bodley Head for Dante *Inferno I* translated by John Sinclair © 1939, John Sinclair, reprinted by permission of Bodley Head; Penguin Books Ltd for Friedrich Schiller, *The Piccolómini*, V.1.3554–67 translated by F. J. Lamport © 1979, F. J. Lamport, reprinted by permission of Penguin Books Ltd; Penguin Books Ltd for 'Correspondences' from *Baudelaire*, translated by Francis Scarfe © 1961, Francis Scarfe, reprinted by permission of Penguin Books Ltd; Penguin Books Ltd for 'Un Voyage à Cythère' from *Baudelaire*, translated by Francis Scarfe © 1961, Francis Scarfe, reprinted by permission of Penguin Books Ltd; Penguin Books Ltd for 'Ma Bohème' from Arthur Rimbaud, *Collected Poems*, translated by Oliver Bernard © 1997, Oliver Bernard, reprinted by permission of Penguin Books Ltd; Penguin Books Ltd for 'Vigils I' from Arthur Rimbaud, *Collected Poems*, translated by Oliver Bernard © 1997, Oliver Bernard, reprinted by permission of Penguin Books Ltd.

Every effort has been made to trace copyright holders but if any have inadvertantly been overlooked, the publishers will be pleased to make the necessary acknowledgements at the first opportunity.

242

Index

Main entries are given in **bold type**; the Further reading sections are not indexed.

Académie Française, 110
adultery, novels of, 98–9, 99n, 101
  see *Ánna Karénina*; *Effie Briest*;
  Madame Bovary; women and adultery
  in the 19th century
Agrigento, 208, 208n
À la recherche du temps perdu, 57, 177n,
  184, 187–90, 237
  title 185n
Alexander I, 77
Alexander II, 77, 80, 121–2, 124, 160–1
Alexander III, 77, 122, 161, 162
Anacreon, 26
Andréeva, María, 168
Ánna Karénina, 10n, 80, 98, 105, 121,
  122, 123, 124n, 127, 129, **130–4**,
  137, 183
Anthès, Georges d', 81, 86
Arouet, François-Marie *see* Voltaire
Arthurian legend, 13n
Arup, Jens, 149
Auden, W. H., 194n
Aufklärung, Die, 60
Aufricht, Ernst-Josef, 214
Augustin, St, 54
Aupick, Jacques, 109, 110
Austen, Jane, 164
Austro-Hungarian Empire, 192
Avignon, 15
Avsey, Ignat, 137n, 140

Bach, J. S., 60
Bakúnin, Mikháil, 123, 161
ballade, 23–5
Ballade des dames du temps jadis, 23–4

Ballade des pendus, 24–5, 215
Balzac, Honoré de, 92–3, **93–7** appearance
  94n, 167
  Comédie humaine, La, 93, 176
  Cousine Bette, La, 93
  Cromwell, 93
  Dernier Chouan, Le, 93
  Eugénie Grandet, 93
  Illusions perdus, Les, 93
  Peau de chagrin, La, 93
  Père Goriot, Le, 93, 94–7, 104; title 94n
Baudelaire, Charles, 108, **109–14**, 115
  'Au lecteur', 110, 111
  'Correspondances', 111–13
  Épaves, Les, 110
  Fanfarlo, La, 110
  Fleurs du mal, Les, 110, 110n, 111–14
  Lesbiennes, Les, 110
  Limbes, Les, 110
  'Voyage à Cythère, Un', 111, 113–14,
  234–5
Bauer, Felice, 201, 203
Baum, Oskar, 200
Beatrice (Portinari), Dante's, 9–10, 12, 16
Beckett, Samuel, 156, 212
Beethoven, L. van, 60, 69n
Behrs, Sófia Andréevna, 129–30, 208n
Belínsky, V. G., 86, 135
Bergmann, Hugo, 200
Berlau, Ruth, 213
Berlin, Isaiah, 128, quoted 130n
Bernard, Oliver, 118–19, 236
Binyon, Laurence, 14
Bismarck, Prince, 108, 173
Bjørnson, Bjørnsterne, 158

Bloch, Greta, 201, 203
Bloom, Harold, 1
Bosse, Harriet, 151
Brandauer, Klaus Maria, 66n
Brecht, Bertolt, 1, 156, **212–16**
   Baal, 213
   Caucasian Chalk Circle, The, 214
   Fear and Misery of the Third Reich, 214
   Good Person of Szechwan, The, 214
   In the Jungle of Cities, 213
   Life of Galileo, 214
   Man is Man, 213
   Mother Courage and her Children, 214
   Threepenny Opera, The, 213, 214–15,
      237; 'Mac the Knife', 215
      see Gay, John, *Beggar's Opera, The*
Briggs, A. D. P., 4n, 82
Brod, Max, 200, 201, 203, 203n
Brooks, Jeremy, 171
Brothers Karamázov, The, 121, 124n,
   132n, 136, **137–40**
   title 137n
Browning, Robert, 124
Búdberg, Móura, 168
Butt, John, 51
Byron, Lord, 61, 87, 88

Candide, **49–51**
canon, literary, 1–2
Calderón, Pedro, 35
Calvin, John, 52
Cameron, Norman, 118, 120, 235
Carey, H. F., 14
Carlyle, Jane and Thomas, 124
Catherine de' Medici, 26
Catullus, 26
Cavalcanti, Guido, 17
Cave, Terence, 105
Cellini, Benvenuto, 54
Cervantes Saavedra, Miguel de, 35, **36–41**
   Don Quixote, 38–41, 105n, 111, 228–9
   Galatea, La, 37
   Persiles y Sigismunda, 38
Cézanne, Paul, 175
characters, reappearing, 96, 176–7
Charles X, 91, 92
Charpentier, Georges, 176
Chassaigne, Françoise de, 29
Châtelet, Marquise du, 47
Chaucer, Geoffrey, 16
Chékhov, Antón Pávlovich, 152, **162–6**,

   168, 197, 208
   Cherry Orchard, The, 163, 164–6
   'Dreary Story, A', 163
   Ivánov, 163
   'Lady with a Dog', 163
   'Peasants', 80, 127, 163
   'Russian Master, The', 163
   Seagull, The, 163
   'Steppe, The', 162
   Three Sisters, 163
   Uncle Vánia, 163
   'Ward Number Six', 163
Cherry Orchard, The, 163, **164–6**
Christiania (Oslo), 142n, 157
Cicero, 15
Cohen, J. M., 41, 58, 228–9
Coleridge, S. T., 2, 69, 73, 232
Colet, Louise, 97–8
Collier, Peter, 181
Commune, Paris, 92, 108, 173
Communism, 206–7, 213–14, 216
Comte, Auguste, 176
Confessions, of Rousseau, **54–8**
Conrad, Joseph, 139, 175, 193, 197
Contemporary, The, 122, 124
Corneille, Pierre, 36
Crawford, M. A., 96–7
Croce, Benedetto, 208

Dante Alighieri, 1, 2, **9–15**, 17
   Divine Comedy, The, 1, 10, 11–15, 111,
      223–5
   Vita Nuova, La, 10
Death in Venice, 195, **196–8**
Denmark *see* Scandinavia
Denny, Norman, quoted 5–6
deterministic positivism, 176
Diamant, Dora, 202
Dickens, Charles, 93, 99n, 130, 167
Diderot, Denis, 47, 52
director, producer, 207n
Disputatio nova contra mulieres, 31n
Divine Comedy, The, 1, 10, **11–15**, 111,
   223–5
divorce *see* women and adultery
Doll's House, A, 2, 102, 145, **146–9**, 150,
   165
Donati, Gemma, 10
Don Quixote, **38–41**, 105n, 111, 228–9
Dostoévsky, Fiódor Mikháilovich, 85, 89,
   122, **134–40**, 155, 162, 167, 193

Brothers Karamázov, The, 121, 124n, 132n, 136, 137–40; title 137n
Crime and Punishment, 121, 136
Devils (The Possessed), 121, 135, 136
Gambler, The, 136
Idiot, The, 121, 135, 136
Memoirs from the House of the Dead, 135
Poor Folk, 135, 136, 162
Writer's Diary, 136
Dostoévsky, Mikháil, 135, 136
Dreyfus, Alfred, 173, 178–9, 178n, 186
Drury, A., 45
Dryden, John, quoted 4–5
Durling, R. M., quoted 4, 17, 18
Duval, Jeanne, 109

Effi Briest, 99, 105n, 182, 183–4, 187
Eliot, George, 93, 94n, 99n, 124
Middlemarch, 130–1
Eliot, T. S., 113, 175, 206n
Encyclopédie, 47, 49, 52
Enlightenment, The, 53, 60, 68
Essays of Montaigne, 30–3
Essen, Siri von, 150
Eugene Onégin, 82–5, 89, 121, 233–4
Everyman Classics, 6
Expressionism, 152, 152n

Falen, James E., 4n, 85, 233–4
Fascism, 206–7, 209
Fathers and Children, 2, 121, 124, 125–8, 132n, 135
Faulkner, William, 193
Faust, 62, 63–7, 70, 111, 198, 230–1
Fen, Elisaveta, 166
Ferdinand II, 70
Ferney, Château de, 49
First Empire, French, 92
Flaubert, Gustave, 93, 94n, 97–8, 103–5, 167, 183n
Bouvard et Pécuchet, 98
Education sentimentale, L', 98
Madame Bovary, 6, 98, 103–5, 110, 183, 217–22
Salammbô, 98
Temptation of St Anthony, The, 98
Three Stories, 98
Fleurs du mal, Les, 111–14
Florence, 8–10
Fontane, Theodor, 175, 181–4

Adulterá, L', 182
Effi Briest, 99, 105n, 182, 183–4, 187
Frau Jenny Treibel, 182
Irrungen Wirrungen, 182
Poggenpuhls, Die, 182
Schach von Wuthenow, 182
Stechlin, Der, 182
Unwiederbringlich, 182
Vor dem Sturm, 182
Foote, Paul, 89
Ford, Ford Madox, 193
Forster, E. M., 193
Fox, John, 24, 25
France
  history of, 19–20, 36, 46–7, 91–3, 107–8, 173–5, 206–7; Commune, 92, 108, 173; First Empire, 92; Franco-Prussian War, 98, 108, 173, 182; July Monarchy, 91, 92; Republics, 91, 92, 107, 173; Restoration, 91, 92; Revolutionary Calendar, 179; Revolutions, 8, 51, 53, 62, 69, 91, 92, 107–8; Second Empire, 107–8, 115, 173; table of governments, 92
  self-esteem of, 36, 108, 175
  see verse, forms of, French
Francis of Assisi, St, 9
Franco-Prussian War, 98, 108, 173, 182
Frayn, Michael, 166
Frazer, Sir James, *Golden Bough, The*, 193
Frederick II, the Great, 48, 59–60, 61
Freeborn, Richard, 127, 128

Garibaldi, Giuseppe, 208
Garnett, Constance, 127, 134, 140, 239
Gaskell, Elizabeth, 93, 99n
Gautier, Théophile, 108
Gay, John, *Beggar's Opera, The*, 214–15
Geneva, 47, 52, 53–4, 54
Germany
  history of, 59–60, 173–5, 181–2, 192, 206–7; Second Reich, 173–4; Third Reich, 195, 206
Germinal, 177, 179–81, 187
Ghibellines, 9
Gide, André, 156, 181
Gielgud, Sir John, 15
Gissing, George, 94n
Goethe, Johann Wolfgang von, 2, 3, 60–7, 70, 71, 81, 193
Egmont, 62

Elective Affinities, 62
Faust, 62, 63–7, 70, 111, 198, 230–1
Götz von Berlichingen, 60
Iphigenie, 62
Sorrows of Young Werther, The, 60–1
Tasso, 62
Wilhelm Meister, 57, 62, 63
Gógol, N. V., 124, 135
Dead Souls, 121
Goncharóva, Natálya, 81
Goncharóv, Iván Alexándrovich, 86, 167
Oblómov, 121
Górky, Maxím, 152, 156, **166–71**
Fomá Gordéev, 168
In the World (My Apprenticeship), 169
Lower Depths, The, 165, 168, 169–71
My Childhood, 169
My Universities, 169
Petty Bourgeois, The, 168
Sketches and Stories, 168
Three of Them, The, 168
Górky (Nízhni Nívgorod), 166, 166n
Grazhdanín, 136
Grigoróvich, Dmítri, 135, 162
Guelphs, 9

Hamsun, Knut, 139, 143, **154–8**, 193
Children of the Age, The, 156
Growth of the Soil, The, 156
Hunger, 57, 155, 156, 157–8
Kareno trilogy, 155
Mysteries, 155
Pan, 155
Ring is Closed, The, 156
Swarming, 155–6
Victoria, 155
Women at the Pump, The, 156
Händel, G. F., 60
Hardy, Emma, 208n
Hardy, Thomas, 80n, 94n
Jude the Obscure, 99n
Woodlanders, The, 99n
Hauptmann, Elisabeth, 213, 214
Haussmann, Baron G. E., 108
Haydn, Josef, 60
Hemingway, Ernest, 156
Henri II, 25
Henri IV, 48
Henry V, 19
Herder, J. G., 60
Hero of Our Time, A, 5, 87–90, 121

Herrick, Robert, 28
Hérzen, Alexánder, 70, 86, 123, 161
Hesse, Hermann, 156
Hingley, Ronald, 163n, 166
Hitler, Adolf, 157, 195, 206, 213
Homer, *Odyssey*, 6
Hopkins, Gerard, 218–22
Horace, 26, 28, 28n
Hugo, Victor, *Les Misérables*, 5–6
Hume, David, 54
Hundred Years' War, 19, 22
Hunger, 57, 155, 156, **157–8**
Hunter-Blair, Kitty, 171

Ibsen, Henrik, 2, 94n, 142, 143, **144–9**,
151, 153–4, 207
Brand, 64, 144–5
Catiline, 144
Doll's House, A, 2, 102, 145, 146–9,
150, 152, 165
Emperor and Galilean, 145
Enemy of the People, An, 145
Ghosts, 145
Hedda Gabler, 145, 153
John Gabriel Borkman, 145
Lady from the Sea, The, 145
League of Youth, The, 145
Little Eyolf, 145
Master Builder, The, 145
Peer Gynt, 64, 144–5
Pillars of the Community, 145
Rosmersholm, 145, 153
When we Dead Awaken, 144, 145
Wild Duck, The, 145, 146
Illiers, 185
Importance of Being Earnest, The, 44, 240
Ionesco, Eugène, 212
Isáeva, Mária, 135, 136
Italy, history of, 8–9, 206
Izambard, Georges, 115

James V, 25–6
James, Henry, 193
Jarvis, Charles, 41
Jesenská, Milena, 201
Joan of Arc, 22, 24
Johnston, Charles, 82–3, 85
Joyce, James, 62, 89, 94n, 113, 139, 175,
193, 197
Portrait of the Artist as a Young Man, A,
57, 197

Ulysses, 94n, 189, 204n
Joyce, Nora, 62, 208n
July Monarchy, 91, 92
Juvenal, 4–5, 4n

Kafka, Franz, 152, 156, 192, **199–204**;
  Jewish identity of, 199–202
  America, 201
  Castle, The, 201
  Country Doctor, A, 201
  Hunger-artist, A, 201
  Meditations, 201
  'Metamorphosis, The', 201
  Trial, The, 201, 202–4
Kafka, Ottla, 199–200, 200n
Kant, Immanuel, 60
Karl August, Duke, 61–3, 67
Karl Eugen, Duke, 67–9
Katkóv, M. N., 122
Keats, John, 115
Kelly, Christopher, 58
Kilmartin, Terence, 188n, 190
Kilmer, Nicholas, 29, 228
Kipling, Rudyard, 193, 197
Knípper, Ólga, 164
Körner, C. G., 69
Krailsheimer, A. J., 96

Lacroix, Albert, 176
la Fontaine, Jean de, 36
Lamport, F. J., 72, 73, 232–3
Laura, Petrarch's, 16–18
Leatherbarrow, W. J., quoted 137–8, 139
Leconte de Lisle, C. M., 108
Leibniz, G. W., 49, 50, 60
leitmotif, 193, 193n
Lenin, V. I., 168
Lepanto, 35, 37
Lérmontov, Mikháil Iúrevich, 85–9, 123
  'Death of a Poet', 86–7
  Demon, The, 87
  Hero of Our Time, A, 5, 87–90, 121
  Novice, The, 87
  Song of Tsar Iván Vasílevich, 87
  Tambóv Treasurer's Wife, The, 87
Lesseps, Ferdinand de, 108
Levasseur, Thérèse, 53
Lewes, G. H., quoted 3–4, 101
Lewis, Wyndham, 175
Linstrum, John, 207n, 210, 212
Lisbon earthquake, 50

Livy, 15
Louis XIV, 36, 41, 42
Louis XVI, 91, 92
Louis XVIII, 91, 92
Louis-Philippe, 92
Lowe-Porter, Helen, 198, 221n
Lower Depths, The, 165, 168, **169–71**
Luke, David, 4n, 64–6, 67, 194n, 198, 221n
Lyngstad, Sverre, 158

McDuff, David, 140
McFarlane, James, 149
McGowan, James, 114
Madame Bovary, 6, 98, **103–5**, 110, 217–22
Mallarmé, Stéphane, 113
Manheim, Ralph, 216, 237
Mann, Heinrich, 194, 194n
Mann, Thomas, 139, 152, 156, 192, **194–8**, 221n
  Buddenbrooks, The, 194, 195, 196; title 194n
  Death in Venice, 195, 196–8
  Dr Faustus, 196
  'Little Herr Friedemann', 194, 197
  Magic Mountain, The, 195, 196
  'Tonio Kröger', 194, 197
  'Tristan', 194, 197
Marber, Patrick, 154n
Marlowe, Christopher, *Dr Faustus*, 63
marriage, position of women in *see* women and adultery
Martýnov, Nikolái, 86
Marvell, Andrew, 28
Marx-Aveling, Eleanor, 218–22
Marxism, 167, 168, 213
Maude, Louise and Aylmer, 134, 239
Meley, Alexandrine, 178
metafiction, 85n, 188
method acting, 208, 208n
Methuen Drama, 7
Meyer, Michael, 148–9, 149, 154
Miller, Henry, 156
Milton, John, 2, 14
Miss Julie, 150, **152–4**, 165
Modernism, 111, 136, 139, 158, 174–5, 193, 207–8, 210–12, 215
Molière, 36, 41–5; name 41n
  Malade imaginaire, Le, 42
  Misanthrope, Le, 42, 44

Tartuffe, 42–5, 229–30
money, value of, 240–1
Montaigne, Michel de, 2, 20, **29–33**
Essays, 30–3
Moscow Arts Theatre, 171, 208
Mozart, W. A., 60, 114
Muir, Willa and Edwin, 204
Munch, Edvard, 152n
Musa, Mark, 11n, 14, 18, 212, 224, 225–6
Musil, Robert, 156
Mussolini, Benito, 206, 209

Nabókov, Vladímir, quoted 5, 88; 85, 89
Napoleon I, 91, 92
Napoleon II, 92
Napoleon III, 92, 98, 107–8
narrator, 84–5, 87–8, 96, 105, 127, 139,
158, 180, 187–9, 197, 204
naturalism, 94n, 176, 197
Nekrásov, N. A., 135
Newman, J. H., *Apologia pro vita sua*, 57
Nicholas I, 77, 81, 89, 122, 135, 160, 162
Nicholas II, 77
Nietzsche, F. W., 152, 155, 193
nihilism, 125n, 151, 162, 180
Nobel Prize for Literature, 195, 209
Norway *see* Scandinavia
Novelle, 196n

Oxford University, 125
Oxford World's Classics, 6–7

Pabst, G. W., 216
Paolo and Francesca, 12–13
Parmée, Douglas, 184
Pascal, Blaise, 36
Pasternák, Borís, 156
Pearson, Roger, 51
Peck, Bob, 15
Penguin Classics, 6–7
Pepusch, Christoph, 214, 215
Père Goriot, Le, 93, **94–7**
title 94n
Peshkóv, Maxím, 166
Petrarch, 1–2, 4, 8, **15–18**
Love Lyrics (*Canzoniere*), 16–18, 225–6
Philip II, 35
Philip III, 35
Phillips, Tom, 14–15, 224
philosophes, 47, 52, 193
Pindar, 26

Pinter, Harold, 212
Pirandello, Antonietta *see* Portulano,
Antonietta
Pirandello, Luigi, **208–12**
Each in His Own Way, 212
Henry IV, 209
Late Mattia Pascal, The, 209
Play of Parts, The, 210n
Rules of the Game, The, 209, 210
Six Characters in Search of an Author,
207n, 209, 210–12
So It Is (If You Think So), 209
Tonight We Improvise, 212
Pitoëff, Georges, 212
Pléiade, 26
Poe, Edgar Alan, 110, 151–2
Poems
of Petrarch, **16–18**
of Rimbaud, **117–19**
of Ronsard, **26–9**
of Villon, **23–5**
Poquelin, Jean Baptiste *see* Molière
Portinari, Folco, 9
see Beatrice (Portinari), Dante's
Portulano, Antonietta, 208–9, 208n
positivism *see* deterministic positivism
Pound, Ezra, 175
Prague, 199–201
Pringsheim, Katia, 194–6
producer *see* director, producer
Proust, Dr Adrien, 184, 185, 186
Proust, Marcel, 175, **184–90**, 193
À la recherche du temps perdu, 57,
177n, 184, 186, 187–90,
237; title, 185n
Albertine disparue, 189
À l'ombre des jeunes filles en fleurs, 187,
189
Du côté de Guermantes, 189
Prisonnière, La, 189
Sodome et Gomorrhe, 189
Swann's Way (*Du côté de chez Swann*),
187–90
Temps retrouvé, Le, 189
translations of Ruskin, 186
Púshkin, Alexánder Sergéevich, **80–5**, 86,
122, 123, 167
Borís Godunóv, 81
Captain's Daughter, The, 81
Eugene Onégin, 81, 82–5, 89, 121,
233–4

Fountain of Bakhchísaray, The, 81
Prisoner of the Caucasus, The, 81
Queen of Spades, The, 81
Robber Brothers, The, 81
Rúslan and Lyudmíla, 81

Quand vous serez bien vieille, 26–9, 228
Quisling, Vidkun, 157n

Rabelais, François, 20
Racine, Jean, 36, 68
realism, 38, 94n, 96, 104, 138, 152, 153, 208
Reed, T. J., 61, 73, 233
Reformation, 20, 59
Renaissance, 8, 15–16, 20, 40
Revolutionary Calendar, French, 179
Revolutions
    French, 8, 51, 53, 62, 69, 91, 92, 107–8
    Russian, 77, 162, 168, 206
Revue des deux mondes, 110
Rimbaud, Arthur, 108, 113, **114–20**
    'Assis, Les', 115
    Bateau ivre, Le, 116
    'Chercheuses de poux, Les', 118–19, 236
    Illuminations, Les, 116, 117
    'Ma Bohème', 115, 117–18, 235
    Saison en enfer, Une, 117
    'Veillées', 119
Rohan-Chabot, Chevalier de, 47
Rome, 15
Ronsard, Pierre de, 1–2, 20, **25–9**
    Quand vous serez bien vieille, 26–9, 228
Rosetti, Dante Gabriel, 17, 227
Rousseau, Jean-Jacques, 2, 47, **51–8**
    Confessions, 54–8
    Discourses, 53
    Émile, 53
    Nouvelle Heloïse, La, 53
    Social Contract, The, 53
Rozerot, Jeanne, 178
Ruskin, John, 186
Russell, Alan, 218–22
Russia
    history of, 75–80, 121–3, 160–2, 206; constitution, 76–80; Estates, 77–80; geography and climate, 75–6; peoples, 76, 78–80; railways, 76; ranks, table of, 79; Revolutions, 77, 162, 168, 206
    names, form of Russian, 238–9
    novel, great age of the Russian, 121–3

see Communism; Slavophiles and Westernists
Russian Herald, The, 122–3

Sainte-Beuve, C. A., 108
Saint-Simon, Duc de, 54
Sakhalín, 164
Salazar, Catalina de, 37
Sávina, 124
Sayers, Dorothy L., 14, 224
Scandinavia
    history of, 142–4; languages, 142–3
Scarfe, Francis, 112–14
Schiller, Friedrich, 60, 62, **67–73**
    Aesthetic Letters, 69
    Bride of Messina, The, 70
    Demetrius, 70
    Don Carlos, 69
    History of the Thirty Years' War, 69
    Maid of Orleans, The, 70
    Maria Stuart, 70
    'Ode to Joy', 69, 69n
    On Naive and Sentimental Poetry, 69
    Piccolómini, The, 71–2, 231
    Robbers, The, 68–9
    Wallenstein's Camp, 71–2
    Wallenstein's Death (Wallensteins Tod), 71–3, 232
    Wallenstein trilogy, 69, 70–3
    William Tell, 70
Schlesinger, Elisa, 97
Schleswig-Holstein, 143, 143n
Schopenhauer, Artur, 193
Scott Moncrieff, C. K., 185n, 188n, 189, 190
Scott, Sir Walter, 160, 167
Screech, M. A., 29, 33
Second Empire, French, 107–8, 115, 173
Second Reich, German, 173–4
Seth, Vikram, *Golden Gate, The,* 85n
sexual morality *see* women and adultery
Shakespeare, William, 2, 13, 16, 28, 60, 68, 71, 72n, 81
    Macbeth, 73
Shaw, G. B., 145–6
Sidney, Sir Philip, 16
Sinclair, John D., 11, 15, 224
Singer, I. B., 156
Sisson, C. J. 14, 224
Six Characters in Search of an Author, 207n, 209, **210–12**

Slavophiles and Westernists, 122, 162
Snítkina, Ánna G., 136
Sonets pour Hélène, 26–9
sonnet, 16–17, 23, 26–8, 82–3, 111–13
Southey, Robert, 69
Spain, history of, 35
Spanish Succession, War of the, 46
Speshněv, Nikolái, 135
Stalin, Josef, 168, 207
Stalin Peace Prize, 214
Stanislávsky, Konstantín, 207–8, 208n, 212
stárets, 138, 138n
Steegmuller, Francis, 219–22
Steffin, Margarete, 213
Steiner, George, 4n
Stellóvsky, F. T., 136
Stevenson, Juliet, 149n
Stidworthy, Kitty, 238n
Stoppard, Tom, 212
Strindberg, August, 142, 143, **149–54**, 155, 193, 207
  Bond, The, 150
  Creditors, 150, 152
  Father, The, 150, 152
  Inferno, 150–1
  Master Olof, 150
  Miss Julie, 150, 152–4, 165
  Playing with Fire, 150
  Red Room, The, 150
  To Damascus, 151
superfluous man, 88
Sully-Prudhomme, R. F. A., 108
Surgères, Hélène de, 26–8
Surrey, Earl of, 16
Súslova, Polína, 136
Swann's Way, **187–90**
Sweden *see* Scandinavia
Swinburne, A. C., 124
Symbolists, 113, 193

Taine, H. A., 108
Tancock, Leonard, 179, 181
Tartuffe, **42–5**, 229–30
Tennyson, Alfred Lord, 124
Terboven, Josef, 157
Terence, 20
Teresa of Avila, St, 54
terza rima, 14
Thackeray, W. M., 93, 99n, 124
Third Reich, German, 195, 206

Thirty Years' War, 36, 69, 70–3
Thomas Aquinas, St, 9
Threepenny Opera, The, 213, **214–15**, 237
  'Mac the Knife', 215
titles
  language of, 7
  translation of, 94n, 177n, 185n, 194n
Tolstóy, Lév Nikoláevich, 2, 85, 89, 122, **128–34**, 162, 167, 168, 183n
  Ánna Karénina, 10n, 80, 98, 105, 121, 122, 123, 124n, 127, 129, 130–4, 137
  Childhood, Boyhood, and Youth, 128
  Confession, A, 129
  Cossacks, The, 129
  Death of Iván Ilých, 129
  Hádji Murát, 130
  How Much Land Does a Man Need?, 129–30
  Kingdom of God is Within You, The, 130
  Kreutzer Sonata, The, 130
  Resurrection, 130
  Sevastópol Sketches, 128
  War and Peace, 101, 121, 123, 124, 129,
Tolstóya, Countess *see* Behrs, Sófia Andréevna
translation, **2–7**, **217–22**
  see titles, translation of
Trial, The, 201, **202–4**
Trollope, Anthony, 93, 99n, 130,
Turgénev, Ivan Sergéevich, 2, 85, 89, 122, **123–8**, 134, 161, 162, 167
  Fathers and Children, 2, 121, 124, 125–8, 132n, 135
  King Lear of the Steppes, 124
  Month in the Country, A, 123
  Nest of Gentlefolk, A, 101, 121
  On the Eve, 121
  Rúdin, 121, 124
  Smoke, 121, 134n
  Sportsman's Sketches, A, 124
  Spring Torrents, 124
  Virgin Soil, 121, 124

Uhl, Frieda, 150

Vega, Lope de, 35, 38
Velásquez, Diego, 35
Verlaine, Paul, 108, 113, 116–17
verse, forms of
  French, 20–1, 23; *see* ballade

German, 65
Russian, 82–3
see *ballade*; sonnet
Viardot, Pauline, 123, 125
Villon, François, 1–2, 20, 21, **22–5**
  Ballade des dames du temps jadis, 23–4,
   226–7
  Ballade des pendus, 24–5, 215, 227
Virgil, 11–12, 15, 16
Vizetelly, Henry, 181
Voltaire, 2, **47–51**, 52, 60, 61, 109; name
  48n
  Candide, 2, 49–51
  Dictionnaire philosophique, 49
  *Essai sur les moeurs et l'ésprit des
   nations*, 49
  Henriade, La, 47
  Letters Concerning the English Nation,
   47
  Oedipe, 47
  Sur le désastre de Lisbonne, 50
Vólzhina, Elizavéta, 168
Vrémia, 135
Vulpius, Christiane, 62

Wall, Geoffrey, 219–22
Wallenstein, Albrecht von, 70–1
Wallenstein trilogy, 70–3
Warens, Madame de, 52
Watts, Peter, 149
Waugh, Evelyn, *Put Out More Flags*,
  103n
Wayne, Philip, 67
Weigel, Helene, 213
Weill, Kurt, 214–15, 216
Weimar, 61–3, 69
Wells, H. G., 156
Weltsch, Felix, 200
Wertherism, 61, 84
Westernists *see* Slavophiles and
  Westernists
Wilbur, R., 45

Wilhelm I, 174
Wilhelm II, 174
Willett, John, 216, 237
women and adultery in the nineteenth
  century, **98–103**, 147
  adultery, 103
  double standards, 101–2
  New Testament, 100
  Old Testament, 99
  opportunities and limitations, 101
  separation and divorce, 102–3
  sexual morality, 99
  women considered inferior to men, 102
Wood, John, 42–4, 45
Woods, John E., 198
Woolf, Leonard, 208n
Woolf, Virginia, 113, 193
Wordsworth, William, 2, 8, 144
World War I, 173–4, 187, 193, 195, 196,
  200, 206–7, 213
World War II, 196, 199, 200n, 206–7
Württemberg, 67–9
Wyatt, Sir Thomas, 16

Yeats, W. B., 28–9

Zoff, Marianne, 213
Zola, Émile, 94n, 175, **175–81**
  Assommoir, L', 177, 181
  Au bonheur des dames, 177
  Bête humaine, La, 177
  Contes à Ninon, Les, 175
  Docteur Pascal, Le, 176
  Fortune des Rougon, La, 176
  Germinal, 177, 179–81, 187
  Nana, 177, 181
  Oeuvre, L', 177
  Pot-bouille, 99n, 177
  Rougon-Macquart novels, 176–7, 176n;
   titles, 177n
  Terre, La, 80n, 177
  Thérèse Raquin, 175